Organizational Behavior Modification and Beyond

An Operant and Social Learning Approach

Management Applications Series

Alan C. Filley, University of Wisconsin, Madison
Series Editor

Performances in Organizations: Determinants and Appraisal
L. L. Cummings, University of Wisconsin, Madison
Donald P. Schwab, University of Wisconsin, Madison

Leadership and Effective Management
Fred E. Fiedler, University of Washington
Martin M. Chemers, University of Utah

Managing by Objectives
Anthony P. Raia, University of California, Los Angeles

Organizational Change: Techniques and Applications
Newton Margulies, University of California, Irvine
John C. Wallace, University of California, Irvine

Interpersonal Conflict Resolution
Alan C. Filley, University of Wisconsin, Madison

*Group Techniques for Program Planning: A Guide to Nominal
  Group and Delphi Processes*
Andre L. Delbecq, University of Wisconsin, Madison
Andrew H. Van de Ven, Kent State University
David H. Gustafson, University of Wisconsin, Madison

Task Design and Employee Motivation
Ramon J. Aldag, University of Wisconsin, Madison
Arthur P. Brief, University of Iowa

*Organizational Surveys: An Internal Assessment of
  Organizational Health*
Randall B. Dunham, University of Wisconsin, Madison
Frank J. Smith, Sears, Roebuck and Company

Managerial Decision Making
George P. Huber, University of Wisconsin, Madison

Stress and Work: A Managerial Perspective
John M. Ivancevich, University of Houston
Michael T. Matteson, University of Houston

Organizational Behavior Modification and Beyond, 2/E
Fred Luthans, University of Nebraska, Lincoln
Robert Kreitner, Arizona State University

Organizational Behavior Modification and Beyond

An Operant and Social Learning Approach

Fred Luthans
University of Nebraska

Robert Kreitner
Arizona State University

Scott, Foresman and Company
Glenview, Illinois   London, England

To Kay and Margaret

ACKNOWLEDGMENTS

Exhibit 1–1. "How to Earn Well Pay," reprinted from the June 12, 1978 issue of *Business Week* by special permission, © 1978 by McGraw-Hill, Inc. **Figure 1–2.** From *Managerial Attitudes and Performance* by Porter and Lawler, p. 165. Copyright © 1968 by Richard D. Irwin, Inc. Reprinted by permission. **Figure 1–3.** From "A Social Learning Approach to Organizational Behavior" by Tim R. V. Davis and Fred Luthans in *The Academy of Management Review*, April 1980, Vol. 5, No. 2, p. 285. Reprinted by permission of the Academy of Management. **Figure 3–8.** F. Luthans and T. Davis, "Managers in Action: A New Look at Their Behavior and Operating Modes," *Organizational Dynamics*, Summer (New York: AMACOM, a division of American Management Associations, 1980) p. 75. Reprinted by permission.

ACKNOWLEDGMENTS CONTINUE ON PAGE 245, WHICH IS A LEGAL EXTENSION OF THE COPYRIGHT PAGE.

Library of Congress Cataloging in Publication Data.

Luthans, Fred.
　　Organizational behavior modification and beyond.

　　(Management applications series)
　　Rev. ed. of: Organizational behavior modification. 1975.
　　Bibliography: p.
　　Includes index.
　　1. Organizational behavior.　2. Behavior modification.　I. Kreitner, Robert. II. Luthans, Fred. Organizational behavior modification.　III. Title.　IV. Series.
HD58.7.L89 1985　　　658.3　　　84-16147　　　ISBN 0-673-15923-X

1 2 3 4 5 6 -RRC- 89 88 87 86 85 84

FOREWORD

The Management Applications Series is concerned with the application of contemporary research, theory, and techniques. There are many excellent books at advanced levels of knowledge, but there are few which address themselves to the application of such knowledge. The authors in this series are uniquely qualified for this purpose, since they are all scholars who have experience in implementing change in real organizations through the methods they write about.

Each book treats a single topic in depth. Where the choice is between presenting many approaches briefly or a single approach thoroughly, we have opted for the latter. Thus, after reading the book, the student or practitioner should know how to apply the methodology described.

Selection of topics for the series was guided by contemporary relevance to management practice, and by the availability of an author qualified as an expert, yet able to write at a basic level of understanding. No attempt is made to cover all management methods, nor is any sequence implied in the series, although the books do complement one another. For example, change methods might fit well with managing by objectives.

The books in this series may be used in several ways. They may be used to supplement textbooks in basic courses on management, organizational behavior, personnel, or industrial psychology/sociology. Students appreciate the fact that the material is immediately applicable. Practicing managers will want to use individual books to increase their skills, either through self study or in connection with management development programs, inside or outside the organization.

Alan C. Filley

PREFACE

Almost ten years ago we attempted to integrate operant learning theory and the established principles of behavior modification with the field of management in general, and human resource management in particular. To recognize this merger, we called our book *Organizational Behavior Modification* and the approach became known simply as "O.B. Mod." In the original book, we consciously tried to provide a new, some would say opposite, direction for managing people at work. Instead of an internal, cognitively based approach that had become so popular with the work of Maslow, Vroom, and Porter and Lawler, we laid out the theoretical foundation, guiding principles, implementation steps, and as many examples and applications as we could muster for an *external*, environmentally based approach.

The results of this new approach speak for themselves. Although the internal, cognitively based approach still dominates the academic side of the study of organizational behavior and, to a lesser degree, the application side, there is little doubt that the gap is closing. Today, most organizational behavior scholars and professional managers would agree that the external, environmentally based approach has made a contribution to the study and understanding of human behavior in organizations. Even more importantly, it is generally recognized that the O.B. Mod. approach can lead to effective employee performance. This was not true ten years ago.

Now the time has come to fine tune the original (i.e., operant) orientation of O.B. Mod. and go beyond (i.e., integrate social learning theory and applications). Thus the title of this new book has been expanded: *Organizational Behavior Modification and Beyond: An Operant and Social Learning Approach*. Whereas the original book was the first to integrate operant theory and principles with human resource management, this book is the first to integrate social learning concepts and principles in a comprehensive approach to the study of organizational behavior.

The social learning emphasis in this revision recognizes the contribution that the cognitive approach can make to the study and management of behavior. However, the social learning approach does not negate the importance of operant concepts and principles. In particular, the social learning approach accepts the importance of environmental contingencies (both antecedent and consequent) as in the operant approach, but then goes *beyond* by recognizing: (1) covert (unobservable), self-evaluative contingencies; (2) cognitive mediating processes (e.g., attributions); (3) imitative learning through vicarious and modeling processes; and (4) the importance of self-control. In other words, by adding the social learning dimension to O.B. Mod., we have built an expanded theoretical foundation that gives more attention to modeling and self-management processes and applications. This is reflected in the significantly revised table of contents of this new book.

Like the earlier book, our goals remain better understanding, prediction and control of human behavior at work. The overriding aim is to increase employee performance effectiveness. We would like to think that this book can serve as a technically sound resource manual for the operant and social learning approaches to behavioral management as well as provide specific guidelines for the successful implementation of O.B. Mod.

There are again ten chapters. The first three chapters provide the perspective, theoretical foundation, and principles of O.B. Mod. Chapter 4 then provides the specific 5-step model for implementation. All these first chapters are modified and updated from the original and now include social learning as well as operant material. Chapter 5 is a completely new chapter on "Antecedent Management." Chapter 6 on "Consequence Management" combines the old chapters on positive and negative control and updates them. Chapter 7 is basically a new chapter giving special attention to the social learning processes of modeling and self-management. Chapter 8, except for one case, contains all new material on actual first-hand applications of O.B. Mod. in a number of manufacturing cases (large and small), a nonmanufacturing case (a large department store), a nonprofit case (a large hospital), and a couple of self-management cases. These applications of O.B. Mod. go into considerable detail and make a comprehensive analysis of the results. Chapter 9 attempts to clarify some of the real and potential misconceptions and ethical issues surrounding O.B. Mod. Finally, Chapter 10 attempts to pull the preceding chapters together into an overall integrative model and looks into the future of O.B. Mod. In total, since it has been almost ten years, this revision in many ways is an entirely new book rather than the usual second edition.

In putting this book together, we owe a great deal to others. First of all we would like to acknowledge the role that Professor Robert Ottemann, University of Nebraska at Omaha, and Dr. David Lyman, a human resources management practitioner, had in shaping some of our first ideas about O.B. Mod. Next, we would like to recognize the many former doctoral students at the University of Nebraska who have given us ideas; for the most part, the various studies conducted on O.B. Mod. applications discussed in Chapter 8 are a direct result of their work. In particular, we would like to mention the following as being particularly helpful: Professors Tim R. V. Davis of Cleveland State University, Diane L. Lockwood of Seattle University, Mark J. Martinko of Florida State University, Jason Schweizer of Northern Arizona University, and Charles A. Snyder of Auburn University. We would also like to acknowledge the late Dr. Peter W. Van Ness, who was a good friend and ardent supporter of O.B. Mod. Last, but by no means least, we would like to thank our wives, to whom we dedicate this book with love and appreciation, for providing us with the necessary positive reinforcement to write it.

Fred Luthans
Robert Kreitner

CONTENTS

A Behavioral Perspective 1

Human resource management is undergoing drastic change. Old approaches to managing employees in today's organizations are no longer adequate. Conventional human relations approaches that attempt to motivate employees with money, conditions, and fringe benefits have fallen way short of meeting the productivity goals for today's organizations. Traditional methods have not resulted in satisfied employees and the assumption that happy employees are productive employees has not been borne out by research or common practice.

Unfortunately, productivity in this country is in bad shape. Starting in the mid-1960s the productivity growth rate began to slip. So far, the 1980s is experiencing the same downward trend. Obviously, there are many reasons for this sad state of affairs (e.g., energy costs, inflation, and a negative balance of trade). The key to understanding productivity problems in this country, however, is to recognize that other countries around the world are also faced with an energy crunch, inflation, and trade problems; but their productivity growth rates are much higher than those in the U.S.

Although the U.S. is still the most productive nation in the world, other nations (e.g., Japan and Western European countries) are rapidly catching up. The U.S.'s problems do not seem to be in technology and equipment. This country has the best; everyone has copied American technological know-how. The difference is that other countries are making this technology work, *through people*, and are getting the job done. Thus, *an* answer, if not *the* answer, seems to be to re-examine the approaches to human resource management. Not that Japanese or European techniques should be copied. They obviously are rooted in much different cultural values and situations. Rather, the commonly used approaches to human resource management and the theory and research that these methods are based upon should be questioned and some alternatives should be explored. Traditional theories and techniques of human resource management may not be entirely wrong, but in light of current productivity problems there seems to be enough justification to explore new theoretical alternatives and develop new techniques. The purpose of this book is to provide such an alternative: specifically, a behavioral perspective as well as some specific behavioral techniques for more effectively managing human resources in modern organizations.

THE SCIENTIFIC PERSPECTIVE IN A BEHAVIORAL APPROACH

A seeming limitation of the old human relations approach to managing people was the lack of a scientific perspective in terms of both theory and practice. In the academic world, meanwhile, the study of human behavior has followed a definite scientific path. This scientific approach is characterized by operational definitions, precise problem formulation, and rigorous data collection, analysis, and interpretation. In the relatively short span of this century, behavioral scientists have carried out what their name implies, i.e., a scientific study of human behavior. Predictably, as with most academic disciplines, behavioral scientists have fragmented into divisions and subdivisions with each group embracing its own theories, tenets, and techniques. Today, the behavioral sciences include psychology, sociology, and anthropology, with respective emphasis given to individual behavior, social behavior, and cultural influences.

The old human relations approach, which made very simplistic assumptions about organizational participants and found solutions in wages, working conditions, and being "nice" to people, generally ignored a scientifically based explanation of complex employee behavior that psychology, sociology, or anthropology could offer. Today, however, the behavioral sciences are receiving much more attention and more complex assumptions are made. Starting almost 25 years ago with the popular writings of Douglas McGregor, a behavioral science approach has become increasingly important and now is the recognized theoretical and research base for the behavioral approach to management. Yet, despite the widespread recognition of behavioral science as a whole, there has been a decided imbalance regarding the possible explanations of organizational behavior.

In behavioral science, and more specifically in psychology, there are two general explanations of human behavior. One approach, which could be called the internal approach, explains behavior in terms of mental states and cognitive processes. In this explanation, the internal states cause behavior. The other approach, which could be called the external approach, explains behavior in terms of environmental consequences. (The internal approach is primarily a "motivational" or need-based explanation of human behavior and the external approach is mainly a "learning" or reinforcement-based explanation.)

To date, the internal approach has dominated the theoretical explanation of organizational behavior. The older expectancy motivation theories of Vroom (1964) or Porter and Lawler (1968) as well as the newer attribution theories (Mitchell and Wood, 1980; Spector, 1982) have been given most of the attention in explanations of organizational behavior. The human resource techniques flowing from these theories (e.g., job design and goal setting) have also dominated the literature. The external approach, on the other hand, has only surfaced in the last ten years. Although some recent attention has been given to the external approach (e.g., see L. Frederiksen [Ed.], *Handbook of Organizational Behavior Management*, 1982, and issues of *The Journal of Organizational Behavior Management*), it still lags far behind the internal approach in terms of emphasis in the field of organizational behavior and human resource management. Yet, the external approach takes a scientific perspective and the evidence so far indicates it has considerable potential for more effective human resource management.

Probably the best position today is to recognize both approaches. Chapter 2 will give detailed attention to a theoretical foundation containing both cognitive and environmental elements. For now, however, the remainder of this chapter will contrast the more widely recognized internal approach with the emerging external approach.

BEHAVIORAL MANAGEMENT: INTERNAL TO EXTERNAL

The behavioral approach to management has spawned a flurry of theory, research, and teaching. Until recently, however, the search has been one-sided, centering on the cognitive causes of employee behavior. Practicing managers, on the other hand, have been faced with the pragmatic realities of managing on-the-job behavior. Our introductory remarks suggest that sole reliance on an internal approach has yielded less than adequate results. Because of this, the time is ripe to get both management scholars and practitioners to give more consideration to behavior and its controlling antecedents and consequences.

Awareness of the external approach

Consider the following depiction of employee behavior as an illustration of the external approach. An individual comes to an organization (large or small, public or private) with the capacity to behave in many ways. Based upon prior experience, training, formal education, and general lifestyle, the person possesses a unique behavioral repertoire. From the organization's viewpoint, some of the employee's behavior may be consistent with formally stated objectives and some of it may not be. Armed with the knowledge of what behavior is desirable (that required to attain organizational objectives), the practicing manager can attempt to accelerate the new employee's desirable behavior and decelerate the undesirable behavior. This important job of behavioral management can be accomplished through the knowledge of some scientifically validated laws of behavior.

At this point it should prove interesting for the reader to take the little test found in Figure 1-1. (Please take the test now.) Regardless of whether the reader has had a lot, some, or no formal management training, there is a high probability that items 4, 5, 6, 8, and 10 will have a higher average score than items 1, 2, 3, 7, and 9. The former group of

FIGURE 1-1.   A Word Recognition Test.

INSTRUCTIONS: After carefully considering each of the following terms as it relates to employee behavior, rate each term with a 2, 1, 0.

2 = Very familiar term
1 = Vaguely or somewhat familiar term
0 = Unfamiliar term

1. Stimulus Cue
2. Extinction
3. Negative Reinforcement
4. Drive
5. Attitude
6. Motive
7. Behavioral Event
8. Need
9. Behavioral Contingency
10. Ability

terms comes from the language of the internal approach of explaining behavior, with its emphasis on mental states, cognitive processes, and hypothetical constructs. The latter group of terms, on the other hand, comes from the language of the external approach, with its emphasis upon behavior and antecedents and consequences. Aware of it or not, most managers speak the cognitive language of the internal approach in explaining employee behavior. Not surprisingly, it is simply the result of steady exposure to the language of the cognitive school of thought — the internal approach. It is a matter of culture and conditioning or, as the behaviorist would say, a matter of the differential reinforcement of the use of mentalistic terminology.

You may want to try the following as a personal experiment. For the next few days listen carefully to yourself, your professors or supervisors, peers, and subordinates and record how many times the words "need," "attitude," "purpose," "desire," "morale," and "ability" are used when the behavior of people, especially organizational participants, is being discussed. Then, going one step farther, shift your attention to the five terms used in the external approach shown in Figure 1-1, "stimulus cue," "extinction," "negative reinforcement," "behavioral event," and "behavioral contingency," and record the number of times each is heard in regard to employee behavior. If our exercise is a reliable indicator, you will end up with many more of the former than of the latter.

Environmental consequences of employee behavior

Employees view the organization as the source of many consequences, some desirable and some undesirable. Some environmental consequences of their behavior include money, security, recognition, social support, formal and informal sanctions, reprimands, and termination. Through instructions, observation of co-workers and supervisors, and, primarily, personal experience with receiving consequences, employees learn which on-the-job behaviors lead to certain desirable consequences and which behaviors result in undesirable consequences. Ideally, the organization obtains the behavior required for organizational goal accomplishment and employees receive personally desirable consequences. Unfortunately, this is not generally the case in today's organizations.

While this initial look at the consequences of employees' behavior is overly simplistic, it is the description itself that is of particular interest to this discussion. Due to the nature of most of the management literature, management theorists and practitioners encounter few analyses and descriptions of employee behavior which contain no allusions to internal explanations of behavior. Words such as those found in the test (drives, attitudes, abilities, motives, and needs) are frequently used to suggest that they are the real "causes" of the employee behavior being analyzed and described.

This latter approach suggests that managers can elicit desirable job performance by somehow getting at the causes of behavior. However, when it is realized that the "causes" of behavior are only hypothetical, then the causal model takes on different meaning. As the famous behaviorist B. F. Skinner (1969) pointed out many years ago:

> "...It is not good scientific practice to explain behavior by appealing to independent variables which have been inferred from the behavior thus explained, although this is commonly done, particularly by psychoanalysts, cognitive theorists, and factor analysts" (p. 264).

Since the behavioral management literature is predominantly steeped in the jargon of the humanistic and cognitive schools of thought, Skinner's observation seems particularly relevant to this discussion.

Going beyond the elusive causes of behavior

In the description of employee behavior in the last section, reference to the explanation and specific causes of behavior was noticeably absent. Rather, the focus was on the relationship between behavior and its environmental consequences, hence giving it an external perspective. Is this saying, then, that the real causes of behavior are nonexistent or unimportant? No, not at all. The point is that management theorists and practitioners have too often gotten sidetracked while pursuing the elusive causes of employee behavior. Thus, the case is being made here for an alternative *external* approach. It involves identifying and managing the external environment which maintains, strengthens, and weakens observable behavior. This external approach suggests that managers can profitably use environment factors rather than just looking "inside" the individual for the complex cognitive causes of job behavior.

Fundamental differences between the internal, cognitive model of behavior and the external, environmental model can be best illustrated from the perspective of science. Scientists' principal goals are to understand, predict, and control phenomena in question. Reliance upon the internal model has definitely contributed to the understanding of organizational behavior but has generally not supplied many practical techniques for controlling employee behavior. When one considers that the very essence of behavioral management is to control employee behavior, relative to attaining organizational objectives, the practical value of looking at this alternative approach becomes clear. The cognitive approach is helpful for understanding human behavior. But the environmentally based external approach is necessary for controlling behavior — the essence of human resource management. For a practical illustration of the "external" approach, see the case study in Exhibit 1.

EXHIBIT 1   "How to Earn 'Well Pay' "

The woman in blue jeans and a logger's shirt looks up from the production line and says grimly: "I can't miss work today. It's almost the end of the month, and I'm going to earn that 'well pay' if it kills me."

At Parsons Pine Products Inc. in Ashland, Oregon, "well pay" is the opposite of sick pay. It is an extra eight hours' wages that the company gives the workers who are neither absent or late for a full month. It is also one of four incentives that owner James W. Parsons has built into a "positive reinforcement plan" for workers: well pay, retro pay, safety pay, and profit-sharing pay.

Beating the tax man. The formula, Parsons says, enables him and his wife to beat the combination of federal and state income taxes that leaves them only 14% of any increase in earnings; it allows them to pass along much of the potential tax money to the workers. Under the Parsons' system, an employee earning $10,000 a year can add as much as $3,500 to his income by helping the plant operate economically.

Parsons Pine employs some 100 workers to cut lumber into specialty items — primarily louver slats for shutters, bifold doors, and blinds, and bases for rat traps. It is reportedly the U.S.'s biggest producer of these items, with sales last year (1977) of $2.5 million.

The company began handing out "well pay" in January, 1977. "We had a problem with lateness," Parsons explains. "Just before the 7 A.M. starting time, the foreman in a department would take a head count and assign three people to this machine and six over there. Then a few minutes later someone else comes in and he has to recalculate and reshuffle. Or he may be so short as to leave a machine idle."

"Well pay" brought lateness down to almost zero and cut absenteeism more than Parsons wanted reduced, because some workers came to work even when they were sick. He dealt with this awkwardness by reminding them of "retro pay." Says Parsons: "I'd say, 'By being here while not feeling well, you may have a costly accident, and that will not only cause you pain and suffering, but it will also affect the retro plan, which could cost you a lot more than one day's well pay.' "

Reducing accidents. The retro plan offers a bonus based on any reductions in premiums received from the state's industrial accident insurance fund. Before the retro plan went into effect in 1976, Parsons Pine had a high accident rate, 86% above the statewide base, and paid the fund accordingly.

Parsons told his workers that if the plant cut its accident rate, the retroactive refund would be distributed to them. The upshot was a 1977 accident bill of $2,500 compared to a 1976 bill of $28,500. After deducting administrative expenses, the state will return $89,000 of a $100,000 premium, some $900 per employee.

The retro plan did not improve the accident rate unaided, Parsons concedes. "We showed films and introduced every safety program the state has," he says. "But no matter what you do, it doesn't really make a dent until the people themselves see that they are going to lose a dollar by not being safe. When management puts on the pressure, they say, 'He's just trying to make a buck for himself,' but when fellow workers say, 'Let's work safe,' that means a lot."

The 'little hurts.' Employees can also earn safety pay — two hours' wages — by remaining accident-free for a month. "Six hours a quarter isn't such a great incentive," says Parsons, "but it helps. When it didn't cost them anything, workers would go to the doctor for every little thing. Now they take care of the little hurts themselves."

As its most substantial incentive, the company offers a profit-sharing bonus — everything the business earns over 4% after taxes, which is Parsons' idea of a fair profit. Each supervisor rates his employees in four categories of excellence, with a worker's bonus figured as a percentage of his wages multiplied by his category. Top-ranked employees generally receive bonuses of 8% to 10%. One year they got 16-1/2%. Two thirds of the bonus is paid in cash and the rest goes into the retirement fund.

To illustrate how workers can contribute to profits, and profit-sharing bonuses, Parsons presents a dramatic display that has a modest fame in Ashland. Inviting the work force to lunch, he sets up a pyramid of 250 rat trap bases, each representing $10,000 in sales. Then he knocks 100 onto the floor, saying: "That's for raw materials. See why it is important not to waste?" Then he pushes over 100 more, adding: "That's for wages." And pointing to the 50 left, he says: "Out of this little pile we have to do all the other things — maintenance, repairs, supplies, taxes. With so many blocks gone, that doesn't leave much for either you or me."

A vote for work. The lunch guests apparently find the display persuasive. Says one nine-year veteran: "We get the most we can out of every piece of wood after seeing that. When new employees come, we work with them to cut down waste."

The message also lingered at the last Christmas luncheon, when, after distribution of checks, someone said: "Hey, how about the afternoon off?" Parsons replied: "O.K., our production is on schedule and the customers won't be hurt. But you know where the cost comes from." Parsons recalls that someone asked him, "How much?" and he replied that the loss would be about $3,000.

"There was a bit of chatter and we took a vote," he says. "Only two hands were raised for the afternoon off. That was because they knew it was not just my money. It was their money, too."

Business Week, June 12, 1978, 143, 146, used with permission.

MOTIVATION: THE TRADITIONAL INTERNAL EXPLANATION

Traditionally, motivation theories have been particularly appealing as explanations of organizational behavior for two major reasons. First, they have helped explain why employees are productive or active, or in other words, what energizes their behavior. Second, motivation theories have attempted to explain the direction organizational behavior takes once it is energized. Generally, two motivational approaches have emerged, commonly labeled the content theories and the process theories.

The content theories of motivation attempt to specify what the energizers of behavior are. In a more sophisticated and comprehensive manner, the process theories of motivation attempt to identify the cognitive processes which give behavior purposeful direction. However, both approaches can be traced back to the concept of hedonism, the seeking of pleasure and avoidance of pain. Hedonism was originally proposed by the ancient Greek philosophers and later was popularized by the English utilitarian Jeremy Bentham. As the dichotomization of events into either pleasurable or painful proved increasingly difficult, more sophisticated extensions and refinements were proposed. Hedonism eventually evolved into the modern content and process theories of motivation.

Content theories

In the content approach, Maslow's famous hierarchy of needs and Herzberg's motivation/hygiene theory are widely recognized. More recently, Clayton Alderfer's ERG model has become a popular way to explain work motivation. These content theories identify the energizers of employee behavior. According to Maslow, behavior is energized by a hierarchy starting with physiological needs and then moving, in turn, from a need for safety or security, to love or belonging, to esteem, and, finally, to a need for self-actualization (Maslow, 1943). Herzberg, on the other hand, proposes two, as opposed to Maslow's five, levels of needs (Herzberg, et al., 1959). Herzberg's hygiene factors (those that prevent dissatisfaction but do not motivate) include company policy and administration, supervision, salary, interpersonal relations, and working conditions. In contrast, the motivators include achievement, recognition, responsibility, advancement, and the work itself. Alderfer identifies three groups of core needs: existence, relatedness, and growth (1972). He presents these needs in terms of a flexible continuum, as opposed to a fixed hierarchy of needs. These content theories of work motivation are particularly appealing because of their relative simplicity and ease of application. Each makes a contribution to both the theory and application of popular behavioral management.

It is important to note, however, that these content theories have generally not stood the test of empirical research. Maslow himself never provided any supporting research for his theory and the few studies that have attempted to test it have produced, at best, inconclusive results (Wahba and Bridwell, 1976). Herzberg's theory is even more questionable. Herzberg himself does provide a great deal of support for his theory by using a critical-incident method of research (subjects recall incidents when they were satisfied and dissatisfied). But, when more rigorous research methodologies are used, the theory is generally not supported (Dunnette, Campbell and Hakel, 1967; Hulin and Smith, 1967; Lindsay, Marks and Gorlow, 1967). Some researchers claim that even the critical incident method, if properly used, does not support the two-factor theory (Schwab, DeVitt, and Cummings, 1971; Schneider and Locke, 1971). Alderfer does provide his own research to test the ERG model (1969), but there is no substantial amount of research so far that validates the model and some actually counters the theory's predictive value (Raushenberger, Schmitt, and Hunter, 1980). At best, based upon the available research evidence, the content theories of work motivation turn out to be explanations of job satisfaction and not motivation and causes of employee behavior.

Process theories

Academicians have generally turned away from the content theories in favor of process theory approaches (e.g., drive, expectancy, and attribution theories) to explain motivation. Drive theories take prior experience into account when explaining behavior. For example, a key concept in Clark Hull's historically important drive-reduction theory was habit strength. According to Hull, habit strength was the result of the number of previously reinforced training trials. Previous reinforcement enabled an organism to learn to satisfy fundamental drives. A major problem with this theory was Hull's failure to distinguish between learned and unlearned responses. He implied that all behavior was a function of drive states. But, getting a drink of water and making a complex management decision are quite different behaviors and require different explanations. Water-drinking behavior usually results from physiological deprivation while decision-making behavior is learned. Modern managers are not driven to make decisions in the same manner that a thirsty organism is driven to get a drink of water.

Another process approach to motivation, but considerably more complex and sophisticated than the drive theories, are the expectancy theories. Whereas drive theories are past-oriented, expectancy theories are future-oriented. Vroom (1964) and Porter and Lawler (1968) developed highly popular expectancy theories of work motivation. Both theories rely heavily upon cognitive processes. Vroom suggests that motivation (force) is a function of the interactions among the value of particular outcomes (valence), subjective behavior-outcome probabilities (expectancy), and beliefs that first-level outcomes (e.g., achieving company standards) will lead to second-level outcomes (e.g., a promotion). This linkage between first level outcomes and second level outcomes is called *instrumentality.*

Porter and Lawler extended the Vroom model. The nine-element model shown in Figure 1-2 is even more future-oriented than the Vroom model. It shows that Porter and Lawler do not equate effort with performance. One's abilities and traits and one's role perceptions intervene between effort and performance. In other words, even though a person places a high value on the reward (1) and perceives a high correlation between the effort and reward (2) and thus puts out a lot of effort (3), this still may not lead to high performance (6). This circumstance may arise because the person just does not have the necessary

FIGURE 1-2.   The Porter and Lawler Model of Motivation.

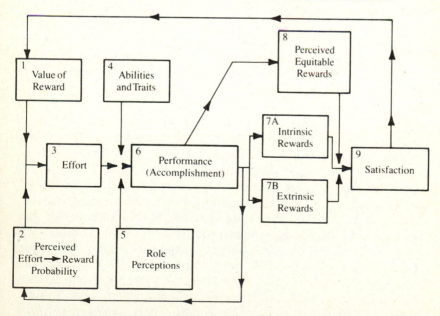

Reproduced with permission from Porter and Lawler, *Managerial Attitudes and Performance* (Homewood, IL: Richard D. Irwin, Inc., 1968, p. 165.

ability or traits (4) to perform well or perceives his or her role wrongly (5) and thus performs poorly.

Even more important, Porter and Lawler reverse the traditional human-relations assumption that satisfaction causes performance. Their model shows that performance, if equitably rewarded, will lead to satisfaction. Although there has been some supportive research evidence provided by Porter and Lawler and others (Kuhn, Slocum, and Chase, 1971; Lawler, 1971; Porter and Lawler, 1968; Schuster, Clark, and Rogers, 1971; Jorgenson, Dunnette and Pritchard, 1973), the model's reliance on unobservable internal cognitive processes such as role perceptions, expectancies, and traits/abilities make isolating and experimentally testing specific cause-effect relationships difficult.

In recent years, Attribution Theory has gained popularity among cognitive theorists. Unlike drive and expectancy theories, attribution theory is more concerned with the relationship between an individual's perception and interpersonal behavior. It is not directly a theory of individual motivation. Kelley (1967) emphasizes that attribution theory is mainly concerned with the cognitive processes by which an individual interprets behavior as being caused by (or attributed to) parts of the relevant environment. Heider (1958) believes that both internal forces (e.g., personal attributes such as ability or effort) and external forces (e.g., environmental attributes such as rules or the weather) combine additively to determine behavior; he also stresses that it is the perceived, not the actual determinants, that affect behavior. In other words, attribution theorists assume humans are rational and are motivated to identify and understand the causal structure of their relevant environment. Accordingly, following a behavior, the person will try to explain why it occurred. This cognitive process of assigning causes to behaviors is called the attribution process.

The concept of *locus of control* (does the person perceive his or her outcomes to be caused and controlled by internal or external attributes) flowing from attribution theory is especially relevant for explaining and predicting employee behavior. For example, Rotter and his colleagues (1961) suggest that the person's perceived locus of control will differentially affect behavior. When applied to work settings, studies produced some very interesting results. One found that employees under internal control are generally more satisfied with their jobs, are more likely to be in managerial positions, and are more satisfied with a participatory management style than are employees who perceive external control (Mitchell, Smyser and Weed, 1975). Other studies have found internal managers to be better performers (Anderson, Hellriegel and Slocum, 1977; Anderson and Schneier, 1978), more considerate with subordinates (Pryer and Distenfano, 1971), and likely to follow a more strategic style of executive action (Miller, Kets de Vries and

Toulouse, 1982). In addition, the general attribution process has been shown to have relevance in explaining goal setting behavior (Dossett and Greenberg, 1981), leadership behavior (Calder, 1977; McElroy, 1982), and the poor performance of employees (Mitchell and Wood, 1980).

Both the content (Maslow, Herzberg and Alderfer) and process (drive, expectancy, and attribution) theories depend on internal, cognitive states and processes to explain behavior. There is no question that they have helped us better understand behavior. In addition, the expectancy models indicate that certain internal states (e.g., valences and instrumentalities) are acquired and modified and the attribution theories even show considerable promise for predicting employee behaviors. These cognitively based theories also recognize the importance that consequences play in affecting internal events and future behavior. However, in dealing with the productivity problems facing today's human resource managers, conceptual understanding and possibly tenuous prediction are not enough. Something must also be done about controlling and changing behavior in organizations. Behavioral control and change require scientifically proven practical application techniques, which are conspicuously absent in the cognitive approach.

AN ALTERNATIVE ENVIRONMENTAL APPROACH

An external or environmental approach to the understanding, prediction, and control of organizational behavior is offered here as an alternative and supplement (not a replacement) to the internal cognitive approach. In the external approach, the control of observable behavior by environmental consequences is the key. This external approach is based primarily on the pioneering work of B. F. Skinner. Among Skinner's many contributions, his distinction between respondent (unlearned) and operant (learned) behavior has proven invaluable. On the basis of scientific research, he concluded that operant behavior is a function of its contingent consequences.

Surprisingly, management scholars and practitioners became so preoccupied with the internal explanations embodied in motivation theory that they overlooked Skinner's possible contribution. This oversight was noted by Nord (1969) as follows:

"Since the major concern of managers of human resources is the prediction and control of behavior of organizational participants, it is curious to find that people with such a need are extremely conversant with McGregor and Maslow and totally

ignorant of Skinner. This condition is not surprising since leading scholars in the field, of what might be termed the applied
behavioral sciences, have turned out book after book, article
after article, and anthology after anthology with scarcely a
mention of Skinner's contributions to the design of social
systems."

In the last few years this void in the study of organizational behavior
and the practice of human resource management has begun to be filled.
Most textbooks in the field now contain some material on the external
approach and an increasing number of applications of behavioral management are being reported in the literature and being tried in actual
organizations. However, compared with the internal approach, the
external approach still receives far less attention in both the theory and
practice of human resource management.

As it is presented in this book, the environmental approach to
organizational behavior is not designed to be another in a long line of
panaceas. It does, however, offer a theoretical base and a set of techniques which, if properly applied, can be a viable alternative or supplement to the internal perspective to human resource management theory
and practice. To refer to the application of the external, environmental
approach to human behavior in organizations, the term organizational
behavior modification, or simply O.B. Mod., was coined.

ORGANIZATIONAL BEHAVIOR
MODIFICATION AND BEYOND

Although the application of behavior modification to human
resource management was suggested by Luthans and White (1971), the
term organizational behavior modification, or O.B. Mod., was originally used by Luthans (1973) and later expanded by Luthans and
Kreitner (1973, 1974 and 1975), Luthans and Lyman (1973), and
Luthans and Ottemann (1973). Our original intent was to integrate the
knowledge embodied in the field of organizational behavior with that
called behavior modification. Our assumption was that despite the primary use of behavior modification on the relatively controllable behavior of children and the behavior of deviant adults, it could be
adaptable to the more complex behavior of organizational participants.
Over the last ten years O.B. Mod. has received increasing recognition in
the management literature and the practice of human resource management. Instead of just providing a relatively in-depth understanding of

the complexities of organizational behavior, which the internal approaches have supplied, the O.B. Mod. approach has given the behavioral approach to management both a sound theoretical foundation and a selection of practical methods for modifying, changing, and directing human resources toward the attainment of objectives in today's organizations.

Control of organizational behavior

As originally formulated, O.B. Mod. was based on operant learning theory and, more specifically, on the body of theoretical and practical knowledge known as behavior modification or applied behavior analysis (see Kreitner, 1982, for a complete discussion of the historical development of O.B. Mod.). Now, especially in light of attribution theory's potential for behavioral prediction, as discussed earlier, and the emergence of social learning theory (Bandura, 1977; Davis and Luthans, 1980) with its potential for more comprehensive understanding and implications for behavioral self-control (Luthans and Davis, 1979), modern O.B. Mod. has gone beyond its original operant premises. Although the original approach and principles are still valid and useful, O.B. Mod. has now gone *beyond* these to hopefully become an even more comprehensive and effective basis for modern human resource management. Our overriding assumption is still that behavior depends on its consequences. But unlike the more pure operant stance, a social learning premise also takes into account cognitive mediating processes (especially attributions which can be used to predict subsequent behavior) and covert (unobservable, nonenvironmentally based events) as well as overt environmental antecedents and consequences.

Succeeding chapters will chart the historical development and contemporary state of O.B. Mod. Conceptually, the O.B. Mod. approach is based on a four-term contingency illustrated in Figure 1-3. Based on a social learning theory foundation (rather than the more restrictive operant theory), the S-O-B-C model shows the interactive relationship of environmental (S and C), intrapersonal, cognitive (O), and behavioral (B) variables. The narrower operant model has a three-term contingency consisting of antecedent cues (A), behaviors (B), and consequences (C). By inserting the "O" we recognize the mediating role that cognitions can and do play in explaining behavior. Moreover, the S-O-B-C model expands upon the traditional operant model by recognizing covert as well as overt contingencies. One could disagree as to which letters to use in representing the four-term contingency, but the S-O-B-C is used here because of our earlier writings (e.g., Luthans,

FIGURE 1-3.   The Four Term Contingency for O.B. Mod.

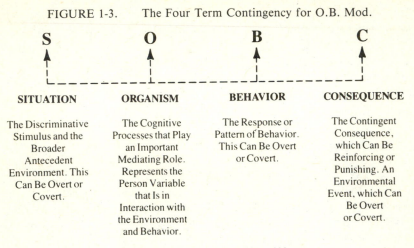

SITUATION	ORGANISM	BEHAVIOR	CONSEQUENCE
The Discriminative Stimulus and the Broader Antecedent Environment. This Can Be Overt or Covert.	The Cognitive Processes that Play an Important Mediating Role. Represents the Person Variable that Is in Interaction with the Environment and Behavior.	The Response or Pattern of Behavior. This Can Be Overt or Covert.	The Contingent Consequence, which Can Be Reinforcing or Punishing. An Environmental Event, which Can Be Overt or Covert.

Source: Davis and Luthans, 1980, p. 285.

1977, 1979, 1981; Luthans and Davis, 1979; and Davis and Luthans, 1979, 1980). We use these letters to represent a combination of the widely recognized, cognitively based S-O-R model (stimulus-organism-response) and the operant-based A-B-C model (antecedent-behavior-consequence). Regardless of the letters used, it should be emphasized that the S-O-B-C model does not abandon the emphasis given to behavior as the unit of analysis or the principles of the operant approach and their value for prediction and control in behavioral management.

In the terminology of Figure 1-3, the stimulus cues set the occasion for the behavior; the cognitions mediate these stimulus cues; and the consequences, in turn, increase, decrease, or maintain the probability that the behavior will occur again. The key to understanding this model centers on determining how and why various cues signal the individual that certain consequences will follow a specific behavior or behavior patterns. To facilitate a better understanding of the simple model in Figure 1-3, a closer look at the relationships between cues, cognitive mediators, behavior, and consequences is needed.

Cues, cognitive mediators, behavior, and consequences

Stimulus cues, as the term is used in the model, represent external environmental or covert events. These cues eventually become paired, through personal or vicarious experience, with various consequences of behavior. Cues take many forms—the behavior of supervisors, co-workers, and subordinates; physical objects, rules, information, formal and informal communications, instructions, schedules, commands, time, and technological instrumentation; or internal goals. Singly or collectively, these behaviors, objects, or covert events serve to cue organizational behavior. Cuing stimuli, in turn, may be mediated by cognitions such as expectancies or perceptions and attributions such as ability or luck. Actual behavior may have many consequences. Money, for instance, is a common consequence of organizational behavior. Social approval, attention, status, privileges, and feedback about performance are positive external consequences, whereas a feeling of accomplishment is a positive internal consequence. Negatively, social sanctions, ostracism, reprimands, demotions, transfers, pay docks, and terminations are common external consequences, whereas a feeling of disappointment is a common internal consequence.

Despite the possible weakening of the link between performance and rewards in contemporary organizations (i.e., most organizations today, except in commissioned sales and a few incentive systems in industry, do not have contingent pay plans based on performance), both the positive and negative consequences supposedly come as a result of performance or lack of performance. Management's intent notwithstanding, these consequences concurrently become associated with antecedent conditions (cues) and control the probability of the related behavior's recurrence. In terms of the predictability of ongoing behavior, it makes a great deal of difference if the stimulus-moderating cognitions-behavior-consequence (S-O-B-C) relationship is systematically managed or simply left to random chance. An O.B. Mod. approach does not leave this dynamic and important relationship to chance; it calls for a systematic analysis and management of all four elements.

Reactions to the foregoing discussion may be: (1) Isn't all this about stimulus cues, cognitive mediators, behavior, and consequences commonsense knowledge? or (2) Why confuse the issue of organizational behavior with cues, mediators, and consequences? These questions can be answered by noting that all organizational behavior is affected by these variables regardless of the knowledge or intent of the organizational participants (supervisors or subordinates).

All too often, the relationships among the S-O-B-C variables are random, unsystematic, inconsistent, or, in short, nonmanaged. In a nonmanaged work situation the supervisor may see a subordinate's particular behavior as related to certain internal events or under the control of a certain cue or consequence. The subordinate, meanwhile, makes different attributions and/or has learned to associate a completely different cue and consequence with the behavior desired by the supervisor. For example, an office manager may feel that a threat will stimulate a clerk's performance when, in fact, the manager's action prompts output restriction. In other words, the manager has failed to consider the dynamic relationship among cues, moderators, behavior, and consequences.

In a work situation where O.B. Mod. is used, the cue-mediator-behavior-consequence relationships are understood by both supervisors and subordinates because they are systematically and consistently identified and managed. Subordinates learn to recognize their cognitions and associate certain cues with certain consequences which are contingent upon or only come as a direct result of desirable performance. Behavior managers, as the direct or indirect controllers of many attributions and environmental consequences, must be systematic and consistent in the management of cue-mediator-behavior-consequence relationships. This behavioral management perspective is our point of departure for what follows. Chapter 2 lays the theoretical foundation for O.B. Mod. in more detail.

Theoretical Foundation

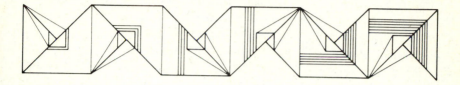

An important variant of the question "What makes people behave?" is the question "How do people learn?" Probably everyone, in varying degrees of sophistication, has their own personal learning theory. Then again, some of us may simply admit to knowing some things and not knowing others without any real idea of how we learned the things we know.

Numerous learning theories have been proposed by behavioral scientists and philosophers as well. There is little agreement among them; there is no single, universally accepted theory of learning. However, one common thread running through the behavioral science definitions of learning is the observation that a change in behavior takes place. After concurring on behavioral change, agreeing upon other aspects of learning becomes more difficult.

This chapter first defines what is meant by learning. The rest of the chapter is devoted to the historical background of learning theory. Without a working knowledge of learning theory, the reader and ultimately the user of O.B. Mod. would be left with a seemingly disjointed array of terms and techniques. A sense of history also enhances the credibility of any subject, including O.B. Mod.

DEFINITION OF LEARNING

One of the most heated controversies about learning centers around the internal versus external approaches discussed in the last chapter. The internal approach or *cognitive* theories explain learning through perception, thinking, judgment, expectancies, reason, and purposefulness. The external approach or *behavioral* learning theories deal with environmental contingencies, especially reinforcing consequences. Fortunately, in recent years, there has been a slow merging (rather than the former polarization) between cognitive and behavioral learning theories. Starting with the work of the famous social psychologist Kurt Lewin, most behavioral scientists today would recognize the importance of both cognitions and environmental contingencies. As was suggested in the opening chapter, there seems little doubt that such a comprehensive approach leads to the best understanding and explanation of learning. Yet, for prediction and control, the behavioral theories of learning seem to still offer more than the cognitive theories.

Behavioral learning theorists or behaviorists first make a careful distinction between *respondent* (reflexive, unlearned) behavior and *operant* (voluntary, learned) behavior. By definition, operant behavior is of major concern in human learning. After giving examples of respondent behavior such as the shedding of tears while peeling onions, Keller (1954) offers the following statement of what is meant by learned (operant) behavior:

> "Operant (voluntary) behavior includes an even greater amount of human activity — from the wrigglings and squirmings and crowings of an infant in its crib to the highest perfection and complication of adult skills and reasoning power. It takes in all those movements of an organism that may at some time be said to have an effect upon or do something to his outside world. Operant behavior operates on this world, so to speak, either directly or indirectly" (p. 2).

This behavior, which operates on and changes the environment, is how operant theorists explain learning. Thus, within this theoretical approach, the term *learning* is defined and used as *any change in behavior that results in a change in the environment.* As Keller (1954) notes, it isn't always easy to determine just how the environment is changed by the operant behavior. "Only when you look into the history of such behavior will you find that, at some time or other, some form of the response in question really did make things happen" (p. 2).

Because learned behavior is defined as having some effect on the environment, behaviorists deal primarily with objective or observable behavior. The cry of a child, the depressing of typewriter keys by a secretary, and the pushing of a turret lathe start button by a machinist are all objective, observable behaviors which have an effect on the environment. On the other hand, the child's need for attention, the secretary's attitude toward work, and the machinist's valence and expectancies of becoming a supervisor are all internal, cognitive events and are unobservable.

A merging of the external and internal approaches to learning seems desirable. The recently popular social learning theories (Bandura, 1976, 1977) are particularly well suited to provide a foundation for the extensions of O.B. Mod. (e.g., into areas such as modeling and self-control covered in Chapter 7). Yet, the radical behaviorism provided by Watson, and especially Skinner, remains a historically important theoretical base for O.B. Mod. After first going through these traditional approaches to behaviorism, the newer social learning theories are presented.

WATSONIAN BEHAVIORISM

In 1913, an outspoken young American psychologist, John B. Watson, opened up a whole new area of thought in the study of human behavior in this country. His article, entitled "Psychology as the Behaviorist Views It," became known as "The Behaviorist Manifesto." He picked up the conditioned reflex or stimulus-response (S-R) approach to behavior where the Russian physiologists, Sechenov and, more notably, Ivan Pavlov, left off. Although the article started a revolution in American psychology, it was not entirely original (Razran, 1965). Watsonian behaviorism and Russian physiology had some features in common, such as using objective behavior as a dependent variable and conditioned reflexes as the explanatory mechanism of objective behavior.

The classic stimulus-response mechanism

The Watsonian doctrine held that consciousness (e.g., thoughts or feelings) belonged in the realm of fantasy; human behavior could best be understood by studying observable, objective, and practical facts. In other words, Watson wanted to approach the study of behavior from the perspective of science rather than conscious experience and introspection. The latter approach had dominated psychology up to that time, but the European structuralists and American philosophers who espoused that approach were now being challenged by Watson to be more scientific.

Watson believed that all learned behavior consisted of responses elicited by prior stimuli. Relevant stimuli supposedly came from
within the organism as well as from the outside environment and continually bombarded the organism. In Watson's (1924) words, "Now the
organism does something when it is assailed by stimuli. It responds. It
moves. The response may be so slight that it can be observed only by the
use of instruments" (p. 13). Typical human responses ranged from gross
motor activity to minute changes in respiration or blood pressure, and
each response could be observed under the proper conditions.

Since Watson felt that most human behavior was learned, he
abandoned the concept of instinct (inborn tendencies to behave in certain ways), the then popular explanation for behavior. He substituted
habit for instinct. A habit was simply a learned response that eventually
became paired with stimuli capable of evoking it. Hence, a trained
behaviorist, according to Watson, was capable of predicting and controlling behavior by identifying the appropriate stimulus-response (S-R)
pairings. Watson's intentions were clear when he stated: "The interest of
the behaviorist in man's doings is more than the interest of the
spectator — he wants to control man's reactions as physical scientists
want to control and manipulate other natural phenomena" (Watson,
1924, p. 11).

Classic stimulus-response experiments

The famous experiment by Watson and Rayner (1920) probably
best illustrates Watsonian behaviorism. The object of the experiment
was to produce a conditioned emotional response in an eleven-month-
old subject named Albert. In proper Watsonian fashion, the subject's
behavior was carefully and systemically observed prior to the experiment. Albert was seen as sluggish but healthy. He responded with no
fear to successive presentations of unfamiliar neutral stimuli such as a
monkey, a dog, a white rat, a rabbit, cotton, wool, masks with and
without hair, and burning newspapers. This alone tended to refute or at
least question some of the popularly held notions about instinctive fear.
However, the experimenters did discover an unconditioned aversive
stimulus when they struck an iron bar with a hammer above and behind
the subject's head. The usually quiet Albert broke into a crying fit after
three such stimulations.

With this background, Watson and Rayner (1920) asked the
hypothetical question: "Can we condition fear of an animal, e.g., a
white rat, by visually presenting it and simultaneously striking a steel
bar?" The experimenters proceeded to present the subject with the
paired stimuli, one naturally aversive and one neutral. After several

pairings, Albert cried at the sight of the white rat alone. He had learned to associate the white rat with the naturally fearful noise of the hammer hitting the iron bar. In Watsonian terminology, an emotional response of fear had been conditioned through the systematic manipulation of environmental stimuli. Moreover, his conditioned fear of the white rat generalized to other furry things such as a rabbit, a dog, and a hairy Santa Claus mask.

In terms of a conditioning or learning paradigm (an ideal model), Watson and Rayner conditioned an emotional response in Albert in much the same manner that Pavlov (1927) had conditioned dogs to salivate at the sight of a luminous circle on a screen. Initially, Albert's crying in the presence of the white rat was as unnatural as a dog salivating at the sight of a lighted circle. But through the systematic presentation of paired stimuli, the child learned to associate the rat with a fearful noise and Pavlov's dogs learned to associate the sight of a luminous circle with food. Figure 2-1 outlines the conditioning paradigm which was operative during Watson's and Rayner's experiment with Albert.

Following the Pavlovian tradition, Figure 2-1 shows that a neutral stimulus (N.S.), the white rat, was paired with an unconditioned aversive stimulus (U.A.S.), the sound of a hammer hitting an iron bar. After a number of stimulus pairings, the previously neutral stimulus (white rat), when presented alone, elicited a conditioned emotional response (C.E.R.), which was crying. The conditioning (indicated by broken lines in Figure 2-1) gave a previously neutral stimulus aversive properties. As hypothesized, the experimenters were able to condition a fear response in Albert.

Watson's contributions

In spite of the legitimate criticism of Watson's somewhat thoughtless choice of an eleven-month-old subject, his relatively crude

FIGURE 2-1.   The Reflex or Classical Conditioning Paradigm.

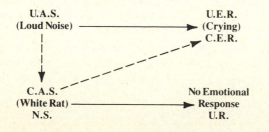

research design, and his overzealous generalizations, there can be little argument that he made some valuable contributions to the study of human behavior. As Watson's work became known, many American psychologists jumped on the Watsonian bandwagon. The popularity was a result of the confident and forceful simplicity with which Watson presented the behavioral constructs. Watson's approach especially appealed to those who had become disenchanted with the structural and functional approaches, which were preoccupied with the study of the elusive mind. As is often stated with tongue in cheek, Watson caused psychology to lose its mind.

In retrospect, Watsonian behaviorism became almost a fad and, like all fads, went out of style about as fast as it came in. Over 20 years ago Hilgard (1962) noted:

> "As enthusiastic supporters of such systems tend to do, they [the behaviorists] went to extremes, but gradually the excitement about behaviorism has subsided. There are still a few ardent behaviorists, but most contemporary psychologists are not extreme about it" (p. 17).

In spite of the fact that modern psychologists are not Watsonian behaviorists, the field of psychology has been greatly influenced by his work. Probably the single greatest impact comes from his recognition of the scientific value of studying observable behavior. Instead of taking hypothetical trips into the mind, Watson offered a viable, scientific alternative. He challenged the field of psychology to be scientific by saying:

> "Why don't we make what we can observe the real field of psychology? Let us limit ourselves to things that can be observed, and formulate laws concerning only the observed things. Now what can we observe? Well, we can observe behavior—what the organism does or says" (Watson and Mac-Dougall, 1929, p. 18).

His challenge to deal only with observable behavior has been heeded by many modern behaviorists. On the other hand, his preoccupation with S-R connections has been questioned. Contemporary behaviorists do not go along with Watson's S-R explanation for all learned behavior. Today, more attention is focused on the effect of consequences on objective behavior than on causal prior stimuli. Reinforcement learning theorists are largely responsible for this shift in focus.

REINFORCEMENT LEARNING THEORIES

Like Watsonian behaviorism, the reinforcement theories deal with objective behavior rather than cognitive processes. However, with the exception of Edwin R. Guthrie, who, like Watson, believed that learning resulted from the pairing of stimuli and responses, Watson's behaviorist successors placed increasing emphasis on the use of *reinforcement* or rewards in learning. This marked a significant departure from Watson's stimulus-response or S-R paradigm in which prior stimuli *evoked* or *elicited* a response.

Generally interpreted, reinforcement can only have an effect if the response comes first. This has meant a reversal of the traditional S-R paradigm. Since a reinforcing event in the environment could be interpreted as a stimulus, a response-stimulus or R-S pairing actually replaced S-R as the dominant theme of behaviorism. Among the learning theorists most often associated with this R-S orientation are Edward L. Thorndike, Clark Hull, Neal Miller, and most notably B. F. Skinner.

Reinforcement theorists argued that Watsonian behaviorism was not an adequate explanation of complex behavior. They saw learned behavior as strengthened or reinforced by rewards. The effect of reinforcement on behavior was initially proposed in the concept of hedonism. However, the reinforcement learning theorists went beyond simple hedonism.

Law of effect

The first comprehensive reinforcement theory of learning can be found in Edward L. Thorndike's famous law of effect. Through years of scientific animal research he discovered the impact of behavioral consequences. Rather than depending exclusively upon prior eliciting stimuli as the causal factor in learned behavior, as Watson had done, Thorndike turned to consequences for explaining behavioral change. The resulting law of effect was described by Thorndike (1913) as follows:

> "When a modifiable connection between a situation and a response is made and is accompanied or followed by a satisfying state of affairs, that connection's strength is increased: when made and accompanied or followed by an annoying state of affairs, its strength is decreased" (p. 4).

Stimulus-response connections, according to Thorndike's interpretation, are reinforced or strengthened by satisfying consequences. His law has had a lasting impact on the understanding and, especially, prediction and control of behavior. For example, Millenson (1967) claims that the law of effect " . . . survives today as a fundamental principle in the analysis and control of adaptive behavior" (p. 10) and even the cognitive motivation theorist Vroom (1964) concluded:

> "Without a doubt the law of effect or principle of reinforcement must be included among the most substantiated findings of experimental psychology and is at the same time among the most useful findings for an applied psychology concerned with the control of human behavior" (p. 13).

Drive-reduction theory

Another pioneering reinforcement theorist was Clark L. Hull. A Yale psychologist with an engineering background, Hull formulated a complex scientific theory of psychology, complete with mathematical postulates, logic, and theorems. Hill (1963) notes that "Hull did not regard his theory as a final statement about the nature of learning. Rather, it was intended as a tentative formulation, always subject to revision to bring it in line with new data or new ideas" (p. 132).

Hull's drive-reduction theory characterized behavior as being caused by the independent variables of deprivation, painful stimulation, magnitude of reward, and number of previously reinforced training trials. He felt that these four independent variables led to three intervening variables: drive, resulting from deprivation and pain; incentive motivation, tied to the magnitude of reward; and habit strength, derived from the number of previously reinforced training trials. Finally, a combination of drive, incentive motivation, and habit strength generate an excitatory potential, i.e., a tendency to respond in a given manner in the presence of an appropriate stimulus.

Despite the fact that it was more sophisticated than Watson's mechanistic interpretation, Hull's theory largely followed Watson's lead by contending that all behavior involves stimulus-response connections. Hull simply considered the effect of reinforcement while Watson did not. It is the habit-strength variable, based upon the number of previously reinforced training trials, that qualifies Hull as a reinforcement learning theorist. Otherwise, because of the central role of drives, he could be considered a motivation theorist.

Neal Miller, another Yale psychologist, extended Hull's theory. Miller divided learning into four basic elements: drive, cue, response, and reward. Like Thorndike and Hull, Miller considered the effects of both prior and subsequent stimuli on behavior. According to Miller, subsequent stimuli in the form of rewarding events have the capacity to strengthen behavior. For example, a small boy may learn to run to his father when he comes home from a trip. Broken down into Miller's elements, the boy likes candy (drive), so when he hears the garage door slam (cue), he runs (response) to his dad to get some candy (reward). If the boy in fact does receive the candy, this will strengthen the probability of running to his father in the future. Miller believed that all learned behavior could be broken down this way.

SKINNERIAN BEHAVIORISM

Like the others discussed above, Harvard psychologist B. F. Skinner could also be considered a reinforcement theorist. But in terms of empirical research, written literature, conceptual formulations, or controversy, Skinner certainly deserves special attention. He is so important that several years ago the American Psychological Association voted him the most influential living psychologist. In an articulate and logical fashion, Skinner has merged his predecessors' and his own work into a practical technology of learned behavior (see: Skinner, 1969; Skinner, 1971).

Watson and Thorndike laid the primary historical foundation for Skinner's work. Conceptually, Skinner's approach can be traced to Watson's preoccupation with objective, observable behavior and Thorndike's emphasis on the effect of the consequences of behavior. Over forty years of exacting laboratory and field research by Skinner, his students, and conceptual adherents have produced an impressive theoretical and empirical base for a comprehensive behavioral learning theory.

At the very heart of Skinnerian behaviorism is a single contention. Behavior is a function of its consequences. This Skinnerian explanation is based on the external approach; it emphasizes the effect of environmental consequences on objective, observable behavior. In Skinner's words (1953):

"The practice of looking inside the organism for an explanation of behavior has tended to obscure the variables which are immediately available for a scientific analysis. These variables lie outside the organism, in its immediate environment and in its environmental history" (p. 31).

The collective influence of both Watson and Thorndike is apparent in this statement. Before discussing more technical aspects of Skinnerian behaviorism, however, it may be interesting to analyze why Skinner and his works are so controversial.

The controversy surrounding Skinner

Find a dozen people who have heard of B. F. Skinner and quite probably a surprising number of them will be critical of him and his work. If the matter is pursued and the critics are asked exactly how familiar they are with Skinner's work, typically the answer will be that they have read excerpts from *Beyond Freedom and Dignity* (1971), Skinner's extrapolation of his research to societal analysis in which he says that the mechanisms for behavior go beyond the mere freedom of choice offered by the cognitive theorists. When one considers the logical sequence of a scientist's career (basic research, formulation, application, publication, and extrapolation), it appears that critics who are familiar with Skinner's work only through a quick reading or a second-hand account of *Beyond Freedom and Dignity* have overlooked the other crucial steps of Skinner's extensive career (see: Skinner, 1938; Skinner, 1953; Skinner, 1969).

Too often, the criticisms of Skinner and his works are based upon misinformation and misunderstanding. The general public and particularly many management practitioners have not been exposed to Skinner's basic premises and the many valuable contributions he has made to the study of human behavior. Instead, most people are familiar only with the extrapolation stage of Skinner's career. All they know of him is that he suggested behavioral control and manipulation of people as ways to change our culture. This, of course, collides with the cherished American concepts of individuality, freedom, dignity, and democracy. The desirability or lack of desirability of Skinner's extrapolation should not be allowed to depreciate the quality, importance, or relevance of his other work. It is his basic research findings and behavioral principles that are of particular interest to the development of O.B. Mod.

Management scholars or practitioners who take the time to carefully study Skinner's fundamental concepts of behavior control should see the potential application to managing human resources in today's organizations. Many of Skinner's concepts and principles have been empirically validated both in the laboratory and in field settings. Even his most ardent critics admit that his behavior principles work.

The position taken by this book is that the behavioral approach to management should study Skinnerian behaviorism and apply its techniques as the situation warrants. Skinnerian behaviorism certainly does not represent the final answer to the behavioral approach to management, but it does deserve special attention and its framework, principles, and applications techniques have, as Chapter 8 will illustrate, been shown to have a real and potential impact on the effective management of human resources.

The essence of Skinnerian behaviorism

In 1938, B. F. Skinner, then an assistant professor of psychology at the University of Minnesota, wrote a book, entitled *The Behavior of Organisms*. This book permanently altered the course of twentieth-century behaviorism and the entire field of psychology. While citing the significance of this book, Skinner (1938) noted: "One outstanding aspect of the present book, which can hardly be overlooked, is the shift in emphasis from respondent to operant behavior" (p. 438). With the publication of this book, Skinner made a break with his behaviorist predecessors by relegating stimulus-response connections to a comparatively minor role in the explanation of behavior.

While previous behaviorists, each to a greater or lesser degree, characterized all behavior as chains of S-R connections, Skinner looked beyond reflexes to demonstrate that environmental consequences are the controlling mechanisms of learned behavior. He attached the label *operant* to learned behavior because it operates on the environment to produce a consequence. He called unlearned or reflexive behavior *respondent* behavior.

Skinner was the first to make the important distinction between operant and respondent behavior. Had he not done so, behaviorists might have spent years developing patchwork formulations intended to explain all behavior in terms of S-R connections. In the Pavlovian tradition, contemporary Russian learning scholars still largely cling to this S-R paradigm; American behaviorists do not. Skinner's respondent/operant distinction has permitted today's behaviorists to portray the environment as a source of both prior and consequent stimuli which influence behavior. The traditional S-R paradigm has been found acceptable for explaining respondent behavior but unacceptable for explaining operant behavior. Operant behavior, as initially conceived by Skinner, is seen as that behavior which is shaped, strengthened, maintained, or weakened by its consequences.

Respondent and operant behavior

Respondent behavior is that behavior which is elicited by a prior stimulus. It most commonly occurs in the form of reflexes. To the extent that reflexive behavior comes naturally, it is unlearned. Healthy human beings do not have to learn to jerk their knee in response to a doctor's tap with a hammer or learn to shed tears while peeling onions. Respondent behavior is a function of our genetic history or endowment. It was this type of S-R scheme that the early behaviorists generalized to all behavior. Operant behavior, on the other hand, is emitted by the organism rather than automatically elicited by a definite prior stimulus; operant behavior must be learned. Most complex human behavior falls into this operant category.

Operant behavior, although it may become paired with prior stimuli, is not caused by the prior stimuli in the sense that the doctor's tap causes the knee-jerk response. For example, if an individual emits behavior appropriate to the successful driving of an automobile only when sitting behind the steering wheel, the steering wheel cannot be called a stimulus which elicits or causes the driving behavior. The driving responses are said to be emitted because of the effects they will produce in the environment, namely, getting quickly and safely from one location to another.

The fundamental difference between respondent and operant behavior may be further illustrated by the functional relationship between a response and the environment. With respondent behavior the environment acts on the organism in the form of a stimulus-response connection. In contrast, the reverse functional relationship is true in operant behavior. Organisms must act on their environment to produce consequences. For example, the doctor must tap the knee to elicit a respondent behavior (reflexive knee jerk) but the individual must drive the automobile in operant behavior. This difference is very important in understanding learned behavior.

Operant conditioning

With the distinction between respondent and operant behavior serving as a point of departure, it is now possible to examine a procedure Skinner called operant conditioning. Skinner (1953) makes the distinction between operant conditioning and respondent or classical conditioning as follows:

"Pavlov . . . called all events which strengthened behavior 'reinforcement' and all the resulting changes 'conditioning.' In the Pavlovian experiment, however, a reinforcer is paired with a stimulus; whereas in operant behavior it is contingent upon a response. Operant reinforcement is therefore a separate process and requires a separate analysis" (p. 65).

The influence of Thorndike's law of effect on operant conditioning is obvious. Essentially, an operant, once emitted by an organism, may be effectively controlled or conditioned (strengthened, maintained, or eliminated) through the systematic management of the consequences of that behavior. It is important to emphasize that this can only occur with operant or learned behavior.

Experiments in recent years indicate there is more accurately a gray rather than a black and white distinction between respondent and operant behavior. Further experimentation will eventually make this important distinction more functional. However, relative to the use of operant conditioning in behavioral management, there is no question that virtually all organizational behavior falls into the operant category. Organizational behavior is largely learned. It follows that the dimensions of learning brought out by Skinner may be relevant to human resource management.

The concept of contingency

The final Skinnerian contribution to be discussed is the concept of a behavioral contingency. Contingencies are specific formulations of the interaction between an organism's operant behavior and its environment (Skinner, 1969, p. 7). A contingent relationship could be simply thought of as an if-then relationship. Learned behavior operates on the environment to produce a change in the environment. Therefore, *if* the behavior causes the environmental change, *then* the environmental change can be said to be contingent upon the behavior. In other words, the specific environmental change only comes when the behavior has been emitted. For example, getting coffee from the office coffee machine is contingent upon inserting the proper coinage in the slot. If the proper coins are inserted, then coffee will come out. In this particular contingency we see an obvious behavior (putting in the coins) and an equally obvious consequence (coffee).

Technically, prior environmental conditions or cues also play an important role in contingencies. The Skinnerian concept of contingency involves three major elements: (1) a prior environmental state or antecedent cue; (2) a behavior; and (3) a consequence. The process of reducing a complex behavioral contingency into these three elements for analysis is termed *functional analysis*. Functional analysis attempts to systematically determine what antecedent cues are present when a specific response is emitted and, more importantly, what consequences are supporting that response.

Skinner (1969) contrasted the behavioral contingency concept (antecedent-behavior-consequence) with the more traditional S-R scheme in the following way:

> "The relationships are much more complex than those between a stimulus and a response, and they are much more productive in both theoretical and experimental analyses. The behavior generated by a given set of contingencies can be accounted for without appealing to hypothetical inner states or processes. If a conspicuous stimulus does not have an effect, it is not because the organism has not attended to it or because some central gatekeeper has screened it out, but because the stimulus plays no important role in the prevailing contingencies" (pp. 7–8).

By viewing all learned behavior in the context of contingencies, Skinnerian behaviorists have been able to study how behavior is learned by systematically managing the contingencies of animals in highly controlled experimental settings and studying humans in less controlled environments. A reliable technology of learned behavior has resulted. Much of the material in the succeeding chapters can be attributed directly or indirectly to the work of B. F. Skinner.

BEHAVIOR MODIFICATION: AN APPROACH TO BEHAVIORAL CHANGE

Watsonian and Skinnerian behaviorism serves as the framework and research base for the actual techniques of behavorial change traditionally called behavior modification. The precise meaning of behavior modification, like learning itself, is difficult to pin down. Goodall (1972) pointed out that in its relatively short lifetime, the term behavior modification has come to mean so many things to so many people that it is fast losing whatever meaning it once had. However, in its broadest interpretation, behavior modification refers to the application of techniques derived from operant conditioning paradigms, principles, and procedures.

An approach called *behavior therapy* is most closely associated with Watsonian behaviorism and classical conditioning. Behavior therapy, based on the work of Wolpe (1958) and others, is used in the clinical psychotherapeutic treatment of maladaptive behavior (for example, see: Sherman, 1973). Skinnerian behaviorism and its operant conditioning paradigm, meanwhile, has been widely applied in an approach commonly referred to as *applied behavior analysis*. It is carried on in natural, real-life settings. The emphasis is upon changing behavior through the management of consequences. Most of the specific behavioral change techniques presented in this book as O.B. Mod. could collectively fall under applied behavior analysis.

Traditionally, behavior modification (popularly known as B. Mod.) is the practical application of Skinnerian operant conditioning. Today, behavior modification has expanded beyond this original formulation. Owing primarily to more comprehensive social learning theory, modern approaches to behavior modification go beyond Skinnerian operant conditioning.

SOCIAL LEARNING THEORY

In circular fashion, behaviorists have criticized the cognitive approach for being too mentalistic and the cognitive theorists have accused the behaviorists of being overly mechanistic. In recent years, it has become increasingly apparent in both camps that both sides can indeed contribute something of value to the study of organizational behavior (Davis and Luthans, 1980). Neither theoretical base was really wrong. Instead, either the cognitive or classical/operant theories alone seemed too limiting and only provided partial answers to the complexities of human behavior. The individual (including internal cognitions), the environment, and the behavior itself all seemed to play important roles in the understanding and analysis of human behavior. Social learning theory has emerged to relate these three factors as interacting, reciprocal determinants.

Social learning theory is a *behavioral* theory. It recognizes and draws heavily upon classical and operant conditioning principles. In addition, however, social learning goes beyond the traditional behavioral approaches. Social learning theorists recognize that there is more to learning than direct learning via antecedent cues and reinforcing consequences. In particular, according to the most widely recognized social learning theorist Albert Bandura (1969, 1977b), social learning theory differs from operant theory because it embraces: (1) the role of vicarious processes (i.e., modeling); (2) the effects of covert cognitive processes; and (3) the role played by self-control processes.

Vicarious learning or modeling

Vicarious or modeling processes constitute the "social" part of social learning theory. Although social learning theory recognizes the operant view that learning takes place as a result of directly experienced response consequences, it goes beyond this by recognizing that learning can also take place by observing or modeling other persons in the social environment. Instead of just learning via the reinforcement of discrete behavioral responses, a person can learn vicariously by observing others.

According to Bandura (1969, 1976, 1977b), this vicarious learning or modeling is regulated by interrelated subprocesses such as attention, retention, motoric reproduction, and reinforcement. Very simply, the person learns by observing how others act and then acquires a mental picture of the act and its consequences. Next the person acts out the newly acquired image and, as in operant theory, if the consequences are positive the person will tend to do it again. If the consequences are undesirable, the person will tend not to do it again. Obviously, this process incorporates traditional operant principles. However, because it also involves cognitive, symbolic representation of the modeled activities, it goes *beyond* the strictly "external" operant approach.

The role of cognitive mediating processes

In addition to vicarious learning and modeling, social learning theory recognizes the role that cognitive mediating processes can play in the behavioral contingencies. For example, Bandura (1977b) states:

"However, most external influences affect behavior through intermediary cognitive processes. Cognitive factors partly determine which external events will be observed, how they will be perceived, whether they leave any lasting effects, what valence and efficiency they have and how the information they convey will be organized for future use" (p. 160).

This role of cognitive mediating processes in social learning theory was presented in the last chapter as the "O" in the four-term S-O-B-C contingency. This S-O-B-C framework represents an expansion of the operant A-B-C functional analysis. By inserting cognitive mediating processes (the "O"), the S-O-B-C contingency becomes a useful tool for functionally analyzing complex social behavior. It serves as a way to integrate and combine the operant and cognitive approaches with an eye toward better understanding and managing of organizational behavior.

The role of self-control processes

Self-regulatory functions become important once the role of cognitive mediating processes is recognized. The operant approach emphasizes the importance of external environmental contingencies, whereas the social learning approach recognizes the importance of both external environmental contingencies *and* internal (or covert) cognitively based antecedents (e.g., goals or expectancies) and consequences (self-evaluative rewards and/or punishers). Thus, the third major way that social learning theory goes beyond operant theory is the recognition of self-control processes.

Bandura (1976) points out that:

> "The notion that behavior is controlled by its consequences is unfortunately interpreted by most people to mean that actions are at the mercy of situational influences. In fact, behavior can, and is, extensively self-regulated by self-produced consequences for one's own actions . . . Because of their great representational and self-reactive capacities, humans are less dependent upon immediate external supports for their behavior" (p. 28).

Such self-control processes, of course, become especially important in organizational behavior modification. But like the other extensions of O.B. Mod. (i.e., vicarious learning or modeling and cognitive mediating processes), self-control is not a substitute for the role of external environmental contingencies for managing behavior. As social learning theorists Kanfer and Karoly (1974) point out, the introduction of self-control processes allows the person *supplementary* cognitive contingencies that are overlaid on the existing environmental contingencies. In essence, self-control processes permit the person to analyze and alter external regulatory contingencies rather than just mechanistically respond to them.

It should be pointed out, however, that simple awareness does not lead to self-controlling behavior relative to an O.B. Mod. approach to human resource management. As Kanfer and Karoly (1974) point out:

> "The degree to which internal stimulation and self-generated reinforcing events take on importance depends on the magnitude

and specificity of these variables, and on the richness and complexity of the person's available covert behaviors as they moderate and interact with the effects and directions of external controlling events" (p. 208).

In other words, the covert contingencies have to be managed in order to change behavior (although it may be self-management). This self-management dimension of O.B. Mod. will be given specific attention in Chapter 7.

O.B. MOD.: A THEORETICAL INTEGRATION

Figure 2-2 graphically and chronologically traces the theoretical foundation for O.B. Mod. As shown, O.B. Mod. is an approach to behavioral management based on several streams of theoretical development. First is the classical behaviorism of Pavlov and Watson that merged with Thorndike's Law of Effect to form "Skinnerian Behaviorism." This stream then merged with the work in cognitive behaviorism (i.e., some of the original notions of Lewin and then more fully developed by Tolman) into Bandura's work on social learning theory. Meanwhile, a different stream of theoretical development was evolving on the human side of management. This evolution can be traced to the early scientific management movement of F. W. Taylor and others who developed a variety of wage incentive systems. Subsequent developments included the famous Hawthorne studies that systematically pinpointed important dynamics of human behavior at work; the human relations movement that fostered personnel departments and more humanistic concern for employees; Douglas McGregor's famous Theory Y participative management; and, finally, modern organizational behavior with its sophisticated behavioral science and research-based approach and specific application techniques (one of which is O.B. Mod.). Thus, O.B. Mod. represents a merging of behavioral learning theory on the one hand and organizational behavior theory on the other.

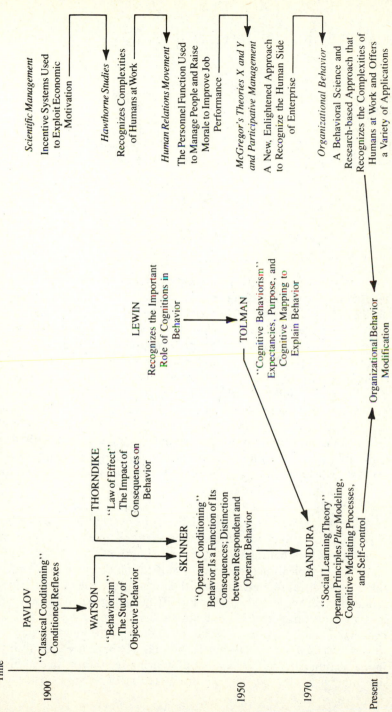

FIGURE 2-2. Historical Development of Organizational Behavior Modification

Behavioral Principles   3

Scientifically derived principles and techniques exist which can be used to effectively manage behavior. These principles and techniques have evolved largely from the work of the behavorial learning theorists discussed in the last chapter. Contrary to the mistaken notion of some people, organizational behavior modification is not a mystical process involving the psychological manipulation of people. Instead, it is a straightforward technology of learned behavior and, like any technology, has underlying principles and procedural methodology. A working knowledge of these principles and techniques will facilitate the development of the technical skills necessary for the successful application of an O.B. Mod. approach to human resource management. This chapter translates a vast amount of theoretical, technical, and empirical literature into workable form and language for human resource management.

At this point, you are asked to examine the following critical incidents which represent fairly typical human resource management situations. A surface analysis will suffice for now, but it would be helpful if you jot down some preliminary observations on each incident. In this exercise you will consider three typical situations, read the "what" and "how" of organizational behavior modification (keeping the incidents in mind as practical references), and then reconsider each of the situations from an organizational behavior modification perspective. The comparison of your analyses of the incidents before and after reading about organizational behavior modification should prove interesting.

Incident 1:   During an annual performance appraisal meeting, a section chief in a heavy manufacturing firm warns one of his first-line supervisors that he may be terminated after six weeks if his general attitude doesn't improve. Six weeks later the supervisor is terminated and complains of not knowing why.

Incident 2: A head nurse in a nonprofit hospital feels she should stay one step ahead of her subordinates by keeping them guessing. She feels that her practice of really raising hell with her entire staff once or twice a month helps keep them in line. While talking with a management consultant, she confides that her staff's overall performance and satisfaction are not what she would like them to be or thinks they could be.

Incident 3: During lunch one day, a secretary for an insurance company relates to a friend her observation that whenever the Claims Department boss comes to work in a bad mood and comes down hard on a couple of people, the mood of the entire office staff takes a turn for the worse. Everyone in the office becomes edgy and nervous and there is a lot of griping about the company.

FUNDAMENTAL BEHAVIORAL PRINCIPLES

Three fundamental principles seem to emerge from the growing literature on behavior management. They include: (1) the necessity of dealing with behavioral events; (2) the use of frequency of behavioral events as the basic datum; and (3) the importance of viewing behavior within a contingency context. An understanding of these principles is the first step toward applying O.B. Mod. to the practice of more effective human resource management.

Behavorial events

Deal in terms of specific behavorial events or responses that have an effect on the environment

Following the tradition of Watsonian behaviorism, organizational behavior modification takes a scientific view of human behavior. To satisfy the scientific goals of understanding, prediction, and control, the study of human behavior only deals with *behavior* as the unit of analysis. In experimental terms, the dependent (effect) variable is always behavior or behavior change which has an effect on the environment. The major independent (cause) variables include antecedents (cues) and consequences (reinforcement and punishment).

These independent variables are given attention later. The

dependent variable, behavior, is the focus of the first principle. However, just noting the importance of behavior is not enough. Realizing that the measurement of a dependent variable is a vital characteristic of a scientific approach, we must break behavior down into workable units. The working unit for organizational behavior modification is the *behavioral event*. Except when applied to modeling or self-control techniques that will be given attention in Chapter 7, it is generally preferable to deal with observable behavioral events and observable impacts on the environment. As Skinner (1969), referring to such behavioral events as responses, pointed out:

> "To be observed, a response must affect the environment—it must have an effect upon an observer or upon an instrument which in turn can affect an observer. This is as true of the contraction of a small group of muscle fibers as of pressing a lever or pacing a figure 8. If we can see a response, we can make reinforcement contingent upon it; if we are to make a reinforcer contingent upon a response, we must be able to see it or at least its effects" (p. 130).

The terms *behavioral event* and *response* are used interchangeably; they are the basic, measurable building blocks of behavior.

Figure 3-1 offers some examples of the difference between behavior and related behavioral events or responses. The behavior manager's basic building blocks are the behavioral events or responses, not overall behavior. Figure 3-1 shows that the behavioral events are much more specific and represent only one instance of a larger class of behavior. Although the identification of overall behavior gets the behavior manager headed in the right direction, it lacks the specificity necessary for a meaningful functional analysis. An effective functional analysis requires the identification, observation, and measurement of specific behavioral events.

Using the illustrations in Figure 3-1 as a general guide, you may want to construct similar examples. Behavior other than that listed may be identified or those in the figure may be reused to identify other possible behavioral events. The behavior listed represents a whole class of typical organizational behavior events. To do the exercise, simply identify a behavior, note its general effect on the environment, and observe and record related behavioral events as emitted by yourself or anyone around you. Then check back to Figure 3-1 and see if each of your listings of the behavior, the general effect, and the behavioral event is somewhat equivalent to those listed in Figure 3-1. You may find that this is not as simple as you thought it would be. Yet, in order to modify behavior, specific behavioral events must first be identified.

FIGURE 3-1. Identifying Behavioral Events

	Behavior	General Effect on the Environment	Specific Response or Behavioral Event
1.	Approving behavior (nonverbal)	Increases the strength of the approved behavior	A floor manager of a department store gives a subordinate a smile and a nod of approval.
2.	Approving behavior (verbal)	Increases the strength of the approved behavior	An Army sergeant tells a private to "keep up the good work."
3.	Disapproving behavior (nonverbal)	Decreases the strength of the disapproved behavior	An office manager shakes her head and frowns in disapproval of a clerk's action.
4.	Disapproving behavior (verbal)	Decreases the strength of the disapproved behavior	After a rough landing a flight instructor tells his student pilot to make a slower approach next time.
5.	Punctual behavior	Increases the probability of getting to designated places on time	An industrial-products salesperson arrives at the outer office of a potential customer five minutes early for an appointment.
6.	Tardy behavior	Increases the probability of getting to designated places late	An assembly-line worker in an automobile plant punches in twenty-five minutes after start-up time.
7.	Disruptive behavior	Disrupts or otherwise interrupts the productive behavior of others	An electrician taps a busy welder on the shoulder and tells him a joke.
8.	Productive behavior (in a work context)	Facilitates the achievement of organizational goals	A secretary rapidly types an error-free letter.
9.	Unproductive behavior (in a work context)	Hinders the achievement of organizational goals	An assistant personnel administrator in a hospital calls in sick and goes golfing.
10.	Instructive behavior	Increases the probability of another's productive behavior	A head bank teller takes time to suggest a more efficient way of handling a transaction to an assistant.

Frequency of behavioral events

Measure behavior in terms of response frequency

Measurement lies at the very heart of any scientific analysis. The dependent variable (observable behavior events, in this case) must be quantifiable so that the effect the independent variable has on it can be measured. Measurement of behavior has taken many forms in the past. Hilgard and Marquis' (1940) classic review of conditioning states: "Among the measures of strength of response used in inferring strength of conditioning may be mentioned magnitude, latency, percentage frequency, total number of responses, and rate of responding" (pp. 136–137).

Importantly, it was not until behavioral scientists started using rate of responding or *frequency* of behavioral events as a dependent variable that a science of behavior became a distinct possibility (Skinner, 1966, p. 16). An important change in emphasis accompanied the shift in focus. What the organism did or how it behaved was relegated to a position of secondary importance; the key lay in *how often* it emitted the response in question. In modern analysis, responses occurring frequently are said to be relatively strong whereas responses with low frequency are considered relatively weak. The important point is not the size or intensity of the behavioral event, but how often it is emitted. For example, it is not how fast the shipping clerk runs from the plant gate to the punchclock, but the frequency of his punching in on time or not that is important to behavior management.

The past dimension of response frequency • There are two important dimensions of response frequency which relate to time. As noted, a record of the frequency with which a given response has occurred during a specified time period indicates its strength. In this case, the time focus is historical or past-oriented. The behavioral events have happened and they are a matter of historical record. Records of such response frequency may be formally recorded on paper or recorded in a person's memory. For example, an employee with a reputation for prompt task completion may have that reputation because his or her personnel folder contains several performance appraisal sheets noting prompt task completions in the past. However, much less formal response records generally are kept.

Whether aware of it or not, most people carry countless response records in their memory. The common practice of labeling people shows this to be true. For example, Mr. A is the office flirt, Ms. B is a hard worker, Mr. C is a golf nut, Mr. D is honest because he pays all his personal debts promptly, and Mr. E is a bug on keeping the shop floor clean. Upon close inspection, each of these statements or labels reflects the strength of a particular response. Response strength is a function of observed response frequency, and response frequency is the basic datum for measurement of behavioral events.

The future dimension of response frequency • A second key dimension of response frequency deals with future time and the prediction of behavior. Probability goes hand in hand with the prediction of the future. Applied to frequency of response, probability is an extrapolation of the past; it is an inference based upon past rate of responding (Skinner, 1969, p. 118). The stronger a response, as indicated by its frequency of occurrence, the greater its probability of reoccurrence. By the same token, the weaker a response, the lower the probability of reoccurrence.

Although the concept of response probability may appear complex, people commonly make use of it. For instance, when a regional sales manager commends a salesperson for making an important sale, she is not attempting to alter the complex chain of behavior just emitted. That behavior has passed inalterably into history. The sales manager hopes that her commendation will increase the probability of similar behavior on the part of the salesperson in the future.

The relationship between the past and future dimensions of response frequency is subtle, but important. With regard to behavior prediction and control (the future), behavior managers attempt to alter the probability of response by systematically and consistently managing the consequences of behavioral events. Unavoidably, the success or failure of such behavior change efforts is revealed in a carefully kept record of response frequency (the past). In this manner, both dimensions of response frequency are appropriate to a science of learned behavior.

Mechanics of measuring frequency • There are certain mechanics of formally recording response frequency. The word *frequency* denotes a link between number of occurrences and time. More specifically, frequency measures the number of times a phenomenon has occurred during a specified period. People often speak in terms of such frequency when describing their daily lives. Some examples include: "I've been to eight conventions in two years"; "My golf game was really on today; I birdied four holes"; and "This word processor has misprinted twelve times today." Each of these statements identifies the frequency of some event over time. In each case something happened a given number of times during a specified time period. Our application of frequency to behavior management is similar except that more attention is given to *specific* responses as they occur over time.

Once a behavioral event has been identified and is under observation, the recording of its frequency of occurrence is made relatively simple through the use of a two-dimensional chart similar to the one shown in Figure 3-2. This procedure is called *charting*. The vertical axis represents number of occurrences and the horizontal axis represents elapsed time.

Inspection of the response frequency chart quickly shows the relative strength of the charted responses. By comparing the slopes or steepness of the three response frequencies charted in Figure 3-2, you can see that A is relatively stronger than B and B, in turn, is relatively stronger than C.

When response frequency is measured prior to attempts to change the behavior, the measurement is called a *baseline*. A baseline measure can tell an observer the natural or unmanaged strength of responses. In experimental terms, the baseline is essentially the control condition. Baseline data play an important role in any systematic approach to changing behavior.

A practical example of charting • Figure 3-3 shows how an on-the-job response such as unauthorized absences from the work area can be charted. Changes in the frequency of a single response such as the one shown in the figure reveal past consequences of that response. During the first month of observation, the response grew steadily stronger which suggests the presence of a favorable environment for such behavior. Also during the first month a pattern in responding seemed to be developing: Smith's unauthorized absences were less frequent on Mondays but increased during the week. Each Friday shows a new high. Evidently, the environment became progressively supportive as each weekday passed. Then suddenly on Monday, May 29, the employee emitted the response only once.

Since other relevant information is missing, one can only make an educated guess as to what caused the reversal. Considering the dramatic drop in frequency, it is very likely that Smith was contingently

FIGURE 3-2.   Charting Response Frequencies

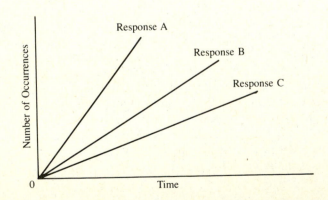

FIGURE 3-3.   Hypothetical Response Frequency Chart

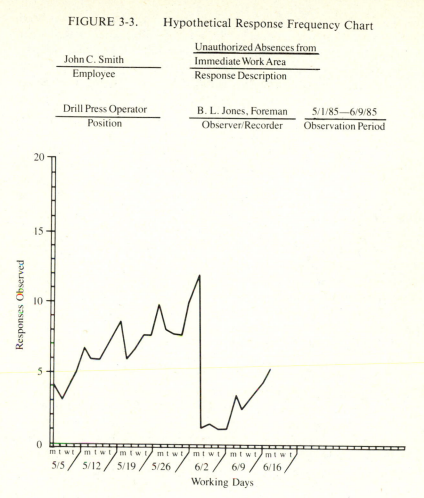

John C. Smith	Unauthorized Absences from Immediate Work Area
Employee	Response Description

Drill Press Operator	B. L. Jones, Foreman	5/1/85—6/9/85
Position	Observer/Recorder	Observation Period

punished for wandering away from his job. Unfortunately, as is frequently the case with punishment, the response dramatically dropped off but only temporarily. Smith's unproductive behavior subsequently re-established itself. Although this example does not cover all the dynamics of behavior change (later chapters are devoted to antecedent and consequence management), it does point out the importance of charting response frequencies when conducting a systematic analysis of behavior.

Our discussion of the response frequency chart had a noted absence of any reference to terms such as "attitudes," "motives," "drives," "desires," "needs," or "purposes." Except when dealing with modeling and self-control, or discussing cognitive mediation within the S-O-B-C framework, these inner states have not been widely used for helping to understand and change behavior. The frequency of observable behavior has been more widely used. Finally, when placed in the context of a behavioral contingency, frequency of response not only tells the behavior manager how strong a particular response is, but it also indicates the environmental conditions responsible for its strength.

Behavioral contingencies

Because behavior is a function of its consequences, the contingency relationship must be identified

Our third and final principle of behavior management is the basic premise that *behavior is a function of its consequences*. The importance of this principle derives from the vital connection between behavior and its consequences. Stated another way, behavior is strengthened, maintained, and weakened by its consequences. Consistent with the second principle, the strength of behavior is always measured in terms of response frequency. At the heart of this third principle is a concept that ties behavior management together: *behavioral contingency*.

Behaviorists use the term *contingency* to identify a dependent relationship between a person's behavior and its immediate antecedent and consequent environments. Consistent with the traditional preoccupation with objective behavior, reinforcement theorist's law of effect or social learning theorist's four terms, this contingent relationship describes how behavior is determined (i.e., controlled in response frequency) by its consequences. Thus, contingencies help isolate the effects of consequences on response frequency. Skinner (1969) identified the three-term contingency, from an operant perspective, as follows:

> "An adequate formulation of the interaction between an organism and its environment must always specify three things: (1) the occasion upon which a response occurs, (2) the response itself, and (3) the . . . consequences. The interrelationships among them are the contingencies . . ." (p. 7).

This three-term contingency was depicted in Chapter 1 as antecedent-behavior-consequence or A-B-C. Since cues represent antecedent events or events occurring prior to a response being emitted, an ANTECEDENT — BEHAVIOR — CONSEQUENCE, or simply an A-B-C model, can be used to identify each term and its relationship to the other two terms in the three-term contingency. Some common organizational examples that can be put into three-term contingencies are listed in Figure 3-4. At this point you may want to pick up where you left off

FIGURE 3-4.   Organizational Behavior Contingencies

	Antecedent	Behavioral Event ⟶	⟶ Consequence
1.	Payday	Opening the mailbox for a paycheck	Receiving a paycheck
2.	A manager enters the work area	Telling the manager how well the work is progressing	Receiving a compliment from the manager
3.	Proximity of the office clown	Asking if he's heard any good ones lately	Hearing a joke
4.	A messy work area	Ordering all machine operators to clean around their machines	A clean work area
5.	A letter in the "In" basket	Answering the letter	An empty "In" basket
6.	A pressure gauge needle nears the danger point	Making an appropriate mechanical adjustment	The pressure gauge needle returns to normal
7.	A computer program fails to run	Rewriting a format statement	The program runs
8.	An exceptionally hectic day at the office	Berating the secretary	The secretary's performance drops
9.	An overhead job needs to be quickly finished before quitting time	Climbing an unsafe ladder	Falling through a broken rung
10.	A position description posted on the luncheon bulletin board	Applying for the position in the personnel office	Getting the position

in identifying behaviors and related behavioral events derived from Figure 3-1 and observe and record some behavioral contingencies. Figure 3-4 can be used as a guide while you work on the "A-B-C's" of behavior management.

The A-B-C model is used in this book to represent the traditional operant three-term contingency. Functional analysis reduces complex operant behavior to A-B-C terms. Once reduced, behavioral events become manageable through the systematic and consistent control of consequences and consequence/antecedent pairings. However, to account for the role of cognitive mediating processes and covert as well as overt variables as in a social learning perspective, a four-term contingency is a helpful extension of the A-B-C model. This four-term contingency will be used throughout this book. As explained by Luthans and Davis (1979):

> "Unlike Skinner's A-B-C analysis, which concentrates on the need to identify observable environmental contingencies (A,C) in order to predict and control behavior (B), our expanded S-O-B-C functional analysis includes the mediating role of cognitive processes (O). When the four-term functional analysis is applied to self-management, the antecedent cues, or discriminative stimuli (S) and the behavior itself (B), and/or the contingent consequences (C) can be either overt (observable events) or covert (inner, private events)" (p. 44).

In response/consequence pairings in either the three- or four-term contingency, where the response must first be emitted before the consequence occurs, the consequence is contingent upon the response. In other words, an if-then sequence exists. *If* the response is emitted by the person, *then* the consequence occurs. Quiet employees, for example, may be contingent in their greeting behavior of co-workers; if someone says hello to them first, then they will reciprocate.

Importantly, as individuals learn to associate certain consequences with certain environmental occasions or even internal predispositions in (cues) self-control, other sets of if-then contingencies evolve. In this case, the "if" becomes a particular situation in the immediate environment such as physical location, commands, instructions, proximity of certain other people, or certain goals or expectations in self-control; the "then" becomes a response. As an example, if an enlisted man walks past an officer, then he will salute. Either by following rules or by actually learning through personal or vicarious experience which consequences are paired with which situations, the behavior of people may actually come to be controlled by environmental situations or internal cues in self-control.

Such so-called *stimulus control*, however, is not functionally equivalent to the classical conditioning S-R connection in spite of the surface similarity. Cues in the contingent relationship do not elicit (cause) learned responses in the manner that onion juice elicits tears; cues only *set the occasion* for the person to emit a response which is, in turn, followed by a consequence. In learned operant behavior cues do not *cause* the response, but they can control the response. More will be said about this important distinction in Chapter 5.

SPECIFIC PROCEDURES AND TECHNIQUES

The basic procedures and techniques of behavior management are primarily derived from the principles of operant learning theory and, to a lesser degree, social learning theory. Behavioral events are the common denominator, frequency of response permits objective quantification and measurement of behavior, and contingencies reveal the person/environment interaction. Each of the three principles was abstracted out of context for the purposes of description and analysis. Now they are placed back into a whole context for a discussion of the "hows" of behavior management. Some of the more important hows include intervention strategies, schedules of reinforcement, discrimination and generalization, chained behavior, shaping, and modeling. Each of these should be considered in light of the three principles of behavior management.

Intervention strategies

Behavioral control basically involves the management of contingencies. However, before contingencies can be managed, the manager must possess a working knowledge of the effects that various consequences have on response frequency. While the principle "behavior is a function of its consequences" speaks of a person/consequence interaction, it is not specific enough for a technology of behavioral change. It fails to describe exactly how consequences come to effect changes in response frequency.

Earlier it was suggested that behavior, in terms of the principles of response frequency, may be strengthened, maintained, or weakened. Yet, like the other principles, this one fails to describe how consequences affect frequency of responding.

Fortunately, there are specific answers to the questions raised by the principles of behavior management. Years of scientific experimentation have produced precise information needed for the control of response frequency with contingent consequences. Four general behavior management strategies have emerged. The four strategies are *positive reinforcement, negative reinforcement, punishment,* and *extinction.* These strategies for behavioral change may be used singly or in various combinations. Each strategy defines a class of consequences which has a particular effect on response frequency. However, it should be remembered that the consequences must be contingent upon a specific behavioral event.

Positive and negative reinforcement, punishment, and extinction may be called strategies if they are systematically applied as consequences to bring about changes in response frequency. But, it is important to note that the four approaches also work when applied in an unwitting, accidental, and unsystematic way. The point is, to varying degrees, everybody is already a behavior manager struggling to control behavior with consequences, but without specific knowledge of the principles and techniques. Hopefully, this book will allow the practicing human-resources manager to turn unsystematic and accidental control of organizational behavior into planned and carefully implemented strategies for more effective goal attainment.

Figure 3-5 illustrates three of the four alternative behavior management strategies and indicates the various effects each strategy has on response frequency. All four strategies share three common characteristics: (1) they are used to change the frequencies of objective behavioral events or responses; (2) in each strategy the consequence must

FIGURE 3-5.   Summary of the Operational Definitions of Positive and Negative Reinforcement and Punishment

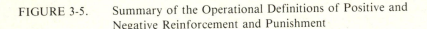
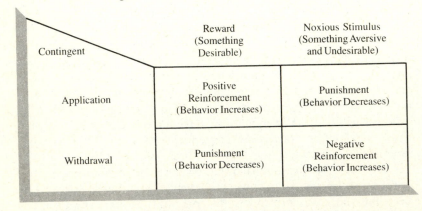

Contingent	Reward (Something Desirable)	Noxious Stimulus (Something Aversive and Undesirable)
Application	Positive Reinforcement (Behavior Increases)	Punishment (Behavior Decreases)
Withdrawal	Punishment (Behavior Decreases)	Negative Reinforcement (Behavior Increases)

Source: Adapted from Luthans, 1981, p. 25.

be contingent upon the specified response, so that immediacy is normally required to ensure a contingent relationship; and (3) the type of effect a particular form of consequence has on a response's subsequent frequency of occurrence determines its strategy category.

To clarify the last point, consequence strategies cannot be labeled subjectively or in an *a priori* manner. Consequences are named for their strategy category, i.e., if the presentation of a contingent consequence weakens a response by decreasing its frequency of occurrence, the strategy is called punishment and the consequence is labeled a punisher. Thus, consequences are not arbitrarily labeled, but are labeled in terms of what impact they actually have on response frequency. This, of course, permits an operational definition of reinforcement or punishment (i.e., if the response frequency increases after presentation of the consequence, then the consequence was reinforcing or if the response frequency decreases, the consequence was punishing). However, by operationally defining a consequence in terms of its effect on subsequent frequency, there is a potential problem with circularity and thus prediction and control.

Using the operational definition, what is a reinforcer (punisher)? The answer is any consequence that increases (decreases) subsequent behavior frequency. If the behavior manager wants to improve performance of an employee by increasing a certain behavior, what does he or she do? The answer is to provide a reinforcing consequence. What is a reinforcing consequence? The answer is any consequence that increases behavior frequency.

This circularity problem is analogous to the problem of defining the construct of intelligence. About the only operational definition of intelligence is "what an intelligence test measures." Definitions such as "ability to think" or "how smart a person is" are nonoperational and essentially useless for precise measurement. So the circularity problem crops up when answering the question: "What does an intelligence test measure?" The answer is intelligence.

The difference between operationally defining consequences in behavior management and defining intelligence is that the behavior manager must observe and count frequencies after trying a consequence to determine if it was a reinforcer or a punisher. In other words, follow-up observation and recording are necessary to define the consequence. In the case of intelligence, though, indirect measures (i.e., a questionnaire) of dubious reliability and validity are used to define an unobservable hypothetical construct (i.e., intelligence). Obviously, there are more problems with defining and measuring intelligence than with defining and measuring reinforcing/punishing consequences.

In addition to determining the nature of the consequence, successful use of the intervention strategies also depends on the ability of behavior managers to efficiently present and withdraw consequences in a contingent manner. It must be remembered that only the *contingent* consequences (i.e., those that link-up or those consequences upon which the behavior depends) will impact on subsequent behavior. The principles of behavior were developed under highly controlled experimental conditions. For instance, there is only one consequence in a Skinner Box. But in less controlled, highly complex settings such as a modern organization, there are many consequences for a given target behavior. Competing contingencies pose a real problem for the behavior manager. For example, he or she may provide a reinforcing consequence for an employee's behavior, while a co-worker provides a punishing consequence for the same behavior. Which one the employee attends to (links up with) will become the contingent consequence and affect subsequent behavior. Ways of overcoming both the circularity and the competing contingency problems are given attention in subsequent chapters. For now, the technical aspects of each strategy summarized briefly in Figure 3-5 are spelled out in more detail in the following sections.

Positive reinforcement • As Figure 3-5 shows, positive reinforcement is the consequence of reward contingently applied that strengthens or increases the frequency or subsequent behavior.

A positively reinforced response has a greater probability of reoccurrence simply because it pays off. For example, a student will repeatedly return to a favorite bookstore because he or she consistently gets good books there. (In this example, the determination of what constitutes a good book is irrelevant.) Since the response of going to the same bookstore is strong, some consequence must be reinforcing it. In this case, a good book is a positive reinforcer which maintains or strengthens the frequency of the student's visits to the bookstore. This entire process is called positive reinforcement and a positive reinforcement strategy is being used by the bookstore owner to attain organizational goals of sales and profits. The more frequently customers are positively reinforced by locating books they desire, the more successful the bookstore will be.

Negative reinforcement • Negative reinforcement is both like and unlike positive reinforcement and is often confused with punishment. It is like positive reinforcement in that it increases the frequency of a response but unlike positive reinforcement in that its reinforcing properties come through the contingent *termination* or *withdrawal* of some undesirable condition. As shown in Figure 3-5, negative reinforcement occurs when a noxious stimulus is contingently withdrawn and the linked behavior subsequently increases in frequency. Thus, negative reinforcement has the same effect on behavior as positive reinforcement and the opposite effect on behavior as punishment.

A simple example of negative reinforcement would be to close the window in a very cold room. Terminating the noxious flow of cold air into the room should increase the subsequent frequency of window-closing behavior in cold rooms. An organizational example would be the draftsman who works harder (emits more productive responses) to get a nagging chief engineer off his back. If, by working harder, the draftsman actually causes the chief engineer to stop nagging, then the hard work is said to be negatively reinforced. Contingent termination of the chief engineer's aversive nagging resulted in an increase in productive responses. Consequently the chief engineer's nagging is labeled a negative reinforcement strategy. Probably the most common negative reinforcer used by supervisors are threats—"If you don't shape up you are going to be in big trouble around here." Employees increase appropriate behavior in order to neutralize the threat of being reprimanded or fired.

An important point to remember is that negative reinforcement *increases* the frequency of behavioral events upon which it is contingent and thus is not the same as a punishment strategy. The term "negative" wrongly implies punishment to many people.

Punishment • As shown in Figure 3-5, punishment can occur in two ways (Kazdin, 1975). Something noxious can be contingently applied or something of value can be contingently withdrawn. Both strategies weaken or tend to decrease the frequency of subsequent behavior. For example, a manager may punish a tardy employee by assigning him or her to an undesirable job or by taking away the employee's morning break. Unfortunately, managers often inadvertently punish desirable behavior: for example, a bright young stock analyst stops telling his boss about new techniques he has developed because every time he has done so in the past the boss admonished him for wasting precious company time. The action of the boss is called a punisher because it served to kill the analyst's creative behavior. Intentional punishment is designed to decrease the frequency of unwanted behavior. Like the other strategies, it must be contingently applied to have the desired impact on behavior.

Extinction • Extinction has the same effect on behavior as punishment. It is a strategy that tends to decrease the frequency of subsequent behavior. But unlike punishment, extinction involves nonreinforcement of behavior. In other words, behavior that is ignored tends to disappear.

Obviously there is a fine line between punishment and extinction. For example, is taking a manager's company car privileges away for a downturn in performance punishment or extinction? Technically it depends on whether the withdrawal occurred before or after the actual behavior in question. It is usually considered punishment if the desirable consequence, that is normally part of the person's environment, is withdrawn *after* the undesirable behavior occurs. This would be akin to applying a noxious consequence. Extinction involves a withholding of normally occurring consequences prior to the person's behavior, i.e., the withdrawal occurs *before* the behavior is emitted. Thus, taking the company car privileges away is more of a punishment strategy (these were part of the normal environment and occurred after the undesirable performance behaviors) than an extinction strategy. Moving the "office gossip" away from co-workers to an isolated part of the room would be more of an extinction strategy. In this latter example, there is elimination of a desirable consequence (co-workers listening) prior to the gossiping behavior.

Importantly, extinction is not a "do nothing" strategy. Rather, it is a deliberate strategy to prevent the reinforcement of undesirable behavior. Since behaviors must be reinforced if they are to remain strong, it is apparent that behaviors that are no longer reinforced decrease in frequency and eventually disappear. Extinguished responses are replaced by alternate behavior that pays off.

If a door-to-door salesperson stops calling on a house after three different tries because he or she consistently finds no one at home, the response of calling on that particular house has been extinguished. The response has disappeared due to a lack of reinforcement (the reinforcer in this case is the answering of the door by a potential customer). If a housewife inside the house has been ignoring the salesperson's knock for whatever reason, she has effectively used a strategy of extinction to terminate the salesperson's calling behavior frequency.

In addition to these "pure" strategies, managers can use the following combination behavior change strategies.

Replacement/positive reinforcement • In behavior management, desirable, goal-oriented behaviors are usually incompatible with undesirable, dysfunctional behaviors. For example, attendance behaviors are incompatible with absenteeism, punctuality is incompatible with tardiness, productive behavior is incompatible with loafing, being courteous to customers is incompatible with being discourteous, and high quality work habits are incompatible with sloppy work habits. In each of these examples, among many in human resource management, both the desirable and undesirable behaviors cannot occur simultaneously. In one's behavioral repertoire, if the desirable behaviors are increasing in frequency, then the undesirable behaviors must be decreasing and, of course, vice versa. A behavior management strategy is needed which accelerates the desirable behaviors and decelerates the undesirable ones.

The simplest, but potentially most effective combination strategy, is to accelerate the desirable behaviors while permitting the undesirable behaviors to be replaced in the natural course of events. This replacement strategy is really a type of "Grandma's Law": "Accentuate the positives and the negatives will take care of themselves." By positively reinforcing a desirable behavior, it will increase. And because the undesirable behavior is incompatible, it will decrease. For example, by accelerating attendance behaviors, absenteeism will decrease.

Replacement is a *deliberate* strategy to decrease the frequency of undesirable behaviors. It is an effective strategy because it is easier to apply than extinction and does not have all the problems and undesirable side effects of punishment. In some situations, however, the replacement strategy may be inappropriate. For example, if the behavior manager observes an unsafe behavior, he or she may not be able to wait for a replacement strategy to decrease this behavior (i.e., positively reinforce the incompatible safe behavior). Other combination strategies can also be used to effectively manage behavior.

Extinction/positive reinforcement • If a replacement/positive reinforcement strategy isn't possible, then the behavior manager may use an extinction strategy to decrease the undesirable behavior and positive reinforcement to accelerate the incompatible desirable behavior. The use of extinction will avoid the problems and undesirable side effects associated with punishment, but it is usually difficult to apply. Consider, for example, the common situation of the overly dependent subordinate. Sometimes subordinates who have been around for a long time will behave like new employees and continually ask superiors for answers to problems they should be solving on their own. Consistent with the strengthening of positive reinforcement, the subordinate becomes dependent on the boss because such behavior has led to the speedy solution of his or her problems in the past. In short, dependent behavior has been positively reinforced and therefore increases in frequency.

Several strategies are open to the boss once he or she observes what is happening and resolves to bring about a change. One effective solution would be to use a strategy of extinction for the dependent responses (stop positively reinforcing them) and, in turn, positively reinforce independent problem-solving behavior. This approach can and should be open and aboveboard. Instructions from the superior may fully prepare the subordinate for a change in contingencies. If effective, the combination extinction/positive reinforcement strategy will weaken dependence and strengthen independence.

Punishment/positive reinforcement • This combination is designed to accomplish the same ends as the replacement and extinction/

positive reinforcement strategies, but through different means. Undesirable responses (i.e., those that detract from goal attainment in an organization) are followed by the application of consequences which weaken them. In other words, they are punished. At the same time, desirable, incompatible responses are positively reinforced and hence strengthened. Punishment may be chosen over replacement or extinction to weaken the undesirable response because it is so unsafe or disruptive that the time required for replacement or extinction to take effect cannot be spared. For example, horseplay by a worker on a dangerous job may require an immediate reprimand. Positive reinforcement of an incompatible attentive work response would constitute the other half of the punishment/positive reinforcement strategy in this case. Punishment is only used as a last resort, as discussed later in Chapter 6, because it is generally ineffective and may lead to more problems than it solves.

Schedules of reinforcement

In analyzing a specific behavioral contingency, a behavior manager must know more than simply "what" a contingent consequence is. "When" or "how often" the consequence follows the response in question is also important. Eventual success or failure of a particular behavior-management strategy frequently depends on the *scheduling* and *timing* of contingent consequences. The administration of reinforcement is as important to behavioral control as what the reinforcer is. For example, whether a consequence is made contingent upon every instance of a particular response or every tenth instance can greatly influence response strength. Similarly, the relation between the passage of time and contingent consequences has its own distinctive effect on response strength.

Empirical research on the effects that various schedules of reinforcement have on response strength has been carried out with animal and human subjects (Ferster and Skinner, 1957; Yukl, Wexley, and Seymore, 1972). Laboratory studies have uncovered some very consistent results on what impact various schedules of reinforcement have on frequency of responding. These studies have found that the timing of positive reinforcement is a fairly reliable causal variable in behavior. In fact, the schedule of reinforcement often has a greater effect on frequency of responding than the size or magnitude of the reinforcer.

For example, Yukl, Wexley, and Seymore (1972) experimentally demonstrated that a group of subjects performing routine tasks who were given the opportunity to earn $1.50 per hour plus the 50/50 chance to earn a 25¢ incentive (determined by a coin flip after the completion of each piece) outperformed an identical group earning $1.50 per hour plus an automatic incentive of 25¢ for each piece. These results point to the significance of how reinforcements are scheduled as opposed to the amount or size of the reinforcer. Other studies in laboratory settings (e.g., Berger, Cummings, and Heneman, 1975) have found similar results and verify what the operant theorists had been saying over the years. However, some field studies using tree planting crews contradicted what the laboratory studies found. Yukl and Latham (1975) and Yukl, Latham, and Pursell (1976) found that continuous schedules led to better performance of the tree planters. These researchers acknowledged some methodological problems with their field studies (e.g., the tree planters had values opposed to gambling and the intermittent schedule was implemented by tossing a coin for the incentive pay) and tried to correct them in a subsequent study (Latham and Dossett, 1978). In the follow-up study it was still found that the employees as a whole performed better under continuous reinforcement, but there were still some limitations in the study and there were some individual differences. Even though on-the-job research results are not yet definitive, an understanding of the basic schedules of reinforcement can be important to effective behavioral management.

As the term schedules of reinforcement suggests, virtually all of the research on the effects of various consequence schedules has almost exclusively depended upon positive reinforcement. This is because most behaviorists favor positive reinforcement and discourage the use of more unpredictable and ineffective strategies such as punishment.

Like the other areas of behavior management, schedules of reinforcement have highly specialized terminology. Continuous, intermittent, fixed ratio, variable ratio, fixed interval, and variable interval are all terms associated with scheduling reinforcements. Figure 3-6 lists the two major types of reinforcement schedules, *continuous* and *intermittent*, and four intermittent subtypes, *fixed* and *variable ratio*, and *fixed* and *variable interval*.

If a secretary is warmly thanked every time she voluntarily gets her boss a cup of coffee, that response is being continuously reinforced. However, because of the nature of a continuous schedule, the secretary's courteous service may stop (undergo extinction) if the boss either deliberately or inadvertently fails to thank her two or three times in a row. A continuous reinforcement schedule, simply known as CRF, is effective at maintaining response strength as long as reinforcement follows every time. Unreinforced responses, whether due to accidental oversight or deliberate plan, stand out in contrast to a continuous stream of reinforcement. Responses on CRF undergo extinction quite easily. In other words, the response stops being emitted shortly after the contingent reinforcement ceases.

Surprisingly, an intermittent reinforcement schedule which does

FIGURE 3-6.   Schedules of Reinforcement

Schedule	Description	Probable Effects on Responding
Continuous (CRF)	Reinforcer follows every response.	(1) Steady high rate of performance as long as reinforcement continues to follow every response. (2) High frequency of reinforcement may lead to early satiation. (3) Behavior weakens rapidly (undergoes extinction) when reinforcers are withheld. (4) Appropriate for newly emitted, unstable, or low-frequency responses.
Intermittent	Reinforcer does not follow every response.	(1) Capable of producing high frequencies of responding. (2) Low frequency of reinforcement precludes early satiation. (3) Appropriate for stable or high-frequency responses.
Fixed ratio (FR)	A fixed number of responses must be emitted before reinforcement occurs.	(1) A fixed ratio of 1:1 (reinforcement occurs after every response) is the same as a continuous schedule. (2) Tends to produce a high rate of response which is vigorous and steady.
Variable ratio (VR)	A varying or random number of responses must be emitted before reinforcement occurs.	(1) Capable of producing a high rate of response which is vigorous, steady, and resistant to extinction.
Fixed interval (FI)	The first response after a specific period of time has elapsed is reinforced.	(1) Produces an uneven response pattern varying from a very slow, unenergetic response immediately following reinforcement to a very fast, vigorous response immediately preceding reinforcement.
Variable interval (VI)	The first response after varying or random periods of time have elapsed is reinforced.	(1) Tends to produce a high rate of response which is vigorous, steady, and resistant to extinction.

not reinforce every response, at least in laboratory studies, tends to promote stronger behavior than does CRF. As Figure 3-6 indicates, intermittent reinforcement leads to stable and frequent responding. The common slot machine serves as a testimony of the tremendous power that intermittent schedules of reinforcement have on behavior. Its potential of a payoff on the next lever pull promotes coin-insertion and vigorous lever-pulling responses. Because slot machines pay off after a varying number of lever pulls, they reinforce money insertion and lever pulling on a variable ratio schedule.

When the reinforcement criterion becomes a fixed number of responses, a fixed ratio schedule is in effect. As Ferster and Perrott (1968) pointed out: "The term *ratio* refers to the ratio of performances to reinforcement" (p. 200). A bonus system in industry follows a fixed ratio schedule if employees can earn an incentive payment after producing a specified number of pieces. Of course, the traditional piece-rate wage system involves such a fixed ratio schedule.

The criterion for an interval schedule of reinforcement is the passage of time: the first response after a stated time interval has elapsed is reinforced. Although many responses may be emitted before the stated interval elapses, they go unreinforced. A common example of administering reinforcement on a fixed interval schedule is the hourly, weekly, or monthly payment of employees. An example of a *variable* interval schedule would be the regional sales manager who randomly drops by a local sales office, without prior notice, to formally recognize outstanding performance.

The various schedules of reinforcement have been largely either taken for granted or unsystematically administered by traditional management approaches. However, with an O.B. Mod. approach, schedules are given a great deal of attention and their vital contribution to more effective human resource management is recognized.

Discrimination and generalization

As discussed earlier, antecedent conditions set the occasion for responses to be emitted. By receiving different consequences in different situations, people learn to associate certain response/consequence relationships with certain antecedent situations. While both discrimination and generalization relate to this association, the mechanics of each are different.

As the word *discrimination* implies, people learn that certain responses are appropriate only in specific environmental settings. This simply amounts to identifying the various environmental cues necessary for certain behaviors to be emitted. We say hello to people we like because they probably will say hello back. Putting this example into functional terms, seeing someone we like sets the occasion for our response of saying hello, which has the consequence of a reinforcing greeting in return.

In a negative light, discrimination also enables a production worker or a clerical worker to look busy when a stern supervisor is in the area. The association between the antecedent cue of seeing the supervisor and the response of looking busy is a function of the worker's past experience. Perhaps at an earlier time, the supervisor punished the worker or punished someone the worker identified with for not being busy. Because discrimination is learned, people can be taught through managed contingencies to respond in appropriate ways in various environmental settings.

Specific environmental settings eventually come to serve as learned cues, telling the individual which responses are appropriate and what consequences are probable. By discriminating among environmental cues, an organizational participant can learn such things as who can be trusted with privileged information, who is good at providing answers to difficult problems, where to eat lunch, how to get to work, where and when to look busy, and where and when it is safe to loaf.

It is also possible for a particular response to *generalize* to more than a single environmental setting or cue. To the extent that cues and the consequences with which they are associated are similar, a person may come to emit the same response in a number of different situations. As with discrimination, the key relationship in generalization is still the antecedent-behavior connection. Generalization, however, broadens rather than narrows the antecedent control of behavior. For example, in vestibule training (duplicating on-the-job situations in a company classroom) trainers count on the trainees' ability to generalize the skills they have learned in the simulated setting to the real work area.

As with discrimination, generalization may be learned through the management of contingencies whereby programmed consequences are systematically and consistently matched with specific antecedents. It would be virtually impossible for people to cope with everyday events without relying on generalization.

Chained behavior

Only careful observation, identification of behavioral events, charting of response frequency, and recognition of response/consequence contingencies (in other words, functional analysis) can reduce complex behavior into the three-term A-B-C contingency. Obviously, this task can be difficult. One of the complicating factors is *chained behavior*.

Through operant conditioning, people build behavioral chains. Linkage occurs at the antecedent and consequences portion of the contingencies involved; a consequence in one contingency may at the same time serve as an antecedent in another. This dual consequence/antecedent relationship can best be illustrated graphically.

Figure 3-7 graphically depicts the chained contingencies of a simple behavior, the typing of a letter. Virtually all organizational behavior consists of such linked contingencies. When functionally analyzing complex organizational behavior, behavior managers should not overlook the dual roles that both consequences and antecedents can play.

When going from a three-term A-B-C functional analysis to the four-term S-O-B-C functional analysis, the chaining of behavior becomes even more complex. Figure 3-8 depicts the actual chains associated with preparing (or not preparing) a daily plan by a manager (Davis and Luthans, 1980b). This manager kept a behavioral diary of both the

FIGURE 3-7.   Chained Behavior in an A-B-C Contingency

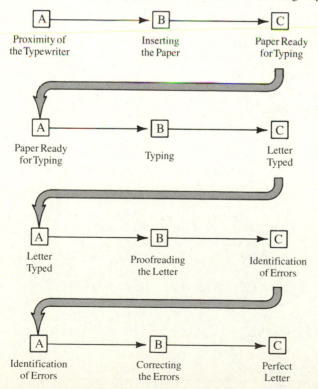

FIGURE 3-8.   Chained Behavior in an S-O-B-C Contingency

Chains of Discrete Behaviors/Activities — Leading to No Plan or to a Plan

The Role of Behavior/Activity (antecedent stimulus S; cognitive mediating process O; rewarding or punishing consequences)	Chain Leading to No Plan	Chain Leading to a Plan	The Role of Behavior/Activity (antecedent stimulus S; cognitive mediating process O; rewarding or punishing consequences)
S	Switch off the alarm	Alarm— 6:30 a.m.	S
	Get up	Get out of bed	
	Go downstairs	Switch off the alarm	
S	Turn on coffee	Go downstairs	
S	Put out dog	Take coffee off timer	S
S	Bring in paper	Put dog out	S
	Go back upstairs	Bring in paper	S
S	Enter bedroom	Drink coffee	C
O	"Will go back to bed for just a few minutes."	Read paper	C
	Get back into bed	Check clock— 6:45 a.m.	S
S	Get up with wife	Go back upstairs	
	Shower, shave, dress, and so on	Shower, shave, dress, and so on	
	Go downstairs	Check watch— 7:15 a.m.	S
C	Drink coffee	Leave home	
S	Look at watch	Leisurely walk	
	Leave the house	Arrive at restaurant— 7:30 a.m.	C
C	Hurry to office	Eat breakfast	C
C	Arrive late	Complete plan	C
C	No plan	Check watch	S
		Leave restaurant— 7:55 a.m.	
		Arrive on time— 8:00 a.m.	C
		Give planning sheet to secretary	C

Source: Adapted from Davis and Luthans, 1980b, p. 75.

events that resulted in no plan and the events that resulted in the preparation of a daily plan. This manager laid out the chained sequence of discrete behaviors that preceded his arrival at the office either with or without the plan. These behavioral events were functionally analyzed relative to antecedent stimulus cues (S), mediating cognitions such as thoughts and feelings (O), and consequences (C).

This chaining process, of course, can become quite tedious. But, as in the example above, if the behavior manager wants to systematically change the behavior in question, chaining can be very helpful in determining appropriate interventions and where they should be applied.

Shaping behavior

The shaping process can be important to behavior management. A given response may be emitted that does not yet meet the specifications of the standard or goal. For example, getting to work five minutes late is almost the same as being on time, but it still does not meet the punctual standard. However, by systematically reinforcing successive approximations, the behavior manager may shape a behavior to reach the desired goal.

The procedure is relatively simple. As closer approximations to the target response are emitted, they are contingently reinforced. Less desirable approximations, including those reinforced earlier in the shaping process, are put on extinction. In this manner, behavior may actually be shaped into what is desired. Shaping solves the problem of waiting for the opportunity to reinforce a desired response. It is a particularly important technique in behavior management if the desired behavior is not currently in the person's repertoire.

Beatty and Schneier (1972) reported an interesting and potentially valuable industrial application of shaping in the training of hard-core unemployed. Since the hard-core unemployed person generally comes from a disadvantaged background, his or her chances of obtaining and holding a regular job are not very good. In behavior management terminology, the behavior repertoires simply are not developed; that is, the person cannot quickly and efficiently emit productive on-the-job responses in order to receive the consequences contingent upon successful performance.

Beatty and Schneier developed a three-stage hard-core training model to counter this problem. The model consists of an off-the-job training stage, an on-the-job training stage, and finally, a complete job performance stage. The first two phases are gradual approximations to reach the third. By progressing through the three-stage sequence, a trainee's work responses are being systematically shaped.

Continuous reinforcement is initially used with weak responses or responses roughly approximating the desired productive responses. Positive reinforcement for satisfactory work is experienced, perhaps for many of the hard-core unemployables, for the first time. As the work responses grow stronger and more accurate, the reinforcement schedule is switched to variable ratio in order to facilitate stable performance and high rates of responding. Improvement is always reinforced.

Thus shaped into adequate performance, the trainees are exposed to the full demands of their new job. As behaviors learned during training generalize to the actual job, they are reinforced with contingent praise, feedback, and higher wages. Importantly, this type of training model also can be used to shape a number of other job behaviors such as punctuality, attendance, quantity, quality, and even initiative.

A side benefit of the shaping procedure, when applied to human resource management, is that it forces managers to look for desirable aspects of subordinate performance. Shaping must start with some approximation of the target or goal response. It works with *ongoing* behavior; it does not actually create behavior. Behavior managers are not preoccupied with what is wrong with their subordinate's performance. Instead, using this approach, managers strive to identify shapable approximations of desirable on-the-job responses and thus start to reinforce desirable behavior instead of commenting and focusing only on undesirable behavior. Once again, this is a case of "accentuating the positive" or catching employees doing something *right*.

Modeling

As was pointed out in the last chapter, besides the recognition of discrete behavior-consequence relationships in the understanding and analysis of behavior, the social learning perspective also recognizes the importance of vicarious and modeling processes. Especially in complex situations like today's organizations, most behavior is learned through modeling. Subordinates, co-workers, and superiors all show one another how to behave, and there are fairly reliable indications of what consequences may be expected when similar behaviors are emitted. Frequently, behavior does indeed speak much louder than words. For example, a safety engineer who smokes in a no-smoking area cannot reasonably expect other members of the organization to observe the rules.

Through modeling, organizational participants learn how to behave, learn relevant response/consequence contingencies, and learn when it is appropriate to respond in given ways. The modeling process is important because it can be managed just as environmental contingencies in the operant approach are managed. An understanding of modeling, like the other procedures and techniques discussed in this section, can lead to more effective human resource management. Chapter 7 will give more detailed attention to modeling.

APPLICATION OF PRINCIPLES AND TECHNIQUES

After reading about the principles, procedures, and techniques presented in this chapter you hopefully have gained an appreciation of the *technology of learned behavior*. It has a special language, its own body of theoretical and empirical knowledge, and a sophisticated collection of interrelated procedures and techniques capable of application to human resource management. However, as with any technical tool, behavior modification can also be misapplied by those who do not fully understand its complexities and subtleties.

To put the principles and techniques of behavior modification into a practical human resource management context, please reconsider the three incidents presented at the beginning of this chapter. Jot down your interpretations of the incidents before reading the following interpretations. Post-interpretations should prove interesting when compared with preliminary interpretations.

Incident 1 interpretation: "Firing the supervisor"

A man has been fired from his job, the severest economic sanction an organization can apply. Termination took place directly or at least indirectly because of factors such as a subjective performance appraisal, the unwitting and unsuccessful application of a negative reinforcement strategy, and failure to formulate specific objective goals for the six-week period.

One key question stands out in this incident. Did the first-line supervisor really deserve to be terminated? It is quite possible that the supervisor performed poorly or, in the "internal" terminology of the section chief, had a bad attitude. But was it the man who was at fault or was it the environment which was not conducive to his performing adequately?

The section chief's strategy was simple; he applied pressure on the man in the form of threatened termination, waited six weeks, and carried out his threat. His actions were those of a passive rather than an active behavior manager. Instead of actively applying his behavior-management skills by structuring the work environment to weaken the supervisor's undesirable behavior and strengthen desirable behavior, he chose to passively apply pressure and shift the entire responsibility for change to his subordinate. The section chief tried to change the person rather than the contingencies controlling the person's behavior.

In behavior management terms, the section chief attempted to use a threat of termination as a negative reinforcer. Removal of the threat was made contingent upon an improvement in the supervisor's general attitude. This action stands as a good example of the unwitting use of behavior management. Even if the manager was familiar with the principles of behavior management and possessed the appropriate skills, negative reinforcement would be very difficult to use effectively. In this case the section chief was not aware of or not able to utilize the principles discussed in this chapter. He was concerned with "attitude" when he should have been focusing his attention on the supervisor's performance-related behavior. Was the supervisor coming in late, overstaying his breaks, being disrespectful to his superiors, turning in unsatisfactory or false production and quality reports, or mistreating his subordinates? These latter possibilities relate to *behavior*, not vague internal states.

A behavior manager would have proceeded in the following manner. After specifically identifying the supervisor's desirable and undesirable behaviors, he would have collected some baseline data and carried out functional analyses to determine what consequences were supporting the behaviors in question.

On the basis of that information, the behavior manager would have met with the supervisor to identify the problem behaviors, mutually determine some realistic behavior improvement goals, and outline the contingencies for the next six weeks. By maintaining response frequency charts on the supervisor's key behaviors or by having the supervisor monitor his own behavior, the manager, after the six-week period had elapsed, would have sufficient objective behavioral data upon which to base a termination/retention decision.

Incident 2 interpretation: "The head nurse's style"

The head nurse has some behavior problems of her own. On the basis of her arbitrary and vague notion of how to manage human resources, she has chosen to rely heavily on the very potent but unpredictable behavior-control strategy of punishment. Compounding her problems is her noncontingent use of punishment. In other words, she is not consistently linking it to a specific behavior. Contingencies exist regardless of a manager's knowledge, intent, or desire. Even the indiscriminate use of punishers creates accidental contingencies that effectively reduce response frequencies. Unfortunately, many of the resulting weakened responses may have been productive or otherwise desirable goals like patient care in the hospital.

In effect, the head nurse is establishing unplanned contingencies with her unsystematic use of punishment. In a noncontingent environment people do not have the opportunity to learn precisely which responses will lead to which consequences. This is because response/consequence connections are random, unsystematic, and unpredictable. A noncontingent work environment generally has little chance of increasing the probability of productive behaviors.

In the final analysis, the head nurse must bring her own behavior under control (i.e., self-management using a S-O-B-C functional analysis as a starting point) before she can possibly hope to control the behavior of her subordinates by managing contingently. She should also move to a positive reinforcement strategy to accelerate the desirable behavior of her subordinate.

Incident 3 interpretation: "The boss's bad mood"

Modeling is the key behavior-management concept in this case, although punishment again enters the picture. Whether the Claims Department head realizes it or not, he is a highly visible behavioral model for his people. His position and status make him a very significant member of the work group. In many respects, as his behavior goes, so goes the behavior of the office. Aside from the effect of simply modeling the department head's behavior, the behavior of every work group member is affected to varying extents by the consequences of his or her relevant co-workers' behavior. When the department head comes down hard on one member of the work group, other members of the group who identify with the punished person may be vicariously punished (see: Bandura, 1971, pp. 47–51).

In other words, even though person A has been punished, person B's behavior may show the signs of punishment — reduced frequency of response. Vicarious punishment may create accidental contingencies that result in the weakening of desirable responses. Punishment often creates unwanted and unpredictable side effects such as anxious or counterproductive responses. Like the head nurse, the Claims Department head must put *himself* under the control of different contingencies and learn how to manage his people in a more contingent manner.

A Model for the Application of O.B. Mod.

4

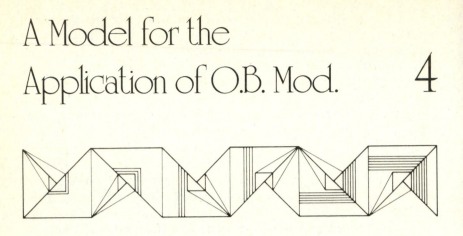

Taken together, the first three chapters can serve as the theoretical and technical foundation for O.B. Mod. and beyond. The term O.B. Mod. (organizational behavior modification), is used rather than just B. Mod. (behavior modification) to emphasize that the application is to organizational behavior and the modern practice of human resource management. Such applications have been largely ignored in the past and are just now beginning to emerge as a widely recognized behavioral approach to management. This chapter focuses directly on O.B. Mod. The others, of course, provide necessary background information.

THE PRACTICING MANAGER AS A BEHAVIORAL MANAGER

Going as far back as the famous Hawthorne studies of the late 1920s and early 1930s, the dialogue between behavioral scientists and those actually responsible for managing human resources has steadily grown in both quantity and quality. At first, the practicing manager, at best, sporadically read reports of behavioral science studies.

However, through the years managers have been exposed to progressively greater amounts of behavioral science theory and research. Knowledge is gained through formal collegiate education, professional organizations, management-development seminars, and numerous professional publications. Still more recently, a burgeoning consulting business has placed behavioral scientists and practicing human resource managers in direct contact with one another.

Generally, this relationship between the behavioral science consultant and the management practitioner has been mutually rewarding. Too often, however, the behavioral scientist, as a management consultant, has prescribed or pushed for one particular approach or technique without the benefit of an adequate diagnosis. This brings to mind the situation of an unsuspecting patient with an earache who retains the services of a doctor who is bent on performing an appendectomy. In an effort to generate more situational sensitivity, full-time applied behavioral scientists and internal change agents are beginning to be employed in personnel or human resource development departments.

Today, the question becomes, how can behavioral science concepts and techniques best be economically and pragmatically applied to improve human resource management? The answer, at least in the long run, is to educate and train practicing managers themselves in the theories and methods of behavioral science. By understanding and applying what is embodied in O.B. Mod., the practicing manager, in a sense, can become a behavioral manager.

This interpretation of a manager is valid to the extent that the manager collects and interprets behavioral data (diagnosis) and selects and applies appropriate behavioral techniques (prescription). While the practicing manager must continue to depend on the academic behavioral scientist for new theoretical concepts, techniques, and tools, an O.B. Mod. approach allows him or her to collect diagnostic behavioral data on the job. Strict reliance on data collected under highly controlled conditions and analyzed and interpreted by academic behavioral scientists is unnecessary. This does not mean that the behavioral scientist is relegated to a dusty academic shelf; much is needed in the way of rigorous theory building and empirical research. However, it does imply that the behavioral scientist is best equipped to carry out original research while the practicing manager, given the appropriate perspective, knowledge, and skill development, is in the best position to carry out the practical applications in managing human resources.

Traditionally, the diagnostic tools proposed by behavioral scientists have been steeped in academic jargon, tied to the internal approach, or dependent upon sophisticated statistical analyses. On the other hand, O.B. Mod., with performance behavior as its basic datum, can provide a workable behavioral technology for the practicing manager. In particular, on-the-job behavior is readily quantifiable when reduced to frequencies of behavior. O.B. Mod. allows the practicing manager to collect behavioral data with relative ease. With the practicing manager collecting and interpreting behavioral data and subsequently applying proven intervention strategies and techniques, the diagnostic/prescriptive circle can be neatly closed within the confines of today's organizations.

ORGANIZATIONAL BEHAVIOR VERSUS ORGANIZATIONAL ACTIVITIES

There is not a one-to-one relationship between an employee's behavior and common measures of organizational effectiveness such as profitability or service. In O.B. Mod., a distinction must be made between individual behavioral events, performance, and organizational consequences. The ramifications of this distinction should be fully understood by the practitioner in order to implement an O.B. Mod. approach to human resource management.

Organizational behavior repertoire

Each employee has a unique set of behaviors or a behavioral repertoire. This repertoire contains all the responses the organizational participant has learned and is capable of emitting, and it is constantly changing. The left-hand side of Figure 4–1 depicts the employee's behavior repertoire. It shows that only part of the repertoire is performance related. The repertoire also contains many potentially dysfunctional or counterproductive behaviors and behaviors unrelated to

FIGURE 4-1.   Matching Organizational Behavior Repertoire with Organizational Activities

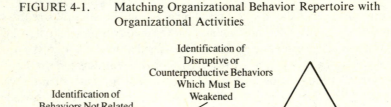
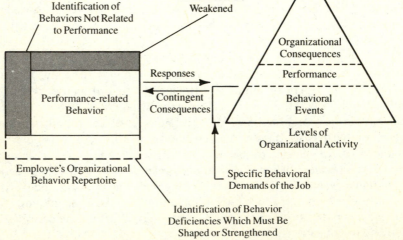

performance. In addition, the repertoire does not contain all the necessary behavioral demands of a particular job. As Figure 4-1 indicates, the process of matching the individual employee's behavior repertoire with the behavioral performance demands of the job necessitates some learning, and occasionally, some unlearning. To facilitate effective matching, the connections between specific behavioral events and more conventional measures of organizational activity need to be identified.

In the traditional approach to human resource management, practitioners do not use the behavioral event as a common denominator. Instead, they typically deal in terms of the organizational consequences of behavioral events. Organizational consequences are really changes in the environment caused by behavior. Terms such as "performance," "effectiveness," "reliability," "efficiency," "profitability," and "service" are commonly heard in descriptions of organizational activity. Performance appraisals are common but *behavior* evaluations are rare. Although performance and other measures of organizational success are certainly important—"the bottom line"—they are of little value to a functional analysis of behavior. "Profitability" cannot be directly placed in the context of either a three-term or four-term contingency. On the other hand, specific behavior leading to profitability, when reduced to behavioral events, plays a vital role in functional analysis. O.B. Mod. concentrates on behavioral events that lead to organizational performance. In practical application, however, it is often sufficient and necessary to deal with what could be called "behavioral products." In the important areas of application such as quantity and quality of performance, identifying and measuring the end result (i.e., the behavioral product) may be sufficient providing that the correctness of the behavior authorship is assured and that there is in fact a one-to-one (or at least known) correspondence between the behaviors and the products being identified and measured (Johnston, Duncan, Monroe, Stephenson, and Stoerzinger, 1978).

A major task for the contingency manager is to identify performance-related behavior in employees' behavior repertoires or their behavioral products. Also, it is important to distinguish between behavior that threatens to restrict performance and behavior that has no impact on performance. Finally, the successful and effective human resource manager must make employees aware of behavior that would lead to improved performance, but that is not currently part of their repertoire.

Figure 4–2 lists some common examples of the varying levels of specificity. These examples show that the behavioral event level is usually necessary for a meaningful functional analysis. For instance, telling a shopworker to be safety conscious is much less specific than telling her or him to immediately clean up any oil spills. Both safety

FIGURE 4-2.   Examples of Behavioral Event, Performance, and
               Organizational Consequence

Very Specific	Intermediate	Very General
Behavioral Event	*Performance*	*Organizational Consequence*
Recording the solution to a complex management problem	Personal effectiveness	Increased productivity Greater return on investment Increased rate of growth
Praising a hard-working subordinate	Rapport with subordinates	Greater job satisfaction Lower absenteeism Lower grievance rate
Replacing a worn-out drill bit	Attention to detail	Cost effectiveness Decreased scrap and rework
Recalculating a capital budget figure after finding an error	Professional knowledge	Lower cost of capital
Working in an extra sales call at quitting time	Personal commitment	Greater share of the market
Immediately cleaning up an oil spill on the shop floor	Safety	Prevention of accidents

consciousness and cleaning up oil spills are intended to have the organizational consequence of fewer accidents, but only the cleaning up of oil spills is a specific behavioral event that can be functionally analyzed and directly changed.

At this point, it will be instructive for you to identify and record some personally observed examples of the various levels of organizational activity, using Figure 4–2 as a guide. Special effort should be made to ensure that each behavioral event identified does in fact lead to the specified organizational consequence. This exercise will help clarify the important distinction between behavioral events, performance, and organizational consequences and will demonstrate the relationship between them.

Naturally, as one proceeds up the organizational hierarchy, from relatively simple and repetitive tasks to more complex executive-level problem solving and decision making, the identification of performance-related behavioral events or their direct products becomes more difficult. But this is not to say that the identification becomes impossible. Behavior can be observed throughout the organizational hierarchy. Problem-solving executives emit behavioral events just as drill-press operators do. The latter are simply more readily observed than the former. In cases where employees work by themselves, self-observation and self-control may also be learned. An O.B. Mod. approach can be applied to all levels with covert self-control processes as well as overt behavioral events related to measurable performance.

EMERY AIR FREIGHT: A WIDELY PUBLICIZED BEGINNING

Over ten years ago, Emery Air Freight's experience with behavioral management was widely publicized in practitioner-oriented journals and a training film, "Business, Behaviorism, and the Bottom Line" (CRM-McGraw-Hill). These write-ups and the film told of the very significant "bottom line" benefits that could be gained from a behavioral approach to human resource management.

Under the general guidance of Edward J. Feeney, who was then vice-president of the company and who currently has his own private consulting firm, Emery was able to save a reported $2 million over a three-year period by identifying performance-related behaviors and strengthening them with positive reinforcement (Performance Audit, 1972). In Feeney's words, "Our end is improved performance, and we've been damned effective in getting it" (At Emery Air Freight, 1973). Feeney put a few basic behavior management techniques to the practical test of modifying on-the-job behavior and succeeded. The emphasis placed on providing feedback to employees about their performance seemed to contribute more than any other single factor to the program's success.

A careful performance audit was first conducted to identify the relatively few job behaviors with the greatest impact on profit. The approach taken by Feeney was then to give specific feedback to those responsible for the high-payoff behaviors. Despite all the information generated by industrial engineering, many employees learned for the first time how they were really doing their job. This feedback was very important to them.

The air-freight container utilization at Emery provides the best example of the value of a performance audit. As a major air-freight forwarder, Emery requires the extensive use of freight containers. Economic, space, and time constraints collectively operate to necessitate maximum utilization of these containers. Emery loses money if a container is not full when the truck leaves for the airport. Because of the importance of maximizing container utilization, the warehousemen who loaded the containers had been thoroughly trained and frequently encouraged to increase their use of empty container space. Because of the extensive effort, both managers and dock workers believed that containers were being used 90 percent of the time (Where Skinner's Theories Work, 1972). However, when put to the test of objective measurement, the performance audit team found the container utilization to be around 45 percent, not 90 percent.

The need for more training was discounted in favor of Feeney's program of feedback and positive reinforcement. Self-feedback was provided by the dockworker as he kept a checklist when his container utilization rate was between 45 percent and 95 percent a day. As a consequence, container utilization jumped tremendously almost immediately and Emery benefited from the program by saving $520,000 in the first year.

Effective simplicity characterized the Emery program. First, the performance audit identified key performance-related behaviors. Second, management established a realistic output goal and gave the relevant employees feedback, mostly provided by the employees themselves, of how they were performing. Finally, increases in performance were systematically strengthened through the use of contingent positive reinforcement (P.R.):

> "In those areas in which Emery uses P.R. as a motivational tool, nothing is left to chance. Each manager receives two elaborate programmed instruction workbooks prepared in-house and geared to the specific work situation at Emery. One deals with recognition and rewards, the other with feedback. Under recognition and rewards, the workbook enumerates no less than 150 kinds, ranging from a smile and a nod of encouragement, to 'Let me buy you a coffee,' to detailed praise for a job well done" (At Emery Air Freight, 1973).

Under this program, Emery employees received accurate and reliable feedback on their performance and positive reinforcement contingent upon improvement. This deceptively simple human resource management approach paid off handsomely for Emery Air Freight. Provided that a program makes effective use of the performance audit, Feeney is confident that his approach can work elsewhere. He states, "I have yet to see any performance area that can function effectively without an effective feedback system and a program of consequences — positive consequences — for the right behaviors" (Performance Audit, 1972).

It is important to remember that Feeney claims that this program saved Emery Air Freight $2 million in three years. These "bottom-line" results are very impressive and understandably received considerable attention by organizations seeking ways to solve their productivity problems. The publicity surrounding the Emery behavioral-management experience served as a stimulus for many companies to try this approach to human resource management. For example, in 1981 alone, Feeney and his staff of 20 full-time consultants worked with over 100 companies (How to Get More from Your Employees, 1981).

Unfortunately, the results at Emery and subsequent claims by Feeney of 200% to 600% return on investment for his work with consulting clients (How to Get More from Your Employees, 1981) have not been subjected to systematic, methodologically accepted evaluations. At least as they are reported in the literature, the results from Emery are mainly based on testimonials by Feeney. Nevertheless, the Emery experience served as an important precedent for modern behavioral management and O.B. Mod. because it was so widely publicized and convinced performance-oriented practitioners that here was finally a behavioral approach *that worked* and could affect the bottom line. Chapter 8 will present O.B. Mod. applications that had similar results to Emery that do use systematic, methodologically accepted evaluations.

THE STEPS OF O.B. MOD.

The authors (Luthans and Kreitner, 1974) formulated a general O.B. Mod. problem-solving model that provides a general methodology for identifying and contingently managing the critical performance-related behaviors of employees in all types of organizations. Figure 4-3 shows the model arranged in its logical flow. Very simply, the approach can be summarized by five one-word steps: (1) identify; (2) measure; (3) analyze; (4) intervene; and (5) evaluate. Each of these five basic steps and related substeps is described and analyzed in the balance of the chapter.

FIGURE 4-3.   O.B. Mod. Model

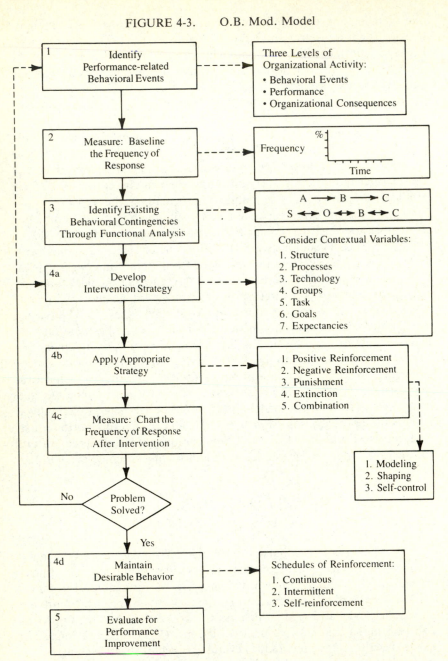

Source: Adapted from Luthans and Kreitner, 1974, p. 13. Reprinted by permission of the publisher from *Personnel*, July-August 1974. © 1974 by AMACOM, a division of American Management Associations.

Step 1: Identify performance-related behavioral events

As discussed earlier, organizational activity may be broken down into three different levels: behavioral events, performance, and organizational consequences. Users of O.B. Mod. need to deal with the most specific level of organizational activity, behavioral events.

From the standpoint of performance, behavioral events may be classified as desirable, undesirable, or irrelevant. Intervention is required when desirable behavioral events occur too infrequently or undesirable behavioral events occur too frequently. Once identified, desirable behaviors must be strengthened and maintained and undesirable behaviors must be weakened and extinguished.

Although value loaded, the term "desirable" is simply used to identify those behaviors which eventually lead to the accomplishment of predetermined organizational objectives. "Undesirable" behaviors, on the other hand, refer to those which directly or indirectly inhibit or detract from the accomplishment of predetermined organizational objectives. The process whereby desirable and undesirable performance-related behavioral events are identified is the focus of Step 1 in O.B. Mod.

As a guide for the practitioner, the following four basic questions should be answered:

1) Can the behavior in question be reduced to observable behavioral events?
2) Can I count how often each behavioral event occurs?
3) Exactly what must the person do before I record a response?
4) Is this a key performance-related behavioral event?

The answers to these questions will lead to the identification of an appropriate behavior for Step 1 of the O.B. Mod. model.

Observable and countable behavior • The importance of dealing only with observable, countable behavioral events has been repeatedly mentioned. A matter that has not received as much attention so far has been the exact meaning of behavioral events. Consistent with a precise technology of learned behavior, the dependent variable (behavior) must be precisely defined. First of all, each behavioral event must have a distinct beginning and a distinct end. Behavioral events are units which change the direction of complex behavior chains. As Brandt (1972) has observed: "No clear-cut standards have been established for determining the size of behavioral units to be measured. These seem to vary primarily with the purposes of the investigation and the specification of variables to be studied" (p. 130).

Often when supervisors and managers are asked what behavioral problems they have with employees, they respond with perceived problems such as "bad attitudes" or "goofing off." Attitudes, of course, are not directly observable and countable and are, therefore, not acceptable for Step 1 of O.B. Mod. Only directly observable behavioral events such as absenteeism, tardiness or staying at the work station, or behavioral products such as quantity or quality of widget-making, or services performed are suitable for this approach. Also, something like "goofing off" needs to be broken down further into more precise, observable and countable behavioral events such as being absent from the work station, returning late from breaks, spending considerable time in the lounge or at the water fountain, or perhaps flirting.

While widget-making activities in today's organizations generally consist of easily observed behavioral events, other service or knowledge-based job activities are not so obviously delineated. For example, consider the case of the manager working on a budget. A typical observation of this activity would be that the manager is sitting there "thinking." The behaviorist, however, does not deal in terms of thinking, instead behavior is the unit of analysis. Looking away from the paperwork, attending to the paperwork, completing calculations, and correctly completing the budget satisfy the fundamental behaviorist requirements. For convenience, an extended behavior, such as attending to a work task, can be readily broken up into minutes or any other time span. One-minute periods of uninterruped attention to a task can be easily recorded, especially on a random time-sampling basis.

Only performance-related behavior • Ensuring that the behavior is performance related is as important as identifying observable, countable behavioral events. Numerous behaviors are emitted in any work situation. Some of these behaviors are related to performance and some of them are not. For example, a supervisor may focus on a subordinate's complaining behavior. However, even though it is irritating to the supervisor, this complaining behavior may have nothing to do with the subordinate's performance. He or she may complain all the time but perform outstandingly on assigned tasks. If so, the complaining behavior is irrelevant.

On the other hand, if the supervisor determines that the complaining behavior is disruptive and counterproductive relative to the subordinate's and/or others' performance, then this would be an appropriate target for change. If the behavior is not performance related, then the subsequent steps of the model become meaningless.

Once again, the purpose of the O.B. Mod. model is to improve performance, not merely to change behavior.

Managers should search for organizational consequences of behavior as an aid to identifying performance-related behavior. For example, the manager might ask the question: What would happen to production records or quality standards if employees did not emit response X? Workers on an assembly line who do not show up for work generally cause lost production time that may not be recoverable. On the other hand, a clerical worker who is absent may have the work sitting on his or her desk when he or she returns, with no lost time production. In the former case, staying at the work station is a critical performance-related behavior, while in the latter case it may not be.

The issue of identifying critical performance-related behavior becomes more complex when collective or group performance is considered. An overriding goal is to identify those behavioral events, individual or collective, with the greatest impact on performance. An example of where collective behavior comes into play would be in the fast-food industry. Heavy emphasis is placed on how long it takes to complete a customer's order. Getting hot, tasty food to customers as quickly as possible is the very essence of their business. Presenting a customer with a properly filled order within a specified period of time would be a critical behavioral event. But this is directly or indirectly the result of the behaviors of several people. In this case, the behaviors must be broken down further and the priority of performance-related behavioral events must be established. As a guideline, human resource managers using this approach should concentrate on the "20–80" behaviors, rather than the "80–20" behaviors. This means that the first step of O.B. Mod. should identify the 20 percent behaviors that impact on 80 percent of performance rather than the 80 percent behaviors that impact on only 20 percent of performance.

Nonbehavioral performance problems • To identify performance-related behavior and assign priorities, managers using this approach may find the framework shown in Figure 4–4 useful. This framework makes a clear distinction between behavioral and nonbehavioral performance problems. Just as not all behavior is related to performance, not all performance problems are related to behavior. Sometimes an employee simply cannot "cut the mustard" because of a lack of the necessary ability to perform adequately; this constitutes a staffing or selection problem, not a behavior problem. Someone with the appropriate ability should be found for the job. On other occasions some training may be necessary to erase a skill deficiency. The employee simply does not know the proper procedures necessary to do the job

FIGURE 4-4.   Framework for Identifying Performance-Related Behavior

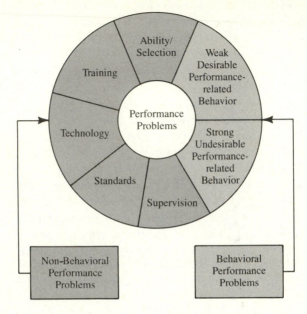

adequately. In other cases, a malfunctioning, outdated, or inefficient machine may be the source of the performance problem. This problem could be labeled technological inefficiencies. The machine portion of the worker/machine interface must be remedied. Behavior management cannot directly remedy performance problems caused by mechanical or technical shortcomings.

        Another source of potential performance problems is unfair output standards. A worker producing at 75 percent of standard may be doing a tremendous job but be working with a standard which was mistakenly set too high. Behavior management will not help this "performance" problem. Unsatisfactory subordinate performance may also be due to improper surpervision or undesirable behavior on the part of the supervisor. Behavior management can be applied in this case, but with the supervisor not the subordinate.

        As with all management techniques, behavior management must be carefully implemented. Ability/selection, training, technology, standards, and supervision problems could rule out the application of behavior management. As the introductory comments of the book pointed out, there are numerous behavioral problems facing today's management. The model presented in this chapter is one systematic approach to help solve performance-related behavior problems. Each manager's ability to identify relevant behavior will largely determine the subsequent success of this approach.

Step 2: Measure the frequency of the behavior

The second basic step in the O.B. Mod. model involves measuring the strength of the performance-related behavioral event(s) identified in the first step. A baseline measure of response frequency indicates how often the behavior is occurring under existing conditions, i.e., prior to attempts to change it. This baseline measure in and of itself is often very revealing. Sometimes the behavior turns out to be very low frequency and the manager realizes that it is not a problem after all.

For example, a supervisor may feel that one of his subordinates has a tardiness behavior problem because "that guy is never on time." Upon objective measurement of tardiness behavior, he finds that the subordinate, on the average, is late once every two weeks. With objective data in hand, the supervisor decides that the tardiness behavior does not significantly affect the performance of his department. In other instances, the reverse is true. In the case of the Emery Air Freight container utilization problem cited earlier, upon measuring the frequency, management discovered that the behavior problem was much greater than was thought. In any case, the measure serves as a baseline for comparative purposes when a manager intervenes in an attempt to change behavior (Step 4 of O.B. Mod.).

There are many ways of measuring frequency of response; the best method depends on many factors. Some methods are more comfortable or natural to managers than others. The key is not in choosing a method of measurement but rather in accurately recording frequencies. In most cases the data for baseline purposes is already available (for example, from quantity or quality records maintained by the engineering or production staff or absenteeism or tardiness records kept by personnel).

In other words, there are all kinds of data being generated by today's computerized information systems. Managers are challenged to ferret out these existing data and use them for this measurement step of behavioral management. The beauty of such archival data is that, because they are generated for other purposes, there are no problems with reactivity or slanting the data for the purposes of behavioral management. Archival data are what researchers call an "unobtrusive measure" (Lockwood and Luthans, 1980; Webb, Campbell, Schwartz, and Sechrest, 1966). Because they are unobtrusive, archival data tend to be more reliable.

If existing data on performance behavior identified in Step 1 are not available, then a measurement scheme must be developed. Two general approaches to recording are to observe and count every response, or to observe and count samples of on-the-job responses. The former technique can be used where the observer can devote considerable time to the measuring task. However, because time is limited for most practicing managers, time-sampling techniques (similar to the common work-sampling techniques of industrial engineering) are more realistic and, if used properly, equally accurate.

Tally sheet • A tailor-made tally sheet is usually first devised to gather the behavior frequency data. Observers should have definite predetermined criteria for the data. For example, what is the criterion for tardiness—punching in one second late on a time clock or five minutes and over? What constitutes being away from the machine—is it any time the operator isn't there or are allowances made for getting material? Criteria can be determined by the relevant manager but, for measuring purposes, must be consistently applied. Another important facet of gathering behavioral data is to attempt to reduce the observation into only two alternatives, yes and no. Yes, the employee is tardy, or, no, he or she isn't. Yes, the operator is absent from the machine or, no, he or she isn't. This greatly simplifies the observer's data gathering and eliminates the possibility of subjectiveness entering the measurement.

Figure 4–5 gives an example of a typical tally sheet. Remember, the tallies usually have to be tailor-made because situations vary.

Awareness of measurement • An important issue in measuring is whether or not the person being measured should be aware of it. O.B. Mod. works best when it is completely aboveboard. However, there is the possibility, in gathering certain types of behavioral data,

FIGURE 4-5.   Sample Tally Sheet for Frequency Data

John Jones	Tardiness (Starting Time, Breaks, Lunch)
Employee	Behavior Description

Bookkeeper	Ruth Smith, Office Manager
Position	Observer/Recorder

6/1/85-6/6/85
Observation Period

Times	Monday		Tuesday		Wednesday		Thursday		Friday	
	Yes	No	Yes	No	Yes	No	Yes	No	Yes	No
8:05										
10:20										
1:05										
2:35										

that the data will be distorted because the person is aware of being measured. Therefore, if the behavior manager feels this is the case, then he or she should devise the tally to minimize this effect. This could be accomplished by keeping a mental record and then recording the data on the tally a short time after, or using counters similar to those used by golfers or supermarket shoppers and then transferring the data to the tally at a later time. Under some circumstances, self-observation may be used. Usable data may be obtained by positively reinforcing accurate self-observation response frequency tallies (this was done successfully at Emery). Also, self-observation may be an effective behavior change strategy. An exact knowledge of how often a person is emitting an undesirable response will often induce him or her to exercise self-control and, of course, provides immediate feedback.

Even with the techniques mentioned above, data distortion due to awareness can still occur. The old approaches to time and motion analysis are an example. Time-study specialists were often frustrated in their efforts to collect reliable data because those being observed could change the normal work environment and thus affect the rate of response. Yet, the awareness problem is not as predominant in today's work environment as it was earlier. The reason is that industrial engineers and supervisors are constantly gathering every kind of imaginable data from today's employees. As a result, employees are relatively immune to being observed and receiving special attention. Thus, distortion stemming from awareness of being measured may not be as big a problem as it appears to be on the surface.

Time sampling • Another practical problem is that busy behavioral managers cannot possibly tally every response of a high-frequency behavior. This, of course, is why the time-sampling technique is so useful. When the behavior occurs regularly throughout the workday, the observer may randomly pick one or more short time periods during which to observe and tally the frequency. For example, suppose a supervisor in a fabricating shop determines that a particular operator's frequent absences from the work area have the effect of reducing output. Being too busy to stand around and inconspicuously record numerous responses per day, the supervisor may choose to randomly pick five minutes during every hour to sample the behavior frequency. While the resulting baseline data do not include all instances of the behavior, if the observations are truly random, there is an accurate indication of the behavior strength. If the behavior is as important to performance as it should be, the time invested should pay off handsomely for managers using this approach.

Transferring tally data to graphs • The same reasoning applies when the tally data are transferred to the actual graph. Normally, the vertical axis of the graph is percentage frequency and the horizontal axis is the time dimension. Percentage frequency is stressed because if the manager misses observing the employee for some reason, he or she can still get a representative frequency from the percentage data.

Figure 4–6 shows a typical graph derived from the tally sheets. Data gathered from existing records should also be graphed. With the avalanche of computer printouts descending on most managers today, graphics are becoming increasingly important. In fact, an insightful adage may be: "A graph is worth a thousand pages of computer print-out." Through visual inspection, managers can quickly obtain an accurate picture of the baseline measure of performance-related behavior. When an intervention strategy is implemented in Step 4, managers can visually see the results in terms of behavior frequency. Seeing this frequency movement in visual, graphic terms in and of itself provides immediate, objective feedback that can be very reinforcing for the behavior manager.

FIGURE 4-6.   Behavior Frequency Chart

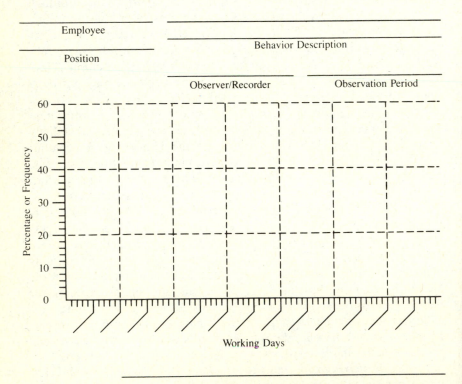

Step 3: Identify existing contingencies through functional analysis

Before the manager can intervene and actually begin to change behaviors, one more preliminary step must be taken. This step involves a functional analysis of the behavior that has been identified and measured. A functional analysis answers two key questions: (1) What are the antecedents to the behavior (i.e., the A in the A-B-C operant contingency and the S-O in the S-O-B-C social learning contingency); and (2) what are the contingent consequences (i.e., the C in both A-B-C and S-O-B-C)? Unless applied to modeling and/or self-control processes (e.g., as will be discussed in Chapter 7), the more simple A-B-C functional analysis is sufficient for the performance behaviors usually identified in Step 1 (Luthans, 1980). For example, Figure 4–7 functionally analyzes attendance and absenteeism behaviors with some representative antecedents and consequences.

The basis for such functional analysis is that the identified behavior (desirable or undesirable) is being maintained by the antecedents and consequences. For example, in the case of undesirable behavior, in order to decrease it, the functional analysis must determine what the consequences reinforcing it are so they can be removed or replaced. It is not enough to simply identify the B's; the antecedents and consequences also need to be identified and analyzed.

One supervisor using the O.B. Mod. model outlined in this chapter determined that his people took an excessive number of restroom breaks (i.e., Step 1 was absence from the work station). He calculated that if the operators devoted the time they spent in the restroom to the task, the unit production record would show a significant increase (i.e., Step 2 of measurement revealed a significant performance deficiency).

In functionally analyzing this behavior, he found that the "A" was the clock. The workers were taking unscheduled breaks almost precisely at 9 A.M., midway between starting time and their first regularly scheduled break, and 11 A.M., midway between their scheduled break and lunch. Thus, the clock served as the antecedent condition (A) for emitting the unscheduled break behavior (B). Significantly, the clock did not cause the behavior; it only set the occasion and served as a cue for the behavior to be emitted.

The consequence of the employees' behavior was not necessarily to relieve themselves at the restroom but instead to socialize with their friends and get away from their boring jobs for awhile. These were the consequences maintaining the behavior at such a high frequency. The antecedent (A) in this case could not be changed. This supervisor could not alter time. If he wanted to change the behavior he had to deal with

FIGURE 4-7.   Functional Analysis of Attendance and Absenteeism

Functional Analysis of Attendance Behavior(s)

| A | → | B | → | C |

Antecedent cue(s)	Behavior(s)	Consequence(s)
Awareness of Any Consequence Advertising Meetings Memorandums Orientation Bulletin Board Observation of Any Consequence Social Status and Pressure Temporal Cues Special Events Weather	Going to Bed on Time Setting the Alarm Waking Up Getting Dressed Getting Children Off to School Leaving Home Getting a Baby-sitter Driving to Work Reporting In to Work	Reward Programs Contingent Time-Off Gifts/Prizes Preferred Jobs Social Attention Recognition Praise Feedback Data on Attendance

Functional Analysis of Absenteeism Behavior(s)

| A | → | B | → | C |

Antecedent cue(s)	Behavior(s)	Consequence(s)
Illness/Accident Hangover Lack of Transportation Traffic No Day-Care Facilities Family Problems Company Policies Group/Personal Norms Seniority/Age Awareness/Observation of Any Consequence	Getting Up Late Sleeping In Staying Home Drinking Fishing/Hunting Working at Home Visiting Caring for Sick Child	Discipline Programs Verbal Reprimands Written Reprimands Pay Docks Layoffs Dismissals Social Consequences from Co-Workers Escape and Avoidance of Working Nothing

Source: Adapted from Luthans and Martinko, 1976, p. 15.

the consequences. In this particular example, changing or replacing the consequences was difficult although not impossible. The next section on intervention strategies and, in particular, the next two chapters on antecedent and consequences management will suggest ways that this supervisor could change the behavior. The supervisor in this instance simply pointed out another consequence besides socializing and escape; namely, loss of the group incentive pay. The supervisor calculated the exact dollar amount it was costing each of the workers in the unit any time any one of them took an unscheduled break.

This monetary contingency was always there but, as most incentive systems tend to be, it was a complex calculation that was not at all clear to the workers. Through the functional analysis the supervisor was able to clarify this overlooked consequence and the workers' unscheduled break behavior went to zero after the facts were revealed. Remember, the supervisor had been on their backs for months about this problem but to no avail. But through the O.B. Mod. process he was able to immediately eliminate the problem and increase the overall performance in his department. Interestingly, the monitoring of this unscheduled break behavior was taken on by the peer group and not the supervisor. The supervisor observed one of the less dependable workers start to wander off the job one day. One of the bigger members of the work team called to him: "Hey, where do you think you're going?" "I have to go to the bathroom!" he announced. The big guy yelled back: "You hold it, man, your going to the bathroom costs me money!"

Potential problems of application • Functional analysis brings out some of the potential problems for attempting to change performance behaviors through O.B. Mod. For example, it may be found that the same consequence may control the frequency of two or more behaviors or a single behavior may have more than one contingent consequence. The following is a good example of how a single consequence may play a role in more than one contingency. A section boss praises a hard-working machine-shop employee as they leave the plant together. Unknown to the boss, the machine-shop worker has a couple of valuable company tools in his lunch bucket. While the section boss intended to reinforce the hard-working behavior, he may have accidently reinforced the theft of company property.

In cases where cooperative effort is involved, a single consequence may simultaneously affect the contingencies of two or more people. When a supervisor compliments one of a pair of equally performing subordinates and the performance of the ignored subordinate drops, the supervisor's action has affected more than one individual's behavior. So we see that a single consequence may at the same time control: (1) two or more behaviors of the same person or (2) the behavior of two or more people.

Another technical problem encountered when functionally analyzing organizational behaviors centers around the manner in which a single response may have two or more contingent consequences. For example, this situation could occur when employee behavior comes under the control of both the formal and informal organizations. Joke telling on the job may be punished formally and at the same time reinforced informally. The jokester is caught in a tug-of-war between competing contingencies. Another example might be a problem employee who is rude to a customer. The supervisor observes this rude behavior and chews out the employee. As soon as the supervisor leaves, however, a co-worker raises her thumb in the air, smiles and calls over: "I really loved the way you treated that snooty customer and I also get a kick out of how you get the supervisor so riled up. His face was so red I thought he was going to pass out. It was great!" So in this case there are two consequences of the rude behavior: (1) the supervisor's negative chewing out; and (2) the co-worker's positive attention and praise for the same behavior. Which of these two competing consequences the employee attends to will determine whether his or her subsequent rude behavior increases or decreases in frequency. If the employee attends to the co-worker's positive consequence, which tends to be quite powerful for most people, then the supervisor, who thinks he is controlling the employee's behavior, really is having little or no impact and the employee behaves exactly opposite from what the supervisor intended. This example points out not only the problems that supervisors often have in trying to control subordinate behaviors (i.e., competing contingencies), but also the value that a functional analysis can have for determining what is really going on in a given situation.

Step 4: Intervention strategies

Steps 1 through 3 provide the necessary background and data for Step 4. Relatively passive identification, measurement, and analysis turn into active intervention and control in Step 4. As Figure 4–3 indicated, Step 4 is the most extensive because it actually consists of four substeps: (4a) developing and (4b) applying intervention strategies; (4c) measuring the impact of the intervention strategy on behavioral frequency; and (4d) maintaining desirable behavioral outcomes.

Variables affecting intervention strategies • When attention shifts to the development of appropriate intervention strategies, certain variables within the work environment should be considered. Organization structure is one such variable. For example, different interventions may be needed for organizations that are mechanistic or centralized than for those that are organic or decentralized (Burns and Stalker, 1961). Self-controlled contingencies would probably be more appropriate in organic, decentralized organizations. On the other hand, carefully delineated and closely controlled contingencies may be more appropriate in the mechanistic, centralized organizations.

Internal organizational processes such as decision making, communication, and control are also variables that need to be considered. These processes may individually or collectively contribute to the eventual success or failure of a particular behavioral management strategy. Technology, which includes knowledge, procedures, and techniques as well as machinery or computers, may also limit or promote the applicability of certain intervention strategies. As stressed earlier, O.B. Mod.

cannot be applied to performance problems caused by lack of knowledge, inefficient procedures, outdated techniques, or malfunctioning machinery. It must also be remembered that organizational environments are largely social environments, and as such they possess all the complexities associated with group dynamics. Before an intervention strategy is implemented, its impact on other members of the work group as well as the impact of other work group members on the intervention strategy should be considered. The complicating nature of groups and co-workers, with all their force and influence on individual employee behavior, cannot and should not be underestimated. Yet, the problems associated with groups and co-workers certainly are not insurmountable.

A final major environmental variable is the nature of the task itself. Some tasks lend themselves to behavioral interventions and some do not. It is becoming increasingly clear that certain task characteristics are more important than others. For example, as discussed in detail in Chapter 5, Hackman and Oldham (1976) have identified skill variety, task identity, task significance, and, especially, autonomy and feedback as related to employee performance in jobs. Feedback is particularly suitable to an O.B. Mod. intervention. Chapters 5 and 6 will suggest many other possible intervention strategies and expand on the use of feedback. The goal is to implement intervention strategies on tasks that have a great deal of behavioral input and, in turn, have a direct impact on performance. In total, these interventions must be related in a contingent manner to the appropriate behaviors. Like the overall theory and practice of contingency management (Luthans, 1976), the goal of this step is to determine the most appropriate intervention strategy that will lead to the greatest performance improvement, given the organization's structure, processes, and technology and group and task constraints.

Selecting and implementing a strategy • After identifying relevant variables in the organizational environment, the behavioral manager must then select and implement an appropriate intervention strategy. The basic strategies are positive and negative reinforcement, punishment, extinction, or a combination of these. Of course, the goal of any O.B. Mod. intervention is to change the frequency of targeted behavior. Once applied, the results of the intervention strategy are monitored and charted on a behavior frequency chart similar to the one shown in Figure 4–8.

This chart is, of course, a continuation of the one started in Step 2. The wavy vertical line marks the beginning of the intervention period. During the intervention period (the area to the right of the intervention line), the target behavior's frequency is continually monitored. Behavior frequency charts, such as the one in Figure 4–8, tell the behavioral manager three things: (1) the baseline strength of the response;

FIGURE 4-8.   Behavior Frequency Chart

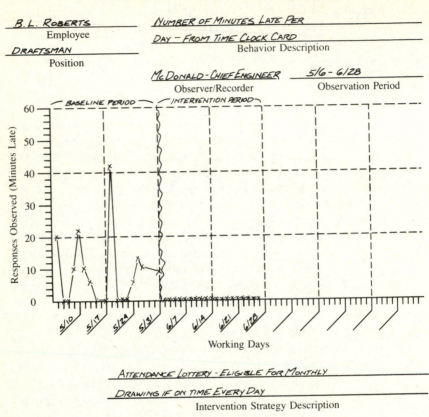

B. L. ROBERTS
Employee
DRAFTSMAN
Position

NUMBER OF MINUTES LATE PER
DAY — FROM TIME CLOCK CARD
Behavior Description

McDONALD — CHIEF ENGINEER   5/6 – 6/28
Observer/Recorder   Observation Period

ATTENDANCE LOTTERY — ELIGIBLE FOR MONTHLY
DRAWING IF ON TIME EVERY DAY
Intervention Strategy Description

(2) the type and date of intervention; and (3) the effect of the intervention strategy on behavior frequency.

During and after intervention, the chart reveals at a glance whether the intervention strategy has worked or not. When the chart reveals that the intervention strategy did not bring about the desired change in behavioral frequency, then the manager must attempt to use another intervention strategy. This points out the value of objective measurement. Managers sometimes think a particular intervention will work one way but objective measurement subsequently proves that it actually had the opposite effect. For example, a supervisor may think that a verbal reprimand is punishing to a subordinate. However, upon contingent application of the reprimand to an undesirable behavior, the data show that the behavior increased instead of decreased in frequency. In other words, the reprimand was actually a reinforcer, not a punisher, for this subordinate. It may be that this is the only time the supervisor pays any attention to the subordinate and, regardless of being "chewed out," this attention reinforces the undesirable behavior. Obviously, in this case another type of intervention strategy must be applied. In some cases, behavioral managers may even have to go all the way back to Step 1 and redefine the behavior.

Maintaining desirable behavioral outcomes • In most cases, however, the result is that the undesirable response is emitted less often or the desired response is emitted more often. When the measurement reveals this intervention is working, appropriate schedules of reinforcement can be employed to maintain the desired behavioral rate. Initially, at least, a weak response may need the steady support of continuous reinforcement. As the behavior gains strength, as indicated by its increase in frequency, intermittent reinforcement should be used. The ultimate goal is to develop a self-reinforcing participant who pursues organizational objectives and maximizes performance. Chapters 5 and 6 will give more detailed attention to intervention strategies.

Step 5: Evaluate

The fifth and final step is the real test of the effectiveness of O.B. Mod. Almost without exception, human resource management techniques in the past have, at best, only conducted sketchy or surface evaluations of effectiveness. The typical approach was to get some informal feedback — "I think it's great" or "The employees seem to be responding" — but make no objective evaluation of the impact on performance and organizational consequences (the "bottom line"). O.B. Mod. is geared directly to performance improvement and bottom-line results. If the evaluation determines that this approach is not positively affecting the performance of the individual or group whose behavior has been identified, measured, analyzed, and intervened, then corrective action must be taken. As emphasized earlier, O.B. Mod. is not attempting to change behavior for the sake of behavioral change. To make it a worthwhile approach to human resource management, O.B. Mod. must be able to improve performance.

The recommended O.B. Mod. process uses four levels of evaluation: reaction, learning, behavioral change, and performance improvement (Cantalanello and Kirkpatrick, 1968). The reaction level simply means that the behavioral manager using this approach, as well as the employees who are having it used on them, should be positive about it: feel that it will work and that it is a good idea. If O.B. Mod. is not well received by all parties concerned, it won't work. In other words, there must be reinforcing consequences for using O.B. Mod. Managers who are able to increase their units' performance by using the steps of O.B. Mod. as outlined in this chapter should be reinforced with attention and, if appropriate, monetary rewards. The same is true for the employees in the unit; they must be reinforced also.

The learning level of evaluation refers to whether the manager using O.B. Mod. understands (i.e., has learned) the underlying principles and specific procedures of the approach. Does the manager understand the type of material covered in the first three chapters? If not, the approach will not work as well, especially in the long run.

As stated throughout, the real evaluation of the O.B. Mod. application is whether the identified behaviors have really changed in the desired directions, and even more important, has performance improved? Objectively charting behavior in Steps 2 and 4 will help in this evaluation phase. However, at least when the approach is first tried, a more systematic evaluation using either experimental designs complete with control groups or reversals/mutiple baseline designs (Luthans, 1981; Luthans and Maris, 1979) should be used. If carefully set up, these designs best support internal and external validity (Cook and Campbell, 1976) and thus provide considerable evidence that the O.B. Mod. approach *caused* the change in behavior and performance improvement. Such causal evidence is quite valuable in the face of today's "show-me" demands, rightfully made by top management, regarding human resource management programs and approaches. Chapter 8 will summarize the results of such evaluations of a number of applications of O.B. Mod. programs in a variety of organizations.

Antecedent Management 5

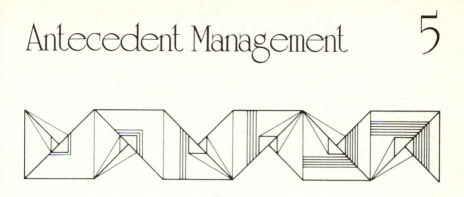

One of the recognized keys to effective management is to be proactive instead of reactive. Inherent in this prescriptive solution is the practical value of managing material and human resources through proactive anticipation instead of reactive firefighting. Relative to behavioral management, the main idea of a proactive approach is to preempt behavioral problems before they get established. In other words, the time to repair the barn door is *before* the prize horse runs away. A broken door is an antecedent (or prior) condition that encourages the horse to run away, whereas a repaired door is an antecedent condition that encourages the horse to remain at home. So, too, there are many antecedents in every work setting that can be managed to encourage productive behavior.

Within the O.B. Mod. framework, *antecedent management* involves increasing the likelihood of productive behavior by systematically managing supportive antecedent cues. Behavioral psychologists use the terms "cue control" or "stimulus control." Antecedent management in O.B. Mod. takes its name from the antecedent→behavior→consequence (A→B→C) model, but it can also be thought of as the S-O portion of the expanded social learning-based S-O-B-C model as well. Like signposts along a highway, these antecedent cues encourage or otherwise set the stage or occasion for productive behavior to be emitted. Perhaps the best way to think of antecedent management in actual practice is in terms of *feedforward control*.

FEEDFORWARD CONTROL

Practicing managers have two basic options for keeping things on track and under control: (1) they can wait for a problem to occur before taking remedial action; or (2) they can anticipate a problem and take preventive steps. An example of option one, appropriately called feed*back* control, would be waiting until a labor strike occurs before attempting to determine labor's unresolved grievances. Oppositely, feed*forward* control would take place if management identified and nipped grievances in the bud to prevent a strike from occurring in the first place. Just as a cardiovascular fitness program is more efficient and less costly than open heart surgery, preventive feedforward control is far and away the preferable option for effective management. According to Koontz and Bradspies (1972), early proponents of feedforward control, "the only way [managers] can exercise control effectively is to see the problems coming in time to do something about them" (p. 27).

Another useful way of viewing the difference between feedforward and feedback control is from the perspective of the S-O-B-C model. As illustrated in Figure 5-1, feedforward control of behavior occurs through management of the prior situation. Reversing the order of things, feedback control of behavior occurs through management of subsequent consequences. Of course, in line with the emphasis on cognitive mediation in the S-O-B-C model, the effects of both feedforward and feedback control are influenced by relevant cognitive processes such as perceptions, goals, and expectations.

The following comments briefly summarize the nature and comparative value of feedforward and feedback behavior control:

"Setting an objective, restructuring a boring task to make it more interesting, and providing skill training all amount to feedforward control because each is carried out *prior to* job performance. On the other hand, favorable consequences such as a pat on the back, permission to go home early, or a bonus amount to feedback control because they tell the individual that

FIGURE 5-1.   The Feedforward Control of Organizational Behavior

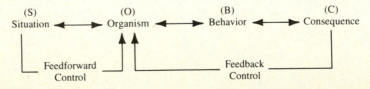

he or she is on the right track. Demotions, criticism, and assignment to disliked tasks also involve feedback control, only negative. Both positive and negative feedback control take place *after* job performance. The feedforward variety is preferable because it helps management anticipate and avoid job performance problems instead of passively waiting for problems to occur and only then taking corrective action to keep those problems from recurring" (Kreitner, 1982, pp. 7–8).

But, despite the practical value of feedforward control, it has been sadly shortchanged in organizational behavior research. In fact, after conducting a comprehensive search of the relevant literature, Frederiksen and Johnson (1981) made the following observation:

"Although it is clear that antecedent [feedforward] control is a ubiquitous technique in business and industrial settings (e.g., memos, policy changes, meetings) there is a lack of systematic research assessing its effectiveness. A review of the literature was unable to pinpoint even a single study where antecedent control was the primary technique in a business or industrial setting" (p. 95).

Hence, the purpose of this chapter is to build an S-O-B-C framework for antecedent management (or feedforward control) of performance behavior in organizations. In essence, this chapter examines the "up front" side of behavioral management and the next chapter is concerned with the "back side" or consequence management.

ANTECEDENTS CUE RATHER THAN CAUSE BEHAVIOR

Considerable confusion surrounds the subject of antecedent management. Specifically, questions arise as to whether or not antecedent stimuli or cues automatically cause or elicit subsequent behavior. Depending upon whether classical or operant conditioning is used as the framework of reference, the answer can be yes or no. Also, Skinner's distinction between respondent behavior and operant behavior is an instructive point of departure for sorting things out. Prior stimulation does in fact automatically cause predictable responses when respondent behaviors are involved. For instance, a squirt of lemon juice in the eye will predictably and automatically elicit a tearful response (i.e., respondent behavior). But things are different when operant behavior is involved.

With operant behavior, certain environmental stimuli can become fairly reliable cues for behavior by being consistently paired with desired consequences. For example, most drivers step on the brake when a green traffic signal turns yellow because it increases their chances of arriving safely without a traffic ticket. This connection is probabilistic rather than automatic, however, because some drivers respond to a yellow traffic light by stepping on the gas, particularly if they are in a hurry or in their experience they have not had an accident or been ticketed. So, unlike a squirt of lemon juice in the eye, yellow traffic lights may cue significantly different behaviors. A professor friend of ours learned this the hard way. This professor and his wife were hurrying to the local airport one day, each driving one of the family's two cars. Upon reaching an intersection where the green light had turned yellow, the professor's wife stepped on the brake while this professor, who was following close behind his wife, responded to the same yellow light by stepping on the gas. By the time he had responded appropriately to a new cue, his wife's brake lights, the costly fender-bender had occurred.

Throughout the balance of this chapter, the antecedents can be thought of and used, as least symbolically, as yellow traffic lights. Antecedents are stimuli that probabilistically rather than automatically control relevant behaviors. For example, a company sales goal may prompt some members of the sales force to work harder while others fail to give it a second thought. In S-O-B-C terms, the potency of antecedents as controllers of behavior is collectively determined (1) by their associated reinforcing consequences, (2) the *value* the individual places on the perceived consequences, and (3) the individual's expectations of success. These processes largely take place in the "O"—the intervening cognitions between the stimulus (S) and the behavior (B) in the S-O-B-C model. Thus, except for the association with the reinforcing consequences which fall within the operant learning framework, much of the background for understanding the role of antecedents in behavior control comes from the expanded social learning theoretical framework and the S-O-B-C model.

GENERAL STRATEGIES FOR MANAGING ANTECEDENTS

Turning from theory to practice, there are two general strategies of antecedent management. As summarized in Figure 5-2, one

FIGURE 5-2. Two General Strategies for Managing On-the-Job Antecedents

Barriers to Performance Behaviors	Aids to Performance Behaviors
Remove barriers that prevent or hinder the completion of a good job	*Provide* helpful aids that enhance the opportunity to do a good job
+ Unrealistic objectives, plans, schedules, or deadlines	+ Challenging, yet attainable objectives
+ Uncooperative or distracting coworkers	+ Clear and realistic plans
+ Training deficiencies	+ Understandable instructions
+ Contradictory or confusing rules	+ Constructive suggestions, hints, or tips
+ Inadequate or inappropriate tools	+ Clear and generally acceptable work rules
+ Conflicting orders from two or more superiors	+ Realistic schedules and deadlines
+ Punitive, destructive supervision	+ Friendly reminders
	+ Posters or signs with helpful tips
	+ Easy-to-use forms
	+ Nonthreatening questions about progress
	+ Supportive, helpful supervision

Source: Adapted from Kreitner, 1983, p. 407.

strategy involves the removal of potential or actual barriers to successful job performance. Removal of seemingly insignificant barriers to performance can sometimes pave the way for significant results.

An example of this strategy is found in an incident reported by Connellan (1978). A telephone company was underbilling its customers about a quarter of a million dollars annually because its equipment installers were not accurately reporting the installation of "ceiling drops," a procedure requiring extra time and materials. Costly training and constant reminders from supervisors only partially and temporarily relieved the problem. The installers soon went back to not reporting their ceiling drop installations and the company's receipts were negatively affected by renewed underbilling. It was eventually discovered through a behavioral analysis that the problem was with an unsupportive antecedent, not a lack of training. Connellan (1978) reports the following took place:

"The form that the installers were required to fill out was extremely complicated and the part dealing with ceiling drops was even more complicated. . . . One small change was made by adding a box where the installer no longer had to fill out an extensive explanation of what took place in the house. Within one week after the change in the form, the number of ceiling drops reported and charged back to the customers had increased dramatically, far above what it was immediately after the training sessions" (p. 27).

The second strategy for managing antecedents involves presenting opportunities. The aids shown in Figure 5-2 summarize some specific ways this strategy can be carried out. For example, setting challenging yet attainable goals, as will be discussed later along with other techniques, can greatly improve the likelihood of effective performance behaviors. Similarly, a person who desires challenging work will tend to perform better when given the opportunity to tackle a stimulating task.

A MODEL FOR ANTECEDENT MANAGEMENT

The S-O-B-C model can serve as a framework to show the relationship between the environmental and cognitive dimensions of antecedent control. Managers can cue performance behaviors by relying on the techniques listed under the "S" in Figure 5-3. Importantly, however, the employee's expectations, self-evaluative standards, and causal attributions found in the "O" must support the antecedents presented if behavior is to change in the desired direction. Because of the critical gatekeeping role played by these cognitive mediators found in the "O," special attention is devoted to them in the next section. After that, our

FIGURE 5-3.   The S-O-B-C Model for Antecedent Management

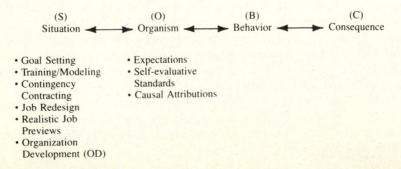

attention will turn to a discussion of the specific antecedent management techniques in the "S" portion of the model in Figure 5-3.

COGNITIVE MEDIATORS IN ANTECEDENT MANAGEMENT

As discussed in the preceding chapters, social learning theorists
(e.g., Bandura, 1977a; 1977b) have gone beyond traditional operant
conditioning theory by weaving in cognitive processes that they maintain will affect person-environment interactions. Whereas Skinner says
that behavior is a function of its consequences, Bandura says that behavior can be a function of *anticipated* consequences as well (Bandura,
1977b, p. 166). Adhering to this social learning proposition, it naturally
follows that individuals can anticipate antecedent-behavior-consequence
contingencies as well. But the reciprocal relationship between environmental cues and behavior is mediated by a number of cognitive processes.
Three of the most significant cognitive mediators that are relevant to
antecedent management in O.B. Mod. are expectations, self-evaluative
standards, and causal attributions. Anticipation of and selective response to one's surroundings are central to each of these cognitive processes. Each cognitive mediator, in effect, is a gatekeeper that either
facilitates or inhibits antecedent-behavior connections.

The role of expectations

An expectation or expectancy is a subjective probability that
one attaches to future events. Quantitatively expressed, such expectancies may range from a low of 0 to a high of 1 (virtual certainty). For
instance, how certain are you that the New York Mets may again win
the World Series, that the price of gasoline will drop below 75 cents a
gallon, or that medical scientists will discover a general cure for cancer
before the year 2000? Different people, depending on their knowledge,
values, and perceptions, would formulate differing expectations for
these events. The same is true for expectations of work-related events.
In fact, cognitive motivation theorists have emphasized the impact of
effort-reward expectations on job performance and job satisfaction
(recall the discussion of the Vroom, 1964 and Porter and Lawler, 1968
models of motivation in Chapter 1).

Within the context of social learning theory, Bandura (1977b)
has drawn the following helpful distinction between *efficacy* expectations and *outcome* expectations:

"An outcome expectancy is defined . . . as a person's estimate that a given behavior will lead to certain outcomes [e.g.,
that sucessfully completing a project will lead to recognition
and a pay increase]. An efficacy expectation is the conviction
that one can successfully execute the behavior required to produce the outcomes. Outcome and efficacy expectations are
differentiated because individuals can come to believe that a
particular course of action will produce certain outcomes, but
question whether they can perform those actions" (p. 79).

Bandura (1977b, pp. 80–82) believes that efficacy expectations
are based on the following four sources of information: (1) the person's
actual performance accomplishments; (2) vicarious experience (modeling); (3) verbal persuasion; and (4) emotional arousal. Firsthand experience, in the form of actual performance accomplishments, is said to
exercise the most powerful influence on one's efficacy expectations. The
adage "nothing succeeds like success" reinforces this notion. For example, completion of a simple but personally relevant exercise on a new
personal computer can wither a manager's resistance to using it by bol-
stering his or her efficacy expectations.

High efficacy expectations are a necessary but insufficient condition if one is to attempt the behavior in question. As indicated in
Figure 5-4, an employee must possess high outcome expectations in
addition to high efficacy expectations before engaging in productive
behavior. Behavioral managers can roughly diagnose these two cognitive hurdles by simply asking individuals what they think their chances
are of (1) completing a given task if they attempt it; and (2) attaining
desired rewards once that task is completed. Outcome expectations are

FIGURE 5-4.   The Impact of Efficacy and Outcome Expectations on
               Behavior

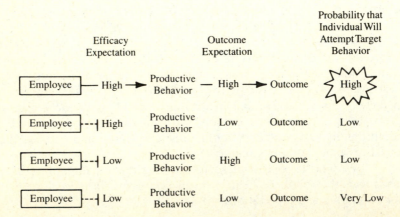

shaped by how consistently and equitably management ties meaningful rewards to performance. Contingency questionnaires such as the one developed by Reitz (1971) and discussed in detail in the next chapter can be used by the behavioral manager to determine his or her people's perceived performance-outcome probabilities.

The role of self-evaluative standards

Because of cognitive symbolic standards, against which people can appraise their conduct, there is the potential capacity for midstream correction and self-control. Self-evaluative standards could be alternatively discussed under the headings of values or ethics. However, primarily because goal-setting is a central feature of modern management prescriptions for effective performance, they are given specific attention here. Edwin A. Locke, the leading proponent of goal setting, and his colleagues have defined a *goal* as "what an individual is trying to accomplish; it is the object or aim of an action" (Locke, Shaw, Saari, and Latham, 1981, p. 126). Cognitive motivation theorists typically use the terms goal, intention, and purpose interchangeably. While discussing cognitive control of behavior within the context of social learning theory, Bandura (1977b) noted:

> "The motivational effects do not derive from the goals themselves, but rather from the fact that people respond evaluatively to their own behavior. Goals specify the conditional requirements for positive self-evaluation. Once individuals have made self-satisfaction contingent upon goal attainment, they tend to persist in their efforts until their performances match what they are seeking to achieve" (p. 161).

Acceptance of organizational goals by the individual is probably desirable if the self-evaluative mechanism is going to work. For example, management-by-objectives (MBO) programs place a great deal of emphasis on participatory goal setting to facilitate goal acceptance by individuals. Locke's research has led him to conclude that "an assigned goal that is rejected can hardly regulate performance" (Locke et al., 1981, p. 126). On the other hand, there is some evidence to indicate there is no difference between the performance of those who were simply assigned goals and those who, through participation, accepted their goals (Latham and Yukl, 1976). In addition, Latham, Mitchell, and Dossett (1978) found that employee participation led to higher goals being set, which in turn led to higher performance. But there was no difference between the performance of those who participated and those who were assigned goals. Regardless of the somewhat mixed research results on some of the specifics of goal setting, it can be concluded that goals do provide a benchmark for self-evaluation and can lead to effective performance behaviors.

The role of causal attributions

Chapter 1 pointed out that attribution theory (Heider, 1958; Kelley, 1967, 1973; Kelley and Michela, 1980) has surfaced in recent years as a major explanation of the way in which individuals interpret their own or others' behavior. Attributions of behavior (the "why" of people's own or other's behavior) is usually dichotomized into internal (ability or effort) or external (luck or the difficulty of the task) dimensions.

There is some evidence, however, that there are other dimensions of attribution. For example, Weiner (1972) suggests that the four perceived causes of success and failure (ability, effort, luck, and task difficulty) can be attributed to two causal dimensions: locus of control (internal or external) and stability (fixed or variable). For example, an experienced employee will have a relatively stable internal attribution about his or her ability and external attribution concerning the difficulty of the task. These are relatively unchanging over time or across situations. On the other hand, attributions of effort (internal) and luck (external) are quite variable and unstable. The employee's effort may vary from hour to hour or from job to job. The same is true of luck. Employees may be really lucky at one time or at doing something, but not at another time or doing something else.

Besides the stability factor, other things may also affect the type of attributions that are made. In assessing others' behavior, Kelley (1973) suggests that consensus (Do others act this way in this situation?), consistency (Does this person act this way in this situation at other times?), and distinctiveness (Does this person act differently in other situations?) will determine whether internal or external attributions are made. Zuckerman's (1978) research has verified Kelley's contention that if these dimensions are all high, then external attributions are made. But if there is low consensus, high consistency, and low distinctiveness, then internal attributions are made. An example would be the union steward who has a disruptive member at a union business meeting. If other members are also disruptive at this meeting (high consensus), this member acts this way at all the business meetings (high consistency), and this person does not act this way in staff meetings held by management (high distinctiveness), the steward would likely make an external attribution of this member's behavior. In other words, the steward would probably conclude that there is something wrong with the way the meeting is being run and this member is not a basically bad person destined to give him trouble. On the other hand, if the other members are not acting this way (low consensus), this member acts this way at all business meetings (high consistency), and this person also acts this way in staff meetings held by management (low distinctiveness), the steward would probably make an internal attribution. He would conclude that he has a real problem union member on his hands.

These attributions that the person makes will, of course, greatly affect how the antecedents are interpreted. For example, a salesperson who believes that luck is the prime determinant of successful selling understandably would be resistant to antecedent management strategies of setting sales quotas or demonstrating selling tactics through a training film. Another, meanwhile, who believes that *ability* is the secret to selling success, may respond quite favorably to the same strategies. As with expectations and self-evaluative standards, causal attributions are highly personalized gatekeepers that may help or hinder the linkage between antecedents and behavior.

ANTECEDENT MANAGEMENT TECHNIQUES

Having identified some of the important cognitive mediating processes, attention now turns to some practical techniques for managing organizational antecedents for effective job performance. Although rules, instructions, and policies are common on-the-job antecedents, the following techniques go beyond these. As listed back in Figure 5-3, goal setting, training/modeling, contingency contracting, job redesign, realistic job previews, and organization development are antecedent management techniques that can cue productive job performance. These techniques are applied from the perspective of feedforward control.

Goal-setting techniques

The goal-setting technique may be applied as a personal cognitive event in self-management (e.g., resolving to have one's in-basket empty by the end of every workday) or as a social process dedicated to improving unit or organizational effectiveness. In either case, personally set goals are ideal because they engender goal acceptance and personal commitment. Realistically, however, when applied to the unit or organization, managers typically have a hand in subordinate goal setting. Management by objectives (MBO) has emerged as the most widely used goal-setting technique for such applications (Odiorne, 1978). Although widely used (probably every organization of any size uses some form of MBO to varying degrees), a recent review of the literature indicates only mixed success (Kondrasuk, 1981). Defining and applying MBO has been a problem.

MBO and goal setting • Amid the many conflicting definitions of MBO, the one offered by McConkie (1979) may be the most complete and instructive. He defines MBO as:

> "A managerial process whereby organizational purposes are diagnosed and met by joining superiors and subordinates in the pursuit of mutually agreed upon goals and objectives, which are specific, measurable, time bounded, and joined to an action plan; progress and goal attainment are measured and monitored in appraisal sessions which center on mutually determined objective standards of performance" (p. 37).

MBO's distinguishing characteristics are goals that are *measurable* and *participatively set*. The participative goal-setting phase of MBO is most closely associated with antecedent management.

How goals affect performance • An exhaustive literature search of goal-setting studies conducted from 1969 to 1980 prompted Locke et al. (1981) to conclude that goals can facilitate task performance in at least four ways:

1. Goals direct one's attention and actions.
2. Goals encourage the expenditure of effort.
3. Goals encourage persistence.
4. Goals motivate one to develop relevant goal-attainment strategies.

Practical guidelines for goal setting • In addition to uncovering the foregoing insights about why goal setting works, Locke et al. (1981) gleaned some practical advice from their review of the studies. Practical guidelines for effective goal setting include:

1. People with *specific* and *challenging* goals tend to perform better than those without assigned goals and those with "do-your-best" goals.
2. Specific *quantitative* goals have more impact on performance than do vague intentions.

3. Trying harder does not improve performance if the individual lacks the necessary *ability*.

4. Performance tends to improve when people are given *feedback* (knowledge of results) relative to goals being pursued.

As discussed earlier, there is at best only mixed evidence that participative goal setting enhances performance. After reviewing this literature, Locke et al. (1981) concluded that:

"There is no consistent evidence that participation in setting goals leads to greater goal commitment or better task performance than assigned goals when goal level is controlled, though it sometimes leads to setting higher goals than the supervisor would have assigned" (p. 146).

In fact, practical experience in situations such as the Emery Air Freight program discussed in Chapter 4 suggests that imposed or assigned goals do indeed facilitate good performance. MBO enthusiasts nonetheless recommend subordinate participation to enhance personal commitment. In the final analysis, quantified and challenging goals appear to be central to effective antecedent management. Subordinate participation appears to be an added luxury that may or may not lead to better performance depending upon the willingness and ability of the parties involved.

Training/modeling techniques

Few, if any, managers would argue that ability is not a key determinant of successful job performance. When an ability deficiency has surfaced, two general courses of action are open to management. An appropriately skilled individual can be hired, promoted, or rotated into the position. Or, the jobholder's skills can be upgraded through appropriate training. In view of the fact that government and business organizations in the United States spend an estimated $30 billion each year on training, this second option has been shown to be very popular ("Worker-training Cost," 1981). Sadly, much of this collective training budget goes for naught because of poorly designed and/or administered training programs. By using the S-O-B-C framework and paying careful attention to antecedent management, behavioral managers can get more mileage out of their training dollars.

Ensuring transfer of learning • A major stumbling block in conventional training programs is transfer of learning. Learning is said to transfer to the job when the training experience actually leads to improved job performance. Getting high grades on a test at the end of a training program is one thing; successfully changing behaviors back on the job and improving performance is quite another. Finding a solution to this problem in antecedent management is brought out by the following observation:

> "A frequently encountered problem with many training programs is that organization members do not remember to put the newly learned behaviors into effect. Arrangements for the cuing of appropriate behavior on those occasions when it is supposed to occur is an aspect of training that has been almost totally neglected" (Luthans and Davis, 1981, p. 24).

In other words, the common tendency to overlook the systematic management of antecedents again is apparent.

Wexley and Latham (1981, pp. 75–77) believe that a training program will maximize retention and transfer of learning if managers adhere to the following guidelines:

1. Maximize the similarity between the training situation and the job situation.
2. Provide as much experience as possible with the task being taught.
3. Provide for a variety of examples when teaching concepts or skills.
4. Label or identify important features of a task.
5. Make sure that general principles are understood before expecting much transfer.
6. Make certain that the trained behaviors and ideas are rewarded in the job situation.
7. Design the training content so that the trainees can see its applicability.
8. Use adjunct questions to guide the trainee's attention.

Except for point 7, each of the above essentially involves feedforward control of learning. If actually applied, these guidelines increase the likelihood that training will change behavior and improve job performance.

A modeling approach to training • Although modeling is discussed at length in Chapter 7, it deserves special mention here for two reasons: (1) modeling in many respects falls into the domain of antecedent management (Manz and Sims, 1981), and (2) behavior modeling has become a widely used training tool ("Imitating Models," 1978). After drawing a distinction between factual learning and skill learning, Wexley and Latham (1981) highlighted the importance of modeling in training by saying: "We believe that effective skill learning should incorporate four essential ingredients: (1) goal setting, (2) modeling, (3) practice, and (4) feedback" (p. 77).

From an S-O-B-C standpoint, the effectiveness of behavior models in formal training can be enhanced by encouraging appropriate cognitive processing of key learning points. For example, on-the-job research by Decker (1982) demonstrated the training value of formalized symbolic coding and symbolic rehearsal processes when using video-taped behavior models. Specifically, twelve experimental subjects (hospital supervisors) and twelve control subjects viewed videotaped models exhibiting correct coaching behavior and complaint handling. Both groups discussed and then practiced the modeled behaviors after viewing the videotapes, as called for in the Goldstein and Sorcher (1974) training protocol. But only the experimental group supervisors were: (1) given learning points (e.g., "listen openly to the complaint") for the modeled behaviors on 3 × 5 cards; (2) encouraged to identify the learning points in the videotaped presentations, remember them, and use them during the practice session; (3) told to write down the learning points after viewing the videotaped models; and (4) instructed to close their eyes and mentally picture themselves performing the learning points. Objective observers later rated the experimental group of supervisors as better able than the control group to apply what they had learned. Thus, in S-O-B-C terms, trainers can facilitate the impact of behavior models (S) on job performance (B) by encouraging symbolic coding and rehearsal (O).

Contingency contracting

Behaviorists discovered long ago the cuing ability of formally spelled-out contingencies of reinforcement (behavior-consequence linkages). For instance, Skinner (1969) observed:

> "The behavior of a person who has calculated his chances, compared alternatives, or considered the consequences of a move is different from, and usually more effective than, the behavior of one who has merely been exposed to the unanalyzed contingencies. The analysis functions as a discriminative stimulus [or cue]" (pp. 121–122).

A direct offshoot of this realization is a technique called *contingency contracting*. Although some prefer the term behavior contracting, the process is still the same. Specifically, in a formal verbal or sometimes written agreement, usually within a specified time frame, one person agrees to behave in a given manner and another person agrees to reinforce that behavior in a specified way. According to Kazdin (1975): "Each party 'gives' something (a reinforcer or performance of a target response) and 'receives' something in exchange (the desired behavior or the desired reinforcer)" (p. 55). In other words, this is a "win-win" contract for both parties.

Contingency contracting in action • A study conducted by Luthans, Paul, and Baker (1981) demonstrates the practical value of specifying behavior-consequence contingencies right from the start. One group of department store clerks who were told that they could earn time off with pay or a cash equivalent and a chance to compete for a free one-week vacation for two by meeting specified performance standards significantly outperformed a control group of clerks who were given the performance standards only. There is, of course, considerable evidence that rewards (such as pay) that are contingent upon performance will have a positive impact on performance (e.g., see: Cherrington, Reitz, and Scott, 1971; Greene, 1973; and Podsakoff, Todor, and Skov, 1982). The next chapter on consequence management will get into more depth on this relationship, but this discussion stresses that contingencies of reinforcement should be spelled out "up front" in a contingency contract.

Goal setting plus contingency contracting • From both conceptual and practical viewpoints, goal setting and contingency contracting are highly compatible. Goals specify what is to be done and when, while contractual contingent consequences provide a clear incentive. Accordingly, O'Banion and Whaley (1981) have suggested:

> "Relations between employers and employees may be greatly improved through a clarification of events. Contracts may state what needs to be done, the deadline for getting it done, and clarify other questions that often must be answered. . . . There is a great deal to be gained by setting down in specific terms what is expected or not expected and by establishing rewards or penalties for such action. The contract may help insure that actions are observed and rewards are presented for correct performance" (pp. 116–117).

Relative to our earlier discussion of expectations, contingency contracts clarify *outcome* expectations. Once again, both high efficacy expectations *and* high outcome expectations are needed to encourage concerted effort on the job. Training and experience promote high efficacy expectations. Contingency contracting can promote high outcome expectations, assuming that the specified rewards are in fact desired by the affected parties.

Job redesign techniques

A valuable legacy of Herzberg's (1968) two-factor theory of employee motivation is the idea that the work itself can be a powerful determinant of job satisfaction and performance. Dull, routine, and monotonous work too often has a stifling effect, whereas challenging work that affords the opportunity for achievement and personal growth can bolster satisfaction and performance. During the 1960s and early 1970s, Herzberg and other proponents of *job enrichment* popularized the notion of enhancing employee motivation by providing meaningful work through job design. In Herzberg's terms, job redesign amounted to incorporating more of the "motivators" (i.e., responsibility, recognition, and, in general, opportunities for growth and achievement). Starting with the work of Turner and Lawrence (1965), identifying specific job characteristics that relate to employee motivation and performance has taken on more importance in job design theory, research, and application. What Herzberg now calls "orthodox job enrichment" (1979) and, even more so, the job-characteristics approach to job design both qualify as antecedent management techniques because they involve feedforward control of job performance and cue (set the occasion for) appropriate performance behaviors.

Hackman-Oldham job characteristics model • The most widely accepted job characteristics model for job redesign has been formulated by Hackman and Oldham (1980). Figure 5-5 highlights the basic components of this model. The five core job characteristics in Hackman and Oldham's model can be summarized as follows:

1. *Skill variety*—How many different activities are performed that require different skills and talents?

2. *Task identity*—To what extent does the individual work on a "whole" piece of work, from beginning to end? Can the job holder readily explain to others what he or she does?

3. *Task significance*—How much does the job in question impact the lives of others, both inside and outside the organization? How important is the task?

4. *Autonomy*—How much freedom, discretion, and independence does the individual have in determining work schedules and procedures?

5. *Job feedback*—How clearly and directly does the work itself tell the individual how well he or she has done?

The first three—skill variety, task identity, and task significance—are said to contribute to the *meaningfulness* one experiences from work. Autonomy relates to the sense of *personal responsibility* one experiences. Job feedback, as the term implies, relates to one's *knowledge of results*. As illustrated in Figure 5-5, increased meaningfulness, personal responsibility, and knowledge of results in turn increase the likelihood of productive job behavior through feedforward control and cuing appropriate behaviors.

Job redesign in action • Experienced meaningfulness can be enhanced by giving people "whole" jobs. For example, Indiana Bell Telephone Company had problems with poor performance among clerks who compiled many directories in a "bits and pieces" fashion. But when each clerk was given personal responsibility for compiling an entire directory for a given geographic area from start to finish, clerks came to view the directories as their *own*, and performance improved significantly (Ford, 1973).

Volvo, the Swedish auto company, took a bold step toward greater employee autonomy (and thus personal responsibility) when it

FIGURE 5-5.   Job Redesign as an Antecedent Management Technique

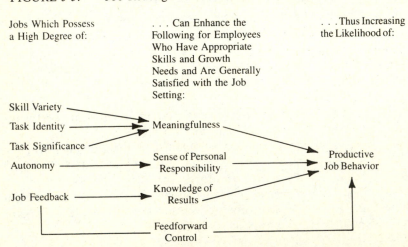

Source: Adapted from Hackman and Oldham, 1980, p. 90.

built a new assembly plant in Kalmar without the familiar assembly lines. In place of traditional assembly lines were movable carts that permitted *teams* of employees to wheel partially assembled autos around to accommodate their own schedules and work assignments. Company production quotas, schedules, and wage incentives facilitated overall control of operations. Absenteeism and turnover dropped at Kalmar while production costs reportedly remained competitive (Gyllenhammar, 1977).

Regarding the redesign of jobs to increase job feedback, auto assemblers at Volvo's Kalmar plant enjoyed greater knowledge of results when they were allowed to conduct quality inspections on their own work. Quality thus became a personal challenge, not a problem to be passed along to someone else down the line. Prompt corrective action also increased under the new arrangement. The much publicized Japanese quality control techniques are along the same line (Schonberger, 1982).

Realistic job previews or RJP technique

Shaping of employee expectations begins before the employment contract is signed. The usual practice of giving recruits a "good news only" preview of what to expect on the new job tends to foster unrealistic and overly optimistic expectations. This is an especially serious problem in organizations where people must perform routine and monotonous jobs. All too often, routine-task employees with unrealistic expectations soon quit because of "reality shock." A promising antecedent management technique called *realistic job previews* (or RJPs) can offer an effective solution to this problem. In essence, an RJP is an honest and frank explanation of what a job actually entails.

Research has demonstrated the practical value of giving applicants for routine jobs a realistic preview of both positive and negative aspects. In one study by Wanous (1973), recruits for positions as telephone operators who viewed a realistic job preview film prior to being hired later reported having fewer thoughts of quitting and did in fact quit with less frequency than a matched group of operators who saw a traditional "good news only" recruiting film. While Wanous (1978) is convinced that RJPs can reduce turnover, he notes that the evidence is unclear as to whether they can improve job performance. However, in routine-task situations where high turnover is a costly problem, RJPs represent an easily implemented tool for the feedforward control of at least turnover behaviors.

Organization development

Organization development (OD) is an overall, systems approach to planned change as well as a loosely defined array of techniques. The purpose of OD is to replace haphazard change with planned change. Rush (1973) defined OD as "a planned, managed, systematic process to change the culture, systems, and behavior of an organization, in order to improve the organization's effectiveness in solving its problems and achieving its objectives" (p. 2). Through traditional OD techniques such as team building, grid training, and survey feedback, and newer techniques such as process consultation or cultural development (e.g., Ouchi's Theory Z, 1981), OD programs strive to achieve the following six objectives:

1. Strengthen interpersonal trust, communication, cooperation, and support.
2. Encourage a problem-solving rather than problem-avoiding approach to organizational problems.
3. Develop a satisfying work experience capable of building enthusiasm.
4. Supplement formal authority with authority based on personal knowledge and skill.
5. Increase personal responsibility for planning and implementing.
6. Encourage personal willingness to change (French, 1969).

To the extent that these objectives become reality, a supportive *antecedent* climate for productive behavior exists. However, like the other antecedent management techniques, the important role of *consequences* should not be overlooked when using OD:

> "Most of the OD techniques, e.g., job enrichment or team building, simply set the occasion or cue appropriate performance behavior. However, . . . these antecedents—an enriched job or a team concept—only become powerful and control behavior to the extent that reinforcing consequences follow the behavior that has been emitted. . . . This OD approach often fails to provide the contingent reward systems to reinforce . . . [desired behavior]. With no reinforcement forthcoming, the OD program loses its controlling power to cause the desirable behavior and soon becomes ineffective" (Luthans, 1982, pp. 260–261).

Recognizing that appropriate reinforcing consequences must accompany all the antecedent management techniques discussed in this chapter, our attention now turns to managing consequences.

Consequence Management 6

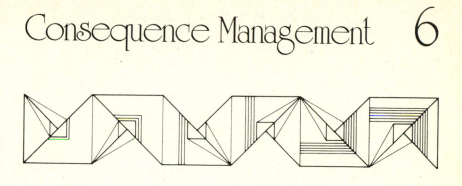

Chapter 5 discussed and presented specific techniques of antecedent management that set the occasion or cue appropriate employee behaviors for performance improvement. It was pointed out that although these antecedents can *control* behavior, they do not cause the behavior and they take on controlling power because of contingently associated consequences. In other words, cue control or stimulus control of behavior occurs because in the presence of these antecedents, desirable or undesirable consequences are known to occur. Thus, in the final analysis, consequence management becomes the key strategy for organizational behavior modification.

Whereas antecedent management depends more on the expanded social learning theoretical base (e.g., the role of cognitive mediators such as expectancies and attributions) and techniques (e.g., goal setting and modeling), consequence management is based more on traditional operant principles of reinforcement and punishment. Reinforcement, of course, is the key to operant learning theory and the single most important principle of behavior management. The simple fact is that positive reinforcement, contingently applied, can effectively control human behavior. In contrast to punishment and negative reinforcement, it is a positive type of consequence management. Understanding and appropriately using positive reinforcement probably is the most important dimension of successful O.B. Mod.

Central to human resource management is the attainment of organizational goals through people. This goal is commonly accomplished through either negative (punishment or negative reinforcement) or positive (positive reinforcement) consequence management. Generally, neither approach is used very effectively in today's human resource management.

A major premise of O.B. Mod. is that positive consequence management is much more effective than negative consequence management. After reading this chapter, the practitioner and student of management will hopefully have a better understanding of and be able to effectively apply the positive approach. Yet, because the negative approach is so widely used, it will also be given attention in the last part of the chapter. But positive reinforcement is the most socially desirable and *effective* method of controlling behavior in today's organizations.

TECHNICAL REFINEMENTS OF REINFORCEMENT

Because positive reinforcement is so important to O.B. Mod., clear distinctions must be made between positive and negative reinforcement, positive reinforcement and rewards, and contrived and natural rewards. An understanding of such distinctions is a necessary prerequisite for identifying and successfully applying positive reinforcement on the job.

Positive and negative reinforcement

As Chapter 3 pointed out, there are two general types of reinforcement, positive and negative. Both positive and negative reinforcement strengthen behavior, but while positive reinforcement strengthens behavior by the presentation of a desirable consequence, negative reinforcement strengthens behavior by the withdrawal of an aversive stimulus.

An organizational example can clarify the distinction. If a key performance-related response of an assistant shipping room manager is strengthened through the use of performance-contingent time off, positive reinforcement is being used. The presentation of time off is made contingent on improved performance. On the other hand, if the boss consistently relies on threats of docked pay, demotion, transfer, dismissal, or just on "chewing out" to stimulate the assistant's performance, negative reinforcement is in operation. In short, the assistant works harder so that the threat will not be carried out. In this latter case, the hard work responses are said to be negatively reinforced because they lead to the withdrawal of threatened undesirable consequences. Negative reinforcement is really a type of blackmail: you behave or else.

Both positive and negative reinforcers are widely used in contemporary behavioral management. Yet, most often they are used intuitively and randomly rather than knowledgeably and systematically. As will be pointed out later, negative reinforcement, like punishment, has many undesirable side effects. With positive reinforcement, on the other hand, about the worst that can happen is its failure to work because of some competing contingency or the inadvertent strengthening of undesirable or otherwise unwanted behavior. Technically, in the case of failure, the consequence cannot really be called positive reinforcement. Remember that only when the behavior is strengthened and subsequent frequency increases has positive reinforcement actually been applied.

Reward and positive reinforcement

Contrary to common belief, reward and positive reinforcement are not one and the same. Although closely related, there is a technical and very important difference. All positive reinforcers can be called rewards, but not all rewards turn out to be positive reinforcers. To clarify this point, we must first distinguish between a positive reinforcer and positive reinforcement. A positive reinforcer is a consequence which, when presented, strengthens a behavior. Positive reinforcement is the name used to identify the entire process whereby behavior is strengthened by the contingent presentation of a consequence. In other words, a positive reinforcer is a consequence and positive reinforcement is the overall process.

The technical distinction between a reward and a positive reinforcer, of course, relates to how the terms are defined. Rewards are commonly defined subjectively while positive reinforcers are functionally and operationally defined. Reward, as the term is commonly used, simply refers to the presentation of something seemingly desirable. The word "desirable" accounts for the subjective nature of the definition. Frequently, employee performance is "rewarded" with consequences that the manager feels are desirable.

A true story demonstrates that employees do not always share management's opinion of what is rewarding. A Christmas tradition at a manufacturing plant in a small Midwestern town had been to invite all personnel to a big dinner at the local country club. Prior to the most recent annual party, much to the surprise of the managers, most of whom were club members, a petition was received which asked if the party could be replaced by equivalent cash. Upon investigation, the managers discovered that many of the hourly personnel felt extremely out of place at the country club. They did not go to the country club during the year and felt awkward going there only at Christmas time. Management saw the Christmas party as a reward while many of the operating personnel found it very aversive. The subjective nature of rewards has led to many such problems.

In contrast to subjectively defined rewards, positive reinforcers are functionally defined. Based on Skinner's interpretation of Thorndike's law of effect, the term positive reinforcement has come to mean something very specific in operant psychology and, in turn, in O.B. Mod. A contingent consequence is called a positive reinforcer because it functions as a positive reinforcer. Positive reinforcers strengthen the behavior upon which they are contingent and make the reoccurrence of the behavior more probable. In other words, a consequence is not a positive reinforcer simply because someone has arbitrarily judged it to be such; it must pass the test of being able to increase response frequency. If the response frequency increases, then, and only then, is it a positive reinforcer. Importantly, this functional definition precludes the subjective or *a priori* definition of positive reinforcers. The key lies in the basic datum of behavior management: behavioral frequency.

The process of defining a positive reinforcer is further illustrated in Figure 6-1. This figure helps clarify the earlier statement that positive reinforcers may be called rewards, but not all rewards turn out to be positive reinforcers. Such a distinction is crucial to successful positive consequence management. Traditional "rewards" may not be positive reinforcers. The difference between rewards and positive reinforcers

FIGURE 6-1.   The Process of Functionally Defining Positive Reinforcers

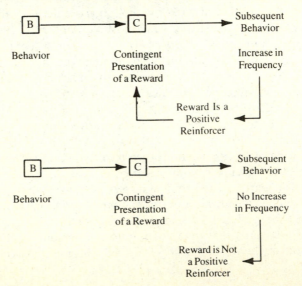

is analogous to the difference between the traditional human relations approach to human resources management and an O.B. Mod. approach.

Another important distinction between rewards and positive reinforcers relates to the contingency concept. Rewards can be and often are presented in a noncontingent manner by managers. Tardiness, dependence, dishonesty, immaturity, output restriction, and other such undesirable behaviors are frequently maintained through the inappropriate use of rewards. In O.B. Mod., positive reinforcers are presented contingent on the successful performance of objectively defined responses. When the store manager says, "I have rewarded Joe with an extra day of summer vacation," two important bits of information are missing: the "if" and the "then" or, the contingency and the effect on behavioral frequency. When the office manager says, "Mary's Monday-through-Thursday performance rating has improved 20 percent since she was given the opportunity to work at her favorite job on Friday, provided she improved her Monday-through-Thursday performance," precise information on both the contingency and the effect on behavioral frequency are given. The store manager's statement is too general for O.B. Mod. purposes, but the office manager's statement presents useful data and is representative of an O.B. Mod. approach.

IDENTIFYING POSITIVE REINFORCERS

The first thing to remember when attempting to identify reinforcers for positive consequence management is that they are unique or idiosyncratic. A true episode illustrates this. After hearing several lectures on the value of positive reinforcement, a student presented one of the authors with a cartoon. It showed a manager picking a sugar cube out of a box and throwing it into the gaping mouth of an employee. The caption read, "He always rewards good work." This cartoon is now prominently posted on the author's door but with an added handwritten notation that reads, "Regarding idiosyncratic reinforcers, not everyone likes sugar."

This comeback helps to make the point that rewards are not necessarily positive reinforcers, and that there is no universal reinforcer. Because all reinforcers must be defined in terms of their effect on subsequent behavioral frequency, there is no single, surefire reinforcer that will effectively control all behavior in a single person or control a single behavior in all people. Technically, the identification of reinforcers becomes a case-by-case proposition. For example, while one employee may work very hard for occasional praise from a relevant supervisor, another will scoff at praise and ask for money. Still another, unimpressed with praise or money, will only be reinforced by the self-evaluation of a job well done. Because of their idiosyncratic nature, a concerted effort is often needed to identify the specific positive reinforcers that work for a particular employee.

The problem of identifying reinforcers is alleviated somewhat by the fact that not every response of every person requires a unique reinforcer. During the socialization process, a person learns to play various socially acceptable roles and consequently comes to behave like many other members of his or her culture (McGinnies, 1970). Consider, for example, the commonality of waking up in a suburban home, having a glass of orange juice, reading the morning newspaper, and joining the morning rush hour. It follows that these common behaviors may come under the control of common consequences. Because of this, many specific reinforcers may be able to strengthen a similar response in a great number of people. Thus, the idiosyncrasy of reinforcers is relative rather than absolute. The collection of reinforcers which positively controls the behavior repertoires of people can be thought of as a kaleidoscope; each person is reinforced by a unique pattern of common parts.

The following discussion summarizes three general approaches that can aid the manager in identifying positive reinforcers on the job. These are: analyzing histories of reinforcement, using self-report data, and using systematic trial-and-error techniques. The use of one, or any combination, of these approaches can help the behavioral manager be more effective in a positive control strategy of consequence management.

Analyzing histories of reinforcement

From a technical standpoint, there is only one correct way to identify positive reinforcers. The correct way involves a historical analysis of contingencies. In Skinner's words (1969), "An experimental analysis permits us to relate behavior to a history of reinforcement" (p. 126). Each behavior in an individual's behavior repertoire has a history of reinforcement. Empirical investigation involves measuring the effect of the managed contingencies on behavior.

A simple functional analysis worksheet as shown in Figure 6-2 could be used. It may be used in conjunction with the response frequency chart illustrated and discussed in Chapter 4 (Steps 2 and 3 of the model). This approach gives the behavioral manager a workable set of tools for systematically analyzing the histories of reinforcement.

FIGURE 6-2.   Functional Analysis Worksheet

Employee

Position   Observer   Observation Period

Note: Describe Each Antecedent Condition, Behavior, and Consequence Carefully

Date/Time   Antecedent ———➤ Behavioral Event ———➤ Consequence

Initially, a particular consequence is made contingent on a performance-related response. Next, a functional analysis worksheet is used to identify all three elements (the A, B, and C) in the contingency. The frequency of the target response can then be charted on the response frequency graph. If the response frequently moves upward, then the consequence in question is a reinforcer. More specifically, the consequence is a *positive* reinforcer if it involves the presentation of some environmental condition and the frequency of response subsequently increases.

In addition to measuring the effect of consequences in experimentally monitored contingencies, this procedure may also be used to identify positive reinforcers in naturally occurring contingencies. Ongoing work environments are not always amenable to experimental manipulation of contingencies for the purpose of identifying positive reinforcers. If such is the case, an alternative method of identifying positive reinforcers is available to the behavioral manager. It involves only observation, as opposed to the management of consequences and observation. Naturally occurring contingencies can be functionally analyzed by use of a functional analysis worksheet, and then recorded on a behavior frequency chart. Observed frequencies can then be analyzed and interpreted. Positive reinforcers which support both desirable and undesirable performance-related behaviors may be identified in this manner. Conceivably, an appropriate intervention strategy, as discussed in Step 4 of the O.B. Mod. model discussed in Chapter 4, could shift the positive reinforcers of undesirable behavior to desirable behavior. This approach represents effective use of data uncovered through the analysis of histories of reinforcement.

Naturally, the farther away one gets from functionally analyzing histories of reinforcement, the less accurate will be the specific identification of true positive reinforcers. An analysis of someone's history of reinforcement reveals the idiosyncratic nature of positive reinforcers. Also, this approach has the advantage of forcing the manager to view organizational behavior in $A \rightarrow B \rightarrow C$ terms and thus use an O.B. Mod. model in consequence management.

Self-reporting of reinforcers

Due to time, or just pragmatic necessity, it may not be possible to technically analyze histories of reinforcement in order to identify on-the-job positive reinforcers. Like any technique which involves the systematic collection of empirical data, the analysis of histories of reinforcement can be very time consuming and tedious for a busy manager. An alternative is to use self-report approaches.

Ask what is reinforcing • The most basic self-report approach would be to simply ask an employee what is reinforcing for him or her. Although this approach can work and is the most straightforward, caution is advised. A verbal self-report stating that a certain consequence is reinforcing is not the same as the result of a history of reinforcment analysis. In other words, verbal opinion is one thing, actual behavior is another. With reference to this point, Skinner (1969) has cautioned that the information derived by asking a person what his or her intentions, plans, or expectations are " . . . may be worth investigating, but it is not a substitute for the behavior observed in an operant analysis" (p. 116). Stated another way, the most reliable indicator of consequences that are positive reinforcers is the history of reinforcement, in which frequency of response is the basic datum. However, because of the realistic limitations of such an approach, self-report techniques may be relied upon in O.B. Mod.

Contingency questionnaires • Questionnaire self-report methods of identifying reinforcers is suggested in a study reported by Reitz (1971). He employed a contingency questionnaire to measure perceived performance-outcome probabilities. Respondents select one of six responses (100 percent certain, very probable, fairly probable, uncertain, fairly improbable, and very improbable) for each of the twenty items. The net result is a self-report selection of contingencies.

Contingency questionnaires can give the practicing manager a reasonably good idea of what types of consequences are important to individual subordinates. Fourteen of the items used by Reitz (1971) identify positive reinforcement contingencies. They include the following:

1) Your supervisor would personally pay you a compliment if you did outstanding work.

2) Your supervisor would lend a sympathetic ear if you had a complaint.

3) You will eventually go as far as you would like to go in this company if your work is consistently above average.

4) You would be promoted if your work was better than others who were otherwise equally qualified.

5) Your supervisor would help you to get a transfer if you asked for one.

6) Your supervisor's boss or others in higher management would know about it if your work was outstanding.

7) Your supervisor's recommendation for a pay increase for you would be consistent with his evaluation of your performance.

8) Your supervisor would show a great deal of interest if you suggested a new and better way of doing things.

9) You would receive special recognition if your work performance was especially good.

10) Your supervisor would do all he could to help you if you were having problems in your work.

11) Your supervisor's evaluation of your performance would be in agreement with your own evaluation of your performance.

12) Your next pay increase will be consistent with the amount recommended by your supervisor.

13) Your supervisor would encourage you to do better if your performance was unacceptable but well below what you are capable of doing.

14) You would be promoted within the next two years if your work was consistently better than the work of others in your department.

While the information generated from this type of self-report instrument is not as precise as that obtained from analyses of histories of reinforcement, this approach can still generate an approximate profile of behavior that requires reinforcement and operative positive reinforcers. Being contingencies, all fourteen of the above statements are if-then statements. The "ifs" refer to performance or results of performance and the "thens" refer to rewards or potential positive reinforcers. Low probability responses to the statements represent areas that probably need attention by the behavioral manager. In other words, the "then" side of the contingency relationship is deficient. Appropriate contingent consequences would then have to be identified and applied.

A close look at the contingency questionnaire reveals that the rewards include a compliment, sympathy, promotion, transfer, recognition from top management, a pay increase, attention, special recognition, help with problems, recognition from the supervisor, and support. Some or all of these rewards may, in fact, turn out to be positive reinforcers that are currently maintaining effective performance. For example, a high-performing employee might indicate low pay and promotion probabilities but a high special-recognition probability. On the basis of such information, the manager could then turn directly to the task of analyzing the histories of reinforcement where special recognition is involved to determine objectively if special recognition is, in fact, a positive reinforcer. Conceivably, a self-report instrument of this nature could be used to identify a general class of potential reinforcers. Subsequent refinements could be carried out with an analysis of reinforcement histories.

Another contingency questionnaire is proposed in Figure 6–3. This test is designed to simply have the respondent fill in the missing if-then contingency elements. The purpose of this test format is to assist in the identification of idiosyncratic reinforcers. It is important to note that this performance/consequence questionnaire is only a suggested prototype. Its validity and reliability have not been tested. Obviously, such an instrument would have very broad applicability. Figure 6–3 is intended to show how a manager using O.B. Mod. can tailor an instrument so that the "ifs" would be key performance-related responses and the "thens" would be rewards (potential positive reinforcers) actually controlled by management. Such a tailor-made instrument could help the manager using O.B. Mod. to measure the degree of contingency in the work environment and help identify positive reinforcers.

"Cafeteria" techniques • Another self-report method for identifying positive reinforcers is cafeteria techniques. Rather than responding to a carefully developed questionnaire, the individual employee chooses his or her own rewards from a broad selection. This approach is really a hybrid evolving from two separate, but not altogether unrelated, trends. The first trend occurred in education. Originally formulated by Premack (1959) and later developed by Addison and Homme (1966), a so-called reinforcement menu technique was designed to involve reluctant schoolchildren in their school work by

FIGURE 6-3.   Sample Performance/Consequence Questionnaire

Directions: After carefully considering your present job, fill in the following blanks as specifically as possible.

            Performance   *Consequence*

If _____, then I will get a raise.

If I ask for a transfer, then _____.

If _____, then I will be complimented by my supervisor.

If I am having problems with my work, then _____.

If _____, then my supervisor will show interest in my work.

If I do my job better than usual, then _____.

If _____, then I will get more sense of accomplishment from my job.

If I make a suggestion, then _____.

If _____, then I will be promoted.

If I take proper care of my equipment, then _____.

If _____, then I will like my job more.

If my work is outstanding, then _____.

If _____, then I will be formally recognized by top management.

If I get to work on time, then _____.

If _____, then I will get some help from my supervisor.

If I save the company some money, then _____.

            Other relationships not mentioned above

If _____, then _____.

If _____, then _____.

If _____, then _____.

If _____, then _____.

allowing them to "pick their own reinforcers." Under this system, the children start working for rewards they desire, not rewards the teacher arbitrarily thinks they desire or should desire. A reinforcement menu typically involves items such as playtime, time away from the task, recess, and favorite curricular and extracurricular activities. Importantly, all reinforcers are contingent upon the achievement of desirable performance criteria. If a student properly completes an assigned activity, then he or she gets to pick a desired reward from the menu. This technique has proven successful for many teachers (Blackham and Silberman, 1971, pp. 128–29).

A trend parallel to that in education has developed in business, particularly in compensation programs. These are the so-called cafeteria compensation plans. This approach involves tailoring the compensation package to fit the individual employee. He or she is allowed to select a total compensation package from a vast assortment of options. For example, an executive may choose more time off instead of cash, or select a deferred income plan instead of immediate cash, or take the cash right now. The total dollar cost is the same in each case but the way it is split up can widely differ. From an O.B. Mod. standpoint, the probability that the selected rewards from such a plan will turn out to be positive reinforcers is greatly increased.

Any personnel manager or compensation specialist will readily admit that the task of employee compensation is getting progressively more difficult. Like everything else, employee likes and dislikes are undergoing drastic change. Much time and effort are being devoted to ensuring equal pay for equal work. In addition, there has been a steady growth in nonwage benefits and services; and tax legislation and Internal Revenue Service interpretations of various types of compensation are continually changing. The base wage or salary has become secondary in many instances. With this type of situation, cafeteria compensation plans take on added appeal. If a contingency relationship between performance and reward is assured, these new approaches to compensation can increase the number of positive reinforcers available on the job.

Admittedly, contingency management in a classroom setting with youngsters and contingency management in a complex organization are two different matters. Contingencies in organizations cannot be as clearcut and time-efficient as the classroom contingencies and some practical, administrative problems have been pointed out (e.g., see: Milkovich and Delaney, 1975; Goode, 1974). There is no question that such an approach to compensation would require considerable planning and administrative tolerance. However, computerization makes this much more feasible and many companies are moving in this direction. For example, American Can created 8,000 individual benefit plans for their staff.

From a reinforcement standpoint, the cafeteria approach has exciting possibilities as a method of identifying positive reinforcers on the job. Successful application for O.B. Mod. depends on establishing contingencies between key performance-related behavior and the chosen forms of compensation.

Identifying positive reinforcers through trial and error

Besides analyzing reinforcement histories and using self-report techniques, managers can turn to systematic trial and error to identify on-the-job positive reinforcers. Though much less precise and efficient than the other two approaches, it is much more convenient and readily applicable and, if done systematically, certainly better than no approach at all. This third approach is very straightforward: make a reward contingent on a particular performance-related response and objectively observe what happens. Increased frequency of response identifies a positive reinforcer and decreased frequency eliminates the consequence as a reinforcer. Once systematically identified this way, positive reinforcers can be made contingent on similar performance-related behavior to see if their ability to positively control generalizes to other behavior.

On the surface, the trial-and-error method appears to be the same as the history-of-reinforcement technique described earlier. They are similar in intent, but that is where the similarity ends. One of the major differences between the two is that in the trial-and-error method the manager relies on rewards to induce performance, without distinguishing between rewards and positive reinforcers. Unlike the analysis of the history of reinforcement, no special attempt is made to ensure a contingency relationship between response and consequence and no accurate response frequency records are kept. With trial and error, the manager often guesses at the reinforcing ability of various consequences. Once again, what reinforces one person may not reinforce another: the idiosyncrasy of reinforcement. A more systematic approach to trial-and-error identification would be the development of a classification scheme of on-the-job rewards.

CLASSIFICATION OF ON-THE-JOB REWARDS

Although practically all managers unwittingly use trial and error, an O.B. Mod. approach requires that it be done much more systematically than is usually the case. The starting point is to categorize all positive consequences available to a given manager. Although most of today's managers cannot directly give more money or time off or a promotion on the spot, they still have many potential reinforcers available to them. To ensure that all possible forms of rewards are considered, a classification framework becomes helpful. Such a classification was proposed by Meacham and Wiesen (1969, p. 46) as follows: (1)

consumables; (2) manipulatables; (3) visual and auditory stimuli; (4) social stimuli; (5) tokens; and (6) Premack. The word *reward* is used to deliberately emphasize that this approach does not necessarily identify positive reinforcers. Only follow-up measures will reveal if the rewards are actually operating as positive reinforcers.

Examples of all the categories are listed in Figure 6–4. The consumables, manipulatables, visual and auditory stimuli, and tokens are placed under the general heading of contrived rewards. The natural rewards, which are much more important to O.B. Mod., are shown to be social stimuli and Premack.

Contrived rewards

Contrived rewards are largely brought in from outside the natural work environment and generally involve costs for the organization over and above the existing situation. It is the contrived rewards which usually come to mind first when practitioners are asked about possible rewards for employees. These are the "jellybeans" that Frederick Herzberg critically refers to in his comment "Jumping for Jellybeans," where he criticizes extrinsic rewards as a way to motivate employees. Although they can be used to positively reinforce behavior, besides being costly, they also tend to lead to satiation rather quickly. An employee can be reinforced by movie passes or wall plaques only so long before he or she becomes tired of these.

An even greater problem with contrived rewards is that they are seldom administered on a contingent basis. The watch given after twenty-five years of "loyal" service to the organization is noncontingent on the individual's performance. About the only thing the watch does is reinforce walking up to the boss and shaking his or her hand as it is presented. A Christmas turkey or even an annual bonus is administered on a noncontingent basis. Even the weekly, biweekly, or monthly paycheck is noncontingent on day-to-day job behavior. Most often the paycheck simply reinforces walking up to a pay window or opening an envelope. In some cases, where employees have their check automatically deposited in their checking account, they never see any money from the organization, let alone establish a contingency with specific job behaviors.

A good example of the use of contrived rewards is the fairly common practice of awarding green stamps or some other reward, such as free dinners or movie tickets, to increase the attendance behavior of employees (reduce absenteeism). Although these programs almost always initially work, they soon begin to fizzle because the employees

FIGURE 6-4. Classifications of On-The-Job Rewards

Contrived On-The-Job Rewards				Natural Rewards	
Consumables	Manipulatables	Visual and Auditory	Tokens	Social	Premack
Coffee-break treats	Desk accessories	Office with a window	Money	Friendly greetings	Job with more responsibility
Free lunches	Personal computer	Piped-in music	Stocks	Informal recognition	Job rotation
Food baskets	Wall plaques	Redecoration of work environment	Stock options	Formal acknowledgment of achievement	Early time off with pay
Easter hams	Company car	Company literature	Movie passes	Feedback about performance	Extended breaks
Christmas turkeys	Watches	Private office	Trading stamps (green stamps)	Solicitations of suggestions	Extended lunch period
Dinners for the family on the company	Trophies	Popular speakers or lecturers	Paid-up insurance policies	Solicitations of advice	Personal time off with pay
Company picnics	Commendations	Book club discussions	Dinner theater/sports tickets	Compliment on work progress	Work on personal project on company time
After-work wine and cheese parties	Rings/tie pins		Vacation trips	Recognition in house organ	Use of company machinery or facilities for personal projects
	Appliances and furniture for the home		Coupons redeemable at local stores	Pat on the back	Use of company recreation facilities
	Home shop tools		Profit sharing	Smile	Special assignments
	Garden tools			Verbal or nonverbal recognition or praise	
	Clothing				
	Club privileges				

become satiated. However, an interesting variation is worthy of mention. One company wrote to each employee's wife announcing the green stamp attendance program, rather than announcing the program to the employees in the normal way by memo or bulletin board. The male-dominated work force in this firm did not seem to be particularly reinforced by green stamps, but the company found out that the wives were. It soon became evident that the wives were getting their spouses to work in the morning in order to receive the green stamps. The behavior used by the wives to induce their husbands to go to work increased in frequency when the contingent consequence was green stamps. As mentioned in Chapters 3 and 4, the administration of the reinforcement may be more important than its content. This company was able to dramatically increase attendance by appropriately administering a contrived reinforcement program.

Natural rewards

Natural rewards are of much more value than contrived rewards in O.B. Mod. These are the rewards that exist in the natural occurrence of events. The social category listed in Figure 6–4 almost always contains natural reinforcers, as do all the existing work procedures, schedules, task assignments, and personnel policies concerning incentive pay, transfer, time off, breaks, etc. Whereas contrived reinforcers generally cost the organization additional money, natural rewards do not. Social reinforcers and existing procedures and policies cost nothing extra. Natural social rewards are potentially the most powerful and universally applicable reinforcers. In contrast to contrived rewards, they do not generally lead to satiation (people seldom get tired of compliments, attention, or recognition) and can be administered on a very contingent basis. The supervisor of any group of employees at any level in the organization is the major source of potential reinforcement. He or she cannot normally dole out consumables, manipulatables, or tokens, but he or she can and does constantly give out social rewards. In the O.B. Mod. approach, however, these social rewards are contingent on desired performance-related behavior and the results are measured to see if they in fact turn out to be positive reinforcers.

The "feedback about performance" listed under the social column of Figure 6–4 deserves special mention. Although this extremely important potential reinforcer could be listed under the "visual and auditory" column in Figure 6–4, it is considered a natural reward here because feedback information is almost always available in the existing situation and is treated as "social" because feedback is contingently administered by the supervisor. Although there is some controversy surrounding feedback as a reinforcer (Ilgen, Fisher, and Taylor, 1979), the studies that have used feedback as an intervention strategy in O.B. Mod. have demonstrated it to have a very positive impact on performance behavior (Prue and Fairbank, 1981). Thus, although the nature of feedback information, the process of using feedback, the individual differences of the recipients of the feedback, and the nature of the task (Nadler, 1979) should all be given attention in the application of contingent performance feedback, it is the most widely used and potentially powerful reinforcer available in O.B. Mod. Chapter 8 will bring this out in some actual applications of O.B. Mod. In general, this feedback should be as *positive, specific*, and *timely* as possible (Kreitner, 1977). Another important guideline is to present performance feedback graphically whenever possible. This, of course, gets away from the "computer printout syndrome" bothering most employees today and provides easy to grasp, instantaneous feedback on trends at a level of specificity not available from verbal or written feedback.

Natural rewards stemming from existing procedures and policies can be made into positive reinforcers by using the Premack Principle. Discussed earlier, this category of rewards involves the use of high probability behavior to reinforce low probability behavior. Undoubtedly, many of us vividly remember our parents saying to us when we were young, "You don't get your dessert until you have finished your dinner" or "You can go out and play with friends after you clean up your room." Whether they realized it or not, our parents were using the Premack Principle. In O.B. Mod., this principle takes advantage of the reinforcing properties of an opportunity to engage in a preferred activity that is already natural to the job. Although frequently overlooked in behavioral management, there are many preferred activities that can be made contingent on less preferred but organizationally important activities.

For example, assume an employee has two tasks to do, A and B. If he or she likes to do B better than A, then the Premack Principle would say that A should be performed first and followed by B. In this manner B becomes a reinforcer for first performing the less desirable A. Performance-contingent time off and rotation to more desirable tasks are some practical examples. Getting off early from work may have strong reinforcing properties for personnel performing tedious, routine tasks such as sorting checks or mail. As an illustration of the reinforcing properties of leaving work, one need only observe and contrast the speed with which employees punch in and start work and later punch out and leave. One manager recently remarked that he wouldn't want to be standing in the exit door when quitting time came around.

The key to taking advantage of the reinforcing properties of leaving the work place lies in making it contingent on performance. More precisely, the work environment must be arranged so that early time off with pay can be earned through improved performance at a given level of quality. In one real case, a bank was having trouble that involved hand counting and calculating checks that the computer rejected. This was a very boring, but nonetheless important job. Turnover was extremely high and costly errors were frequent. The manager of this operation decided to use a contingent time off (CTO) approach with the employees in this job. Extremely high standards of performance were set (higher than actual performance had ever been in the history of this job) and a very demanding level of quality (no detected errors). The contingency contract was that once the employee reached these very high levels of performance, he or she was permitted to go home for the day. What happened, of course, was that the CTO turned out to be a powerful positive reinforcer: the employees in this job were going home very early every afternoon.

MONEY AS A CONSEQUENCE MANAGEMENT STRATEGY

There are two major reasons for giving special attention to money as a reward in the positive control of organizational behavior. First, the extensive use of money makes it the closest thing there is to a universal reward in behavioral management. Second, the use of money as a reward for performance is as controversial as it is widespread. Discussing money as a consequence management strategy will certainly not end the controversy, but it will give emphasis to the dual role of money as a reward and a positive reinforcer.

The complexity of money

Human resource management experts such as Lawler (1981) have generally agreed that monetary reward should be tied to performance in order to get the most "motivational" impact. The generally advocated solution is a variety of individual or group incentive pay for hourly workers and some type of merit or bonus plan for salaried personnel. For example, some operations management experts, citing the successful use of piece-rate pay plans since the time of Frederick W. Taylor's scientific management movement at the turn of the century, recommend the use of incentive wage plans (McManis and Dick, 1973).

On the other hand, some organizational behavior theorists stress the administrative, technical, and psychological problems associated with piece-rate compensation. Some of the important "human" problems mentioned are output restriction (Vroom, 1964, p. 258), diminished intrinsic motivation (Deci, 1973; Mawhinney, 1979), and reduced satisfaction (Schwab, 1974). There is also strong evidence to suggest that incentive pay plans are not used as widely as is supposed (Evans, 1970; Lawler, 1971, p. 158). Most recently, Lawler (1981) reports that the trend in large companies is to have more than one performance-based pay plan. For example, TRW, General Electric, and Borg-Warner have multiple plant-level bonus systems. The net result is general confusion and few useful guidelines for the behavior manager in tying pay to performance and using money as a reward for performance.

Money is the best example of a generalized conditioned reinforcer. In spite of being the most common reward for organizational performance, it is not necessarily a positive reinforcer. Once again, money is not a positive reinforcer until its performance-contingent presentation demonstrably increases response frequency. This fundamental point is often overlooked by those advocating wage-incentive plans or by the expectancy motivational theorists who are concerned with valence, expectancy, and instrumentality. While these latter terms may help us to understand the psychological process of motivation and, more specifically, the role of money as a motivator, they have done little to explain how to control employee behavior with money. Only situation-specific experimentation on a case-by-case basis will tell the behavioral manager whether money is a reward and a positive reinforcer or just a reward with no known impact on performance. The key from an O.B. Mod. perspective lies in analyzing the histories of reinforcement for money and gauging its impact on performance-related behavior.

The changing social, technological, and economic environment suggests that the reinforcing potential of money may be diminishing. First, unemployment insurance and other forms of social welfare have diminished the significance of money earned through work (Conversation with B. F. Skinner, 1973). Second, and perhaps more important, as we pointed out earlier, the contingency connection between performance and pay is slowly but steadily eroded mainly through the increased use of time-based pay plans. For example, a weekly, biweekly, or monthly paycheck is administered on a fixed interval schedule of reinforcement (described in Chapter 3 as being one of the least efficient reinforcement schedules). Thus, the reward of money is weakened as a positive reinforcer because of the diminution of its reinforcing properties (for example, because of less materialistic social values) and the inefficient manner in which it is typically administered in today's organizations. Economic factors like inflation also do little to enhance the reinforcing properties of money as its purchasing value is eroded. Many kids today will not even bother to pick up a penny or nickel on the sidewalk.

Making money contingent

As far as conventional pay plans are concerned, with the possible exception of sales commissions, the piece-rate method is the most contingent. An increment of pay is given for a defined increment of work. During the scientific management era, dramatic improvements in performance were attained through the use of such piece-rate incentive plans. They appeared to be one of the keys to greater human productivity. Workers were generally very poor economically, the tasks were relatively simple to perform, and the key variable was the speed at which the individual worked. However, as twentieth-century technology pervaded and began to dominate industrial organizations, the resulting human/machine interface began to complicate the conventional piece-rate plans. As a result of this new technological variable and administrative problems with establishing and maintaining meaningful standards, piece-rate plans fell into a state of limbo and confusion, where they seem to remain today.

The best means of getting piece-rate incentive plans out of their current state is to start making money truly contingent on key performance-related behaviors. The same holds true for merit pay plans for managerial personnel, although the process would be more difficult. At the minimum, some portion of the paycheck should always be made contingent on performance (Cummings and Schwab, 1973, p. 53). Appropriate consideration must also be given to task, technology, personal, group, and other relevant work-environment variables. By identifying key performance-related behavior and then making monetary rewards as contingent as possible upon improvement, at least part of the paycheck becomes a reward for more than simply showing up at work. Performance improvement is also rewarded.

A study reported by Hermann et al. (1973) illustrates the practical utility of making money contingent on a specific on-the-job response. In this study money was more than a reward; it became a positive reinforcer. Chronic tardiness was the behavior problem. The subjects were workers at a Mexican division of a large U.S. corporation. Several workers with chronic tardiness records were experimentally exposed to some systematic positive consequences. The target behavior was punctuality—defined as punching a time clock card on or before the designated starting time. Punching in later was the incompatible, undesirable response of tardiness. Each worker in the experiment was instructed that every day he arrived on time the plant guard would give him a slip of paper saying he was entitled to a small cash bonus (approximately 3 percent of an average day's pay). At the end of each work week the workers could exchange their punctuality bonus slips for cash. This arrangement had the effect of making the slips of paper conditioned reinforcers; they had value because of their association with money.

Baseline punctuality figures covering the previous year were obtained from punch-card records. All together, there were three experimental treatment periods and three baseline periods. This reversal design was discussed in the last chapter as meeting the threats to reliability and validity. To ensure that any changes in tardiness were due to the presence or absence of the punctuality bonus plan, an equivalent control group which did not receive the plan was also selected and observed. Tardiness increased during the baseline periods (the control periods) when the bonus plan was not in effect and clearly decreased during the treatment periods when the workers were able to earn a bonus for punctual arrival at work. The last treatment period covering thirty-two weeks demonstrated the durability of the bonus effect. More tardy arrivals at work were recorded for the control group which was not under the punctuality bonus plan than for the experimental group which was. Clearly, the punctuality bonus plan helped this company overcome its tardiness problem with the workers studied.

The primary value of the above reported study is the manner in which it demonstrates how management can turn rewards like money into positive reinforcers. Consistent with the whole O.B. Mod. approach, the techniques and application of performance-contingent pay must necessarily be objective and precise which, of course, takes time. The benefits accruing to the organization in the form of greater effectiveness, however, can make the effort worthwhile. This or any other consequence management approach must include continual monitoring of the results to make sure the desired change is being maintained and aimed toward performance improvement.

NEGATIVE CONTROL IN CONSEQUENCE MANAGEMENT

So far, positive control in general and reinforcement techniques in particular have dominated the discussion. We strongly feel that this is the most effective form of consequence management. On the other hand, we are also realistic enough to recognize that negative control in general and punishment in particular are a common consequence management strategy. Thus, the remainder of this chapter is devoted to developing an understanding of and effectiveness in using this "dark side" of consequence management.

The functional definition of punishment

Realistically, punishment probably plays as much a role in the control of human behavior as does reinforcement. As with reinforcement, punishment should be operationally and functionally defined. In other words, the consequences involved in the process called punishment must be labeled in terms of their effect on frequency of behavior. In a punishment contingency, the effect is a reduction of behavioral frequency; punishment weakens behavior. As in the other O.B. Mod. concepts discussed thus far, this definition centers around the action of the individual, the reaction of the environment, and the subsequent effect on behavioral frequency.

An important distinction to make is the one between the subjective use of the term punisher and what is meant here by functional punishment. Like a reward, a punisher is often a subjectively defined consequence. But like positive reinforcement, punishment is a functionally defined process. The term punishment is used to identify a consequence that has demonstrably weakened a particular response (its frequency has decreased). A subjectively defined aversive consequence could be called a punisher while a functionally defined consequence is called punishment.

The example of a manager publicly berating a subordinate helps clarify this distinction. From the manager's viewpoint, the public berating was felt to be a punishment for the subordinate, supposedly possessing the power to weaken the undesirable behavior. However, precisely the opposite may occur. The subordinate in this case may go out of his way to misbehave to "get the manager's goat" or, perhaps, he may see misbehaving as the only way to receive any attention from his boss. In this example, the assumed punisher actually turns out to be a positive reinforcer. The use of negative control commonly backfires this way when managers fail to make the important distinction between subjective punishers and functional punishment. An O.B. Mod. approach centers on behavioral frequency when defining punishment. Again, punishment weakens behavior and decreases its frequency. If the consequence does not have this effect, punishment has not occurred.

A last point in functionally defining punishment is to recognize that, like reinforcement, punishment is idiosyncratic. Using the example cited above, a manager's public berating of an employee because of performance deficiencies may be punishing for some but not for others. Only the decreased frequency of a particular response stands as an accurate and reliable indicator of the effects of various so-called punishers. Because punishment is idiosyncratic, thus producing different effects in different people, a hard and fast list of universally effective punishers is just as difficult to formulate as a list of universally effective positive reinforcers. Consequences are not punishing simply because the manager feels they should be punishing. However, punishers can be identified in much the same manner as is used for reinforcers.

The role of negative reinforcement

Some may argue that negative reinforcement contributes to positive rather than negative control of behavior. As we pointed out earlier in this chapter and in Chapter 3, negative reinforcement has the opposite effect of punishment on behavior. It strengthens behavior, only negatively. But because punishing consequences are a threat in negative reinforcement, it is considered a form of negative control in consequence management.

Like punishment, negative reinforcement is widely used and abused. Most discussions of human behavior either ignore it or lump it together with positive reinforcement or punishment. One major reason for the confusion surrounding negative reinforcement is that it is a concept that is much more difficult to explain verbally or in writing than it is to apply in the actual control of behavior. Although much of everyone's behavior is a function of negative reinforcement, most people, including managers who greatly depend on it, do not understand it. Negative reinforcement and punishment are not the same. Behavior is strengthened rather than weakened through negative reinforcement. When a behavior prevents or terminates a punishing consequence and is thereby strengthened, negative reinforcement has occurred. Put into everyday terms, when certain behavior gets or keeps us out of trouble, we tend to repeat that behavior when we are again faced with the same situation.

Negative reinforcement starts to control behavior at a very early age. Once a child learns that his or her parent will finally give in to various demands after a period of progressively louder crying, the process of negative reinforcement begins to control both the child's and the parent's behavior. The tantrum-throwing child who is pacified with a cookie is being positively reinforced for throwing tantrums. More importantly, however, the behavior of the parent (the response of giving her misbehaving child a cookie) is negatively reinforced by the prevention or termination of the bothersome crying. Thus, the child gets a cookie for the parent's *negative* reinforcement. It is interesting to note who the real behavior modifier is in this example. Learning from experience, the child makes greater and greater demands. Later, as an adult, the individual possesses a whole repertoire of disruptive behavior with which to exact compliance from others regarding personal demands.

In a technical sense, there are normally two key roles in the use of negative reinforcement: (1) the person who controls the aversive situation and stands to gain if the other person behaves in a certain manner; and (2) the person who is negatively reinforced for emitting the appropriate behavior which terminates or prevents the aversive situation. In the following discussion, these two roles are simply referred to as Role 1 and Role 2. In effect, from the standpoint of the Role 1 person, a negative reinforcement strategy constitutes a form of social blackmail. The Role 2 person must do something or continue to be punished. The reason for labeling negative reinforcement as a form of negative control should now be clear.

Examples of negative reinforcement in human resource management are plentiful. A nagging head nurse (Role 1) is positively reinforced by a staff nurse's return to a necessary but distasteful task. The staff nurse (Role 2), meanwhile, is negatively reinforced for returning to the task because the head nurse stops nagging. Similarly, a busy executive (Role 2) is negatively reinforced for answering the phone. When a manufacturing company's collective bargaining team (Role 2) yields to the demands of the striking union (Role 1), its action is negatively reinforced by the termination of the strike. In each case, the Role 2 person(s) had to behave in a prescribed manner in order to escape an unpleasant situation.

Negative reinforcement has many of the same undesirable side effects as punishment. These will be mentioned later. For now, it is hoped that the reader has a clearer understanding of this relatively *difficult* area of negative reinforcement. Because of its prevalence, this understanding is important when using the O.B. Mod. approach to behavioral management.

The role of extinction

Whereas negative reinforcement has the opposite effect of punishment on behavior, extinction has the same effect. Both punishment and extinction reduce behavior frequency and weaken behavior. Notably, each reduces the response frequency—punishment through the presentation of noxious or withdrawal of positive consequences, and extinction through the termination of rewards, or simply the failure to provide any type of contingent consequence. Angrily telling someone that his opinion has offended you would constitute punishment while ignoring or not paying any attention to his opinion would constitute extinction. Both strategies attempt to prevent further expression of the offending opinion. However, undesirable side effects are much less probable with an extinction strategy. On the other hand, an extinction strategy generally takes much longer to decrease frequencies than does punishment and is more difficult to accomplish.

As Chapter 3 pointed out, there is a very fine line between punishment and extinction. According to Bandura (1969): "In extinction, consequences that ordinarily follow the behavior are simply discontinued; in punishment, behavior results in the application of aversive consequences through forfeiture of positive reinforcers" (p. 338). Thus, the failure to formally or informally recognize an employee's superior performance could be construed as extinction. The withdrawal of recognition, pay, or privileges because of substandard performance would be punishment. In the former case a desirable behavior is unintentionally weakened. Regardless of the intent, both extinction and punishment weaken behavior. As an intervention strategy, extinction may be effectively employed as an alternative to punishment for weakening undesirable behavior.

Escape and avoidance behavior

Much of the day-to-day behavior that occurs in today's organizations involves escaping from or avoiding punishing situations. Modern work environments are literally filled with potential and actual punishing consequences. Criticism, undesirable tasks, nagging, unsatisfactory performance evaluations, layoffs, pay docks, and terminations are common punishing consequences of employee behavior. Each of these real or imagined consequences may lead to escape behavior. When a harried executive leaves work a few hours early to play tennis, she is emitting escape behavior. She is escaping the stress and pressure of her job by playing tennis. In this case, the aversive situation is both physiologically and psychologically based. In a more social context, the securities broker who snaps at a complaining client after the stock market goes down again may also be emitting escape behavior.

A careful functional analysis generally reveals that a person who punishes others is exhibiting escape behavior. In other words, punishment begets more punishment. Recalling the earlier discussion of negative reinforcement, it is easy to see why escape behavior is so common. People in punishing situations are negatively reinforced for behaving in a way that will terminate the punishment.

The unfortunate aspect of escape behavior is that it usually detracts from rather than facilitates effective job performance. For a government welfare agency employee, the short-run personal objective of expeditiously passing along a troublesome case may take precedence over the organizational objective of efficient, thorough service. Immediate negative reinforcement resulting from escape behavior is very appealing, particularly when the pressure is on, as it is in most organizations. Unfortunately, high-pressure situations often demand problem solvers who can persevere and resist the negative reinforcement associated with expedient escape behavior. To the extent that performance-related behavior is at the same time escape behavior (employees performing to escape punishing situations), many aggressive, emotional, and otherwise dysfunctional behaviors will emerge. Performance in the name of placating a punitive boss will tend to be reluctant, marginal, and of relatively short duration. Furthermore, the desirable goal of self-control is highly improbable when organizational participants must perform in order to escape negative consequences.

Avoidance is conceptually different from escape behavior. As a result of experience with punishing consequences, people learn to associate environmental cues (the antecedent of the behavioral contingency) with punishment. These cues, through their association with past punishing consequences, take on aversive properties and serve as warnings of impending punishment. Threats of various undesirable consequences such as layoff, unsatisfactory performance ratings, and termination signal impending punishment. These threatening cues serve as antecedent events which set the occasion for avoidance behavior. Employees living under expressed or implied threats work to avoid having the manager carry out the threats.

As will be discussed in greater detail later, punitive managers themselves often become so closely associated with the punishment they inflict that their mere presence in the work environment cues or sets the occasion for all sorts of avoidance behavior. For example, subordinates will look busy to avoid being reprimanded. A manager with this stigma has little hope of being viewed as a source of positive reinforcement for desirable performance. Like escape behavior, avoidance behavior is not typically associated with efficient and highly productive behavior. With escape and avoidance behavior, employees are literally looking over their shoulders for trouble or signs of trouble rather than straight ahead at what must be done in order to get the reinforcing consequences associated with effective performance. This type of inefficient behavior is symptomatic of the use of negative control.

THE CASE AGAINST NEGATIVE CONTROL

An entirely distinct combination of variables goes into action every time an individual is faced with a negatively based if-then behavioral contingency. The behavior modifiers, in turn, operate under their own if-then contingencies. In general, results may be unpredictable if punishment is used.

To build a case against the use of negative control, it is initially important to note that punishment does not weaken behavior as efficiently as positive reinforcement strengthens behavior. This disparity is due to the possibility, with punishment, of undesirable and unpredictable side effects. This is not to say that punishment does not work, but rather that it does *more* than work.

In the following discussion, specific attention is focused on the four long-run side effects of punishment: temporary suppression of behavior rather than permanent change; the generation of emotional, anxious behavior; the possibility of behavioral inflexibility; and the generalization of aversiveness to the controller of the punishing consequences. These side effects are so counterproductive that they present an effective case against punishment. Conceivably, if more managers were aware of the undesirable side effects of punishment, they would not rely so heavily on it for changing the behavior of organizational participants.

Temporary suppression of behavior

As many parents, teachers, and managers have discovered, the old adage that "when the cat's away, the mice will play" is all too often true. Punishment will eventually operate against the person using it. Once a behavioral manager depends on punitive control, he or she will have to continue to rely on it to exact compliance. Punishment only temporarily suppresses rather than permanently changes behavior (Skinner, 1953, pp. 183–84). Empirical research shows that punishment initially reduces response frequency, but once the aversive consequence is withdrawn or not salient (in the forefront of awareness), the punished response reemerges. Continued negative control becomes necessary for sustained suppression and, hence, punishment leads to more punishment.

Consider, for example, the undesirable response of wasting time by telling stories on the job. After warning her subordinate a number of times about idly standing around telling stories, a food service manager catches a glimpse of the subordinate distracting three co-workers with a story. Knowing the subordinate is sensitive to criticism, the food service manager decides to really "chew out" the subordinate right in front of her co-workers. Besides, the manager feels her action will serve as a warning to the other members of the work group. So the manager proceeds to berate her subordinate for stealing valuable time and keeping others from their work. As soon as the manager finishes talking, everyone goes back to her own job and the food service manager returns to her desk with the feeling that she has put things back on the straight and narrow.

Now let us take a look at what has happened from a behavioral management perspective. The manager's action, as intended, put an immediate stop to the unproductive storytelling behavior. What the manager does not realize, however, is that the action has just begun rather than ended. A functional analysis may reveal that the storytelling behavior has been punished and the incompatible behavior of returning to work has been negatively reinforced, the former through the contingent presentation of a punisher (chewing out) and the latter through the contingent withdrawal of the same punisher. In other words, the food service manager's aversive berating started because of the storytelling and did not stop until the subordinate returned to work. Both responses, storytelling and the immediate return to work, were followed by contingent consequences controlled by the manager. If the food service manager has some reliable way of accurately measuring the frequency of her subordinate's storytelling behavior, she will probably discover one or both of two things. First, after the "chewing out" the storytelling will initially diminish and then return to its former strength. Second, when she (the manager) is in the general vicinity, the subordinate will refrain from telling stories—but in the manager's absence, the subordinate's storytelling will go on as usual.

In the example, social learning has taken place as a result of behavior/consequence interaction. Unfortunately for the manager, the subordinate has learned more than initially meets the eye. In short, the subordinate has learned not to tell stories when the manager is around. In functional analysis terms, the food service manager has become an antecedent condition (A) in the subordinate's work environment signaling the high probability of punishment (C) for storytelling (B). Accordingly, the subordinate has learned that storytelling is safe and will go unpunished as long as the boss is not around. The food service manager, meanwhile, is tied to intermittently punishing her subordinate's deviant behavior to keep it suppressed. Unfortunately, an employee who actively pursues organizational goals because of the positive reinforcement associated with such pursuit is a far cry from an employee who passively works to achieve organizational goals in order to avoid the punishment associated with not pursuing those goals.

Generation of emotional behavior

Emotional behavior is very complex and, frankly, not fully understood at this time. Some behavioral scientists feel that emotion lies in a gray area somewhere between respondent and operant behavior. For example, McGinnis (1970) suggests that emotion is more than a unique set of cognitive, physiological, and behavioral manifestations; he feels that emotion is most appropriately viewed as a reaction that disrupts or otherwise interferes with ongoing behavior. The commonly heard terms used by psychologists and laymen such as anger, aggression, frustration, regression, fear, withdrawal, and especially anxiety are examples of what is meant in this discussion by emotional behavior. Angrily yelling back or perhaps striking at a superior, kicking a candy machine which will not work, loudly announcing the intention to quit, sabotaging an important piece of equipment or a production run or computer program, getting drunk after work, and storming out of the office and crying after a conference with the boss all qualify as behavioral manifestations of what we commonly call emotion. This type of behavior is considered here to be mainly dysfunctional behavior which may inhibit the achievement of personal mental health and adjustment and organizational objectives.

What does emotion have to do with punishment? Simply stated, punishment appears to increase the incidence of emotional behavior. Skinner (1953) has noted that behavior temporarily suppressed with contingent punishment is commonly replaced by an emotional reaction. Returning for the moment to the example of the storytelling subordinate cited earlier, the subordinate's immediate cessation of storytelling after the food service manager's punishment could easily have been accompanied by emotional behavior. Emotional reactions to the food service manager's public censure could have taken the form of angrily snapping back at the boss, ripping up some worksheets, damaging equipment back at the work station, or telling the other members of the work group what a so-and-so the boss is. Importantly, each of these emotional displays threatens to diminish rather than enhance personal performance effectiveness and organizational goal attainment. People in this anxious state may likely want to "get even."

Possibility of behavioral inflexibility

A third undesirable side effect of punishment has particularly important implications for today's human resource managers. Bandura (1969) and others have noted that punishment may sometimes permanently stifle behavior. In light of the first side effect (punished behavior is only temporarily suppressed rather than permanently changed), this observation may seem to be a favorable turn of events. The catch, however, is that behavior that is viewed as undesirable at one time but highly desirable at another may be permanently repressed by ill-timed punishment. For example, a child severely punished for sex-related behavior may suffer problems later in life when sexual behavior becomes both appropriate and desirable. In other words, punishment may permanently suppress the wrong responses.

Extended to an organizational context, important performance-related behaviors involving decision making, creativity, or problem solving may be severely weakened by early punishment. Suppose, for instance, that a new management trainee with the ink still wet on his MBA degree is subjected to embarrassing derogatory comments from his superiors and peers for making a seemingly creative suggestion at a management meeting. Not stopping to realize how sensitive new employees are to reinforcement and punishment, his critics may permanently stifle his creative contributions in the future. Later on, when the management team actively solicits creative contributions, they should not be surprised to hear none from the now "experienced" trainee.

In a similar manner, the consequence climate of most subordinate positions does not tend to prepare one for eventually assuming a responsible superordinate role. To assure that superiors are responsible, take-charge people, it is necessary that the relevant behavior of subordinates be nurtured and shaped with positive consequences instead of permanently damaged with indiscriminate punishment. With the dynamic change facing today's organizations, inflexible behavior created by punitive control seems highly undesirable.

Generalization of aversiveness to the administrator

A fourth undesirable side effect of punishment is very common in contemporary organizations. The aversiveness of a punisher may generalize through frequent and close association between the punisher and the supervisor who administers it. The behavioral manager who uses punitive control becomes a cue for punishment; i.e., when the punitive manager is present, the probability of punishment increases. In effect, the punitive manager becomes what is technically called a conditioned aversive stimulus (Skinner, 1953). We have all had experience with this type of individual. All he or she has to do is appear on the scene and everyone is suddenly hard at his task. As long as the punitive manager is breathing down people's necks he or she is effective at stimulating performance — or at least what outwardly appears to be performance.

In the long run, the punitive manager actually turns out to be quite ineffective. It is almost impossible to assume the dual roles of punisher and reinforcer. As a conditioned aversive stimulus, the punitive manager's ability to positively reinforce is eroded by fear and distrust. Also, once the punitive manager leaves the work area, the now unrestrained subordinates get the all-clear cue and control begins to break down. Self-discipline and self-control in the absence of authority are not usually associated with a punishing environment.

Steady exposure to punishment typically leads to a stressful climate of aggressiveness, defensiveness, dependence, passivity, and immature, anxious, emotional behavior. Moreover, the productivity stimulated by the presence of a manager who relies a great deal on punishment may be just a masquerade. The behavior which the punitive manager's presence creates is defensive; its goal is to avoid rather than to seek. Organizational goals are not efficiently and effectively achieved through such defensive behavior. Unfortunately, this tends to be the rule rather than the exception in most modern organizations and can help explain the productivity problems we have in this country today.

A final word on negative control as a consequence management strategy

The four undesirable side effects just discussed provide a strong case against the use of punishment. Punishment is not merely less effective than positive reinforcement in controlling human behavior; in some cases, punishment may create permanent inflexibility where it can least be afforded. On the other hand, when permanent change is desired, punishment may produce only temporary suppression. Punitive control may not only fail to weaken undesirable behavior, it may actually facilitate the emergence of emotional behavior which generally erodes human performance and thus organizational effectiveness.

Negative reinforcement is subject to many of the same problems and limitations attributed to punishment. Although the person who controls the aversive situation may exact the compliance de-manded, such pressure tactics may eventually breed ill feelings and threaten superior-subordinate openness and rapport. Also, since a punishing situation is first created and later terminated, punishing contingencies may accidentally be established with other prior behavior. As an example of this last problem, take the case of a supervisor who started criticizing an operative employee for standing around and talking with a friend without first checking on the operator's performance. Suppose the operator has exceeded the production standard all day. While the criticism for standing around has the immediate effect of get-ting the operator back to his or her machine, a long-run effect may be lower performance as the operator resolves to get back at his or her boss by doing less work. High performance has been accidentally punished through the inappropriate use of a negative reinforcement strategy.

In summary, whether punishment or negative reinforcement is used, the result can be very ineffective in managing behavior. Con-sequently, practicing managers should actively rely more on positive and less on negative consequence management. If negative control is used, special effort must be made to avoid or diminish as much as possible its undesirable side effects and, as the discussion of intervention strategies in Chapter 3 pointed out, should always be used in combination with positive reinforcement.

Modeling and
Self-Management 7

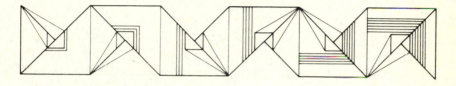

Whether systematically managed or not, human behavior in organizations is constantly being shaped into new and varied forms. However, as pointed out in Chapter 2, direct learning through contingent consequences or the shaping process does not account for the learning of all organizational behavior. In contrast to shaping, whereby simple responses eventually evolve into complex behaviors through selective reinforcement, some complex job behaviors appear rather suddenly. Social learning theorists such as Albert Bandura (1970, 1971, 1977b), working in the areas called vicarious learning (or modeling) and self-control (e.g., see: Thoresen and Mahoney, 1974), have formulated some insightful explanations of how complex behavior can appear without benefit of a long trial-and-error shaping process. Consequently, this chapter goes beyond a purely operant approach to O.B. Mod. It focuses on a social learning perspective of modeling and self-management. Although some would consider this chapter to be outside the mainstream of O.B. Mod., it serves to point out how social learning theory can supplement and extend the operant model in a practical manner.

MODELING

A significant portion of what we call organizational behavior is learned through modeling or, more simply stated, through imitation. As discussed in Chapter 5 on "Antecedent Management," models can and

145

often do serve as antecedents or cues for performance. Sims and Manz (1981/1982) have explained this important aspect of models as follows:

> "Models are an important class of antecedents. The influence of models in the acquisition of new behaviors stems from the fact that individuals are frequently rewarded for imitating others. This learning history leads to the development of imitation as a generalized response class" (p. 56).

To the casual observer, modeling is a straightforward and apparently simple process. One person, such as a respected manager or co-worker, behaves in a certain manner, another person observes and then imitates that behavior. Indeed, in any social setting, much of our behavior is a function of behaving like those around us. This, of course, is where the term "social learning" comes from. We commonly pattern our behavior after live or symbolic models which exemplify potentially reinforceable behavior standards. But there is more to this apparently simple process called modeling than initially meets the eye.

According to Bandura, "One of the fundamental means by which new modes of behavior are acquired and existing patterns are modified entails modeling and vicarious processes" (Bandura, 1969, p. 118). In addition to the terms *modeling* and *vicarious learning*, terms such as "copying," "matching," "imitation," "observational learning," and "social facilitation" are often used in connection with the process of learning by observing others. The following definitional framework captures the essence of the term *modeling*, relative to O.B. Mod.:

> "The fundamental characteristic of modeling is that learning takes place, *not* through actual experience, but through observation or imagination of another individual's experience. Modeling is a "vicarious process," which implies sharing in the experience of another person through imagination or sympathetic participation" (Sims and Manz 1982, p. 58).

In our discussion of modeling, we will review three basic modeling effects, examine the modeling process, outline the use of modeling as a training tool, and present a modeling strategy for O.B. Mod. This discussion should be especially appealing to those who prefer "practical techniques" because, among the many areas of applied psychology, modeling represents one of the most successful translations of behavioral science theory to practice.

THREE BASIC MODELING EFFECTS

Bandura (1969, p. 120) identified three effects of exposure to modeling influences. They are: (1) an observational learning or modeling effect, (2) an inhibitory or disinhibitory effect, and (3) a response facilitation effect.

In O.B. Mod. terms, the first effect is concerned with the learning of new responses by imitation; the second effect relates to the manner in which the consequences of one individual's behavior may vicariously affect the behavior of another individual; and the third effect identifies the process whereby one individual's behavior cues a similar behavior in another individual. Each of these modeling effects, despite only subtle differences, plays a unique and important role in day-to-day organizational behavior. Understanding the three basic modeling effects can contribute to successful behavioral management.

Learning through imitation

This first effect occurs when an individual learns a new behavior by identically reproducing a response observed in another individual. Prior to acquisition, this behavior would have a very low or zero probability of occurrence in the presence of appropriate stimuli (Bandura, 1969, p. 120).

An example of such a behavior (actually a collection of closely related behaviors) in an organization would be the efficient operation of a personal computer by a manager who has never touched one before. With no prior "hands on" experience, the behaviors associated with successful computing are not part of the manager's behavior repertoire. But suppose that this manager is observed turning on the machine, properly inserting the floppy disks, and successfully keying in commands and data. While these behaviors may have resulted from trial-and-error/success shaping, assume for the moment that shaping was not the operative process. Instead, a series of related but novel behaviors has suddenly appeared. No successive approximations have been emitted and systematically reinforced. Evidently, an alternative learning process — namely, modeling — has taken place.

In the case of the personal computer operator, assume that he or she has just finished watching a training film supplied by the computer manufacturer. The modeling effect that has occurred in this example is *imitation*. In a sense, a long and otherwise time-consuming shaping process has been replaced by a fast-acting modeling approach involving imitation.

New behaviors may be learned from both live and symbolic models. A supermarket manager who takes time to show a stock clerk how to operate a labeling machine is acting as a live model. The personal computer operator mentioned above made use of a symbolic model (a film). Symbolic models may be presented pictorially (Bandura and Walters, 1963, p. 49) in the form of movies, television, still pictures, slides, or videotape, or can be presented in the form of textbooks, records, cassette tapes, manuals, graphic presentations, charts, and common verbal or written directions. This book you are reading qualifies as a symbolic model for effective behavioral management techniques.

Regardless of whether the model is live or symbolic, however, imitation helps explain how a significant amount of complex organizational behavior, both desirable and undesirable, is learned. The challenge for O.B. Mod. is to understand and manage the imitative effect of modeling rather than passively watch models facilitate the learning of dysfunctional as well as functional organizational behavior.

Learning from others' consequences

As in direct learning from operant conditioning, consequences also play an important role in modeling. With regard to the learning of novel behavior through imitation, successful imitation, by itself, seems to have very strong reinforcing properties. In addition, consequences experienced by others, especially relevant behavior models, play an important role in determining what behavior is imitated and what behavior is ignored. The inhibitory (discouraging) or disinhibitory (encouraging) effect comes into play when we witness a model experiencing negative or positive consequences. Tempered by the extent to which we identify with the model, the status of the model, and the nature of the consequence(s), we tend to imitate behavior which pays off for the model and avoid imitating behavior which does not pay off or has negative consequences for the model.

Television advertising of personal care products such as toothpaste, deodorants, perfumes, and shave creams rely heavily on this modeling effect. For example, an advertisement implies that if we buy and use "Toothy Grin" toothpaste we will enjoy the same consequences (affection, friendship, love, or esteem) received by the model in the advertisement. Magazine ads and billboard displays also bombard us with an endless stream of models experiencing widely desired consequences.

Many people in democratic societies feel that what one person gets, everyone should get, and what one person avoids, everyone should avoid. Given these cultural values, the inhibitory or disinhibitory effect of modeling takes on added meaning. If properly handled, the reinforcing quality of equitable treatment can become a powerful management tool. This contention is bolstered by equity theory (e.g., see Adams, 1965; Carrell and Dittrich, 1978) which holds that perceived inequity motivates individuals to readjust inputs/outcomes relationships. Publicly giving generalized positive reinforcers to those who display desirable organizational behavior can have a two-stage impact on performance, as Sims and Manz (1981/1982) have observed:

> "Leaders should recognize that rewards given to one employee as a consequence for achievement-oriented behavior can have an impact on other employees because a model is established. Performance-contingent rewards such as compliments, favored job assignments, and material rewards can act as an incentive to employees who observe the reward, in addition to those who receive the reward. Modeling is indeed a means of diffusing knowledge about reward contingencies among employees" (p. 61).

Thus, members of the work group can become constructive behavior models for their peers.

Using the behavior of others as a cue

Whereas new behaviors may be learned by imitating others, responses already in an individual's behavior repertoire may be cued by a model's behavior. Some typical examples would be: at a top management meeting everyone sits down when the CEO sits down; dinner guests begin eating when the hostess begins; and everyone in the mail room loafs when the supervisor loafs.

In each instance, the behavior in question did not have to be learned by imitating the model. Each behavior was already part of the individual's present repertoire. Previously acquired behaviors may be cued by similar behavior on the part of relevant others. In A-B-C or S-O-B-C terms, the model's behavior serves as an antecedent condition which sets the occasion for the performance of a matching behavior by the observer. Applied to organizational environments, the behavior exhibited by relevant models serves as a reminder or cue for organizational participants to behave in a similar fashion.

THE MODELING PROCESS

While pointing out that learning through modeling is an efficient process, because needless errors are avoided, Bandura (1977b, pp. 22–29) instructively reduced the modeling process to four subprocesses: (1) attentional processes, (2) retention processes, (3) motor reproduction processes, and (4) motivational processes. These modeling subprocesses will be referred to here simply as *attention, retention, reproduction,* and *reinforcement* in this chapter. Before modeled behavior can manifest successful imitation, each of these four subprocesses must be operative (see Figure 7-1).

Attention

Employees would literally go mad if they attended to every single one of the countless stimuli that constantly bombard them each workday. In fact, one of the significant factors that differentiates successful organizational members from less successful ones is that the former can selectively attend to information, people, and problems that really matter. It is very important that appropriate behavior that will enhance organizational effectiveness be modeled, attended to, and

FIGURE 7-1.   The Modeling Process. Adapted from Bandura (1977b, p. 23)

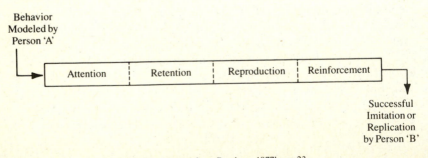

Source: Adapted from Bandura, 1977b, p. 23.

imitated. Otherwise, ineffective or unsatisfactory performance will result. For instance, if a clerk does not even see his or her supervisor model the office-safety behavior of removing tripping hazards, then the probability of successful imitation is low because the subprocess of attention was inoperative.

Three variables that can either encourage or discourage an observer's attention are: (1) the model, (2) the modeling display, and (3) the observer. Goldstein and Sorcher (1974, pp. 28–29) have called these three variables "modeling enhancers" because all three variables must work in concert if observers are to attend to and successfully imitate modeled behavior.

Characteristics of the model • Bandura has pointed out that "models who possess engaging qualities are sought out, while those lacking pleasing characteristics are generally ignored or rejected" (Bandura, 1977b, p. 24). Simply stated, we tend to imitate those we identify with or relate to in some personally significant way. According to Goldstein and Sorcher (1974, p. 28), a model who possesses the following profile of characteristics has a good chance of gaining the observer's requisite attention and influencing his or her behavior:

1. evidently is competent and an expert relative to the behavior being displayed.
2. has high status.
3. has control over resources that the observer desires.
4. is the same race and sex as the observer.
5. models, in a friendly and helpful manner, behavior that seems important to the observer.
6. is rewarded for the behavior being modeled with consequences that the observer desires.

Field research has provided partial validation for this list of model characteristics. For instance, Weiss (1977; 1978) found in his studies that subordinates tended to imitate their immediate superiors when the subordinates perceived their superiors to be competent and successful. Interestingly, however, the subordinates' perception of their superiors' reward power was not positively correlated with imitation.

Characteristics of the modeling display • Generally speaking, some media have a much better track record than others for getting and keeping our attention. Our imagination can be fired by a dynamic and informative training film, whereas a monotone lecture on the very same subject can lull us to sleep. Television, for example, is a compelling medium in itself. A surefire way to kill group conversation is to switch on the television set. It is not surprising, therefore, that videotape technology has become so popular in organizational training. Goldstein and

Sorcher (1974) have offered some practical advice for getting the most out of the modeling display:

> "Greater modeling will occur when the modeling display depicts the behaviors to be modeled: (a) in a vivid, and detailed manner, (b) in order from least to most difficult behaviors, (c) with sufficient frequency and repetitiveness to make overlearning probable, (d) with a minimum of irrelevant detail (behaviors *not* to be [imitated]), and (e) when several different models rather than a single model are utilized" (p. 28).

These pointers are equally useful for both live and symbolic (i.e., videotape or film) modeling.

Characteristics of the observer • In terms of the S-O-B-C social learning model, the characteristics of the model and the modeling display are antecedents within the "S." But, as discussed in Chapter 5, the person's perception serves as a critical gatekeeper in the "O" portion of the S-O-B-C model. In fact, referring once again to Weiss' (1977; 1978) research, subordinates tended to imitate superiors who were *perceived* to be competent and successful. Whether their superiors were objectively competent or incompetent or successful or unsuccessful remained to be determined. Just as beauty lies in the eye of the beholder, managers must be perceived as competent and successful in their subordinates' eyes if they are to serve as potent models.

Along with perceptual predispositions such as expectations, self-evaluative standards (goals), and causal attributions, individuals bring aptitudes, abilities, and other individual differences to the situation. These individual differences may facilitate or inhibit the ability of the model to, first, gain and hold the observer's attention and, second, influence his or her behavior in a constructive direction. Once again referring to Weiss' (1977; 1978) research, it was found that subordinates with low self-esteem were more amenable to imitating their immediate superiors than were high self-esteem subordinates.

Retention

Owing to the typical time lag between viewing a model and engaging in the behavior, some sort of cognitive mediation, as represented by the "O" portion of the S-O-B-C model, is required to help one remember the modeled behavior. According to Bandura (1977b):

"In order for observers to profit from the behavior of models when they are no longer present to provide direction, the response patterns must be represented in memory in symbolic form. Through the medium of symbols, transitory modeling experiences can be maintained in permanent memory. It is the advanced capacity for symbolization that enables humans to learn much of their behavior by observation" (p. 25).

The retention of modeled behavior is facilitated by symbolic coding (in the form of visual imagery or verbal coding) and mental rehearsal (Bandura, 1977b, pp. 25–26). Although visual imagery is hard to objectively describe because it involves personal cognitive events, we all can call up mental pictures of loved ones, pleasant situations, or traumatic events. And sayings such as "A stitch in time saves nine" would not have been passed from generation to generation if verbal coding was not a useful memory device.

Regarding the practical value of mental rehearsal, Sims and Manz (1982) offer an interesting example:

"The sports announcer was interviewing the high-jump star who had just broken the world high jump record. The performance of this athlete was quite remarkable in that his own height was only about 5 feet 8 inches, but he had high-jumped over seven and one-half feet. 'What do you think about just before you make your jump?' asked the announcer.

'Well,' replied the young star, 'I just have this picture of myself in my mind, and in this picture, I slowly run up to the bar and just float over the bar. When I can get this image fixed in my mind, I know I can make the jump'" (p. 61).

As discussed in Chapter 5, research by Decker (1982) demonstrated the training value of (1) giving trainees specific learning points relating to a videotape presentation, (2) instructing them to identify and write down the learning points in the videotape presentation, and (3) telling them to close their eyes and mentally picture themselves performing the learning points. Since the trainees in this field experiment were later judged to be better able than a control group (who did none of this) to apply what they had learned from the videotape presentation, it is reasonable to assume that their *retention* of the modeled behavior was facilitated by the symbolic coding and mental rehearsal.

Reproduction

If an employee is to translate mental symbols into actual behavior, he or she must possess the requisite skills and/or abilities. For example, a secretary must know how to type if a sales representative's demonstration of a new electronic-memory typewriter is to pay off in improved performance. Skill or ability deficiencies need to be diagnosed early and remedied through appropriate training or selection. Within the context of structured training, role-playing has proven to be a good vehicle for encouraging successful reproduction of modeled performance. Beyond that, a supportive, reinforcing climate back on the job for the performance of newly acquired behaviors is essential.

Reinforcement

This subprocess gives recognition to the operant principle of reinforcement. In other words, even though modeling goes beyond the operant process of learning, it is still grounded in the importance of reinforcement. While drawing a distinction between acquiring (learning) a behavior and actually performing it, Bandura (1977b, pp. 28–29) identified three sources of motivation or reinforcement to perform given behaviors: (1) performance of the modeled behavior results in desired rewards for the observer, (2) the observer sees the model receive desired rewards for performing the target behavior, and (3) the observer finds performance of the target behavior self-rewarding. When acting in combination, these three potential sources of reinforcement can prompt productive and timely imitation.

MODELING FOR EMPLOYEE TRAINING

Modeling, as mentioned earlier, has an excellent track record in terms of its successful transition from theory to practice (e.g., see: Kraut, 1976; Moses, 1978; Imitating models, 1978). The use of videotaped behavior models for training supervisors in a variety of interpersonal skills ranging from handling minority employees to recognizing good workers has accounted for the most notable successes. This highly effective application of modeling theory was initiated in 1970 at General Electric by Melvin Sorcher, a personnel psychologist. According to Burnaska (1976):

"The objective of this first course was to reduce the turnover of hard-core employees by helping them to develop skills that would allow them to adapt to and cope with a job in industry. Both hard-core employees and their first-line supervisors were trained in parallel but separate sessions on how to take and give constructive criticism, how to ask and give help, and how to establish mutual trust and respect. After six months, 72% of the 39 hard-core employees who had been trained, and who worked for supervisors who had also been trained, remained on the job; only 28% of the 25 hard-core employees who had not been trained and who worked for untrained supervisors did not leave" (p. 329).

Encouraged by this early success, General Electric broadened the application of Sorcher's approach to thousands of supervisors in many different business situations.

Applied learning

After being refined and labeled "Applied Learning," Sorcher's modeling approach to supervisory training evolved into the following four-stage sequence:

"1. *Modeling*, in which small groups of supervisor-trainees watch filmed supervisor and employee models interact in effective ways in a problem situation.

2. *Role-playing*, in which the trainees take part in extensive practice and rehearsal of the specific behaviors demonstrated by the models. As their role-play behaviors become more and more similar to the model's,

3. *Social reinforcement* (praise, reward, constructive feedback) is provided by both the trainers and other trainees. These three procedures are implemented in such a way that

4. *Transfer of training* from classroom to job setting is encouraged" (Goldstein and Sorcher, 1974, p. ix).

Importantly, Sorcher and his colleagues emphasize the systematic relationship among these four stages. If a stage is ignored, the chances of successful training are said to drop significantly. This contention was partially validated by Krumhus and Malott's (1980) study which showed that modeling plus feedback produced better results than either modeling alone or instructions alone. Of course, as discussed earlier, much of the power of Applied Learning derives from the use of relevant and convincing behavior models and an appealing modeling display (videotape or film).

Strong empirical support

Unlike the evaluation of most training protocols, where objective behavior change is promised but rarely documented, the Sorcher approach has been rigorously evaluated in a number of different settings (Burnaska, 1976; Moses and Ritchie, 1976; Byham, 1976; Smith, 1976; and Decker, 1982). In one representative study of Goldstein and Sorcher's Applied Learning (Latham and Saari, 1979), forty first-line supervisors received training in nine interpersonal skill areas (e.g., orienting a new employee, reducing absenteeism, and overcoming resistance to change). One year later, they were judged, by objective observers, to be significantly more effective than a matched control group. When the supervisors in the control group were subsequently trained in the same manner, their performance improved to the level of the first group of trainees.

An important aspect of this study that deserves mention here is the use of "learning points" to facilitate retention:

> "In each of the practice sessions, one trainee took the role of the supervisor and another trainee assumed the role of an employee. No prepared scripts were used. The two trainees were simply asked to recreate an incident, relevant to the film topic for that week, that had occurred to at least one of them within the past 12 months. The spontaneity of each practice session was designed to parallel that which occurs on the job.
>
> The learning points shown in the film were posted in front of the trainee playing the role of supervisor. For example, the learning points on handling a complaining employee included the following: (a) Avoid responding with hostility or defensiveness; (b) ask for and listen openly to the employee's complaint; (c) restate the complaint for thorough understanding; (d) recognize and acknowledge his or her viewpoint; (e) if necessary, state your position nondefensively; and (f) set a specific date for a follow-up meeting" (Latham and Saari, 1979, p. 241).

In addition to facilitating the modeling subprocess of *retention*, behaviorally specific learning points such as the foregoing also focus the trainee's *attention* and encourage successful *reproduction*. Moreover, valid learning points conceivably even enhance the learner's *motivation* to try the new skills back on the job, thus increasing the chances of training transfer.

A modeling strategy for O.B. Mod.

Using accepted principles of modeling and successful training applications involving modeling, it is possible to derive a generally applicable strategy. The key considerations are model selection, media selection, target behavior specification, display, and consequence programming. An on-the-job modeling strategy generally should include the following steps:

1. Precisely identify the goal or target behavior(s) that will lead to performance improvement.
2. Select the appropriate model(s) and modeling medium, i.e., live demonstration, training film, videotape, etc.
3. Make sure the employee is capable of meeting the technical skill requirements of the target behavior(s).
4. Structure a favorable and positive learning environment to increase the probability of attention and reproduction and to enhance motivation to learn and improve.
5. Model the target behavior(s) and carry out supporting activities such as role playing. Clearly demonstrate the positive consequences of engaging in the modeled target behavior(s).
6. Positively reinforce reproduction of the target behavior(s) both in training and back on the job.
7. Once reproduced, maintain and strengthen the target behavior(s), first with a continuous schedule of reinforcement and later with an intermittent schedule.

If situational refinements and adaptations are made, this O.B. Mod. strategy for modeling can lead to more effective behavioral management.

SELF-MANAGEMENT

Self-management, also referred to as self-control, certainly deserves more attention than it has traditionally received in human resource management. Luthans and Davis have framed the issue by noting:

"Research and writing in the management field have given a great deal of attention to managing societies, organizations, groups, and individuals. Strangely, almost no one has paid any attention to managing oneself more effectively. . . . Self-management seems to be a basic prerequisite for effective management of other people, groups, organizations, and societies" (1979, p. 43).

Modern managers and their subordinates alike stand to benefit from improved self-management.

Taking the top-down view, managers need to engage in a good measure of self-control if they are to effectively apply the behavioral principles presented in this book. For example, an offhanded nasty remark from a construction supervisor who is having a particularly bad day may cancel out weeks of shaping and goodwill built through performance-contingent positive reinforcement. Also, productive self-management is much less expensive than close supervision or elaborate control schemes. From the subordinate's standpoint, the opportunity for self-control generally means greater autonomy, signifies management's trust, and enhances what Argyris (1957, p. 50) believes is a natural striving for psychological maturity. Moreover, proponents of self-control contend that it is more ethically defensible than externally imposed behavior control techniques when used for job enrichment, behavior modification, management by objectives, or organization development.

Most of us have a pretty good intuitive notion of what self-management involves. But because of the widespread use of cognitive explanations, we tend to use referents like willpower, resistance to temptation, self-discipline, and struggling between the forces of good and evil. Unfortunately, each of these popular explanations really tells us very little about the mechanisms of behavioral self-management. This is where operant and, to a greater extent, social learning theory have made and can continue to make a contribution.

First, from the operant perspective, Skinner provided a useful foundation and the precise meaning of self-control. He stated:

> "When a man controls himself, chooses a course of action, thinks out the solution to a problem, or strives toward an increase in self-knowledge, he is *behaving*. He controls himself precisely as he would control the behavior of anyone else — through the manipulation of variables of which behavior is a function" (1953, p. 228).

In other words, in operant A-B-C terms, one controls one's own behavior by exercising control over relevant antecedents and consequences.

More recently, social learning theorists such as Bandura (1976),

Thoresen and Mahoney (1974), and Kanfer (1980) have instructively extended Skinner's operant approach to self-control by including cognitive mediation and covert processes, while still retaining the operant emphasis on functional behavior-environment interaction. Thus, because it is more comprehensive and suitable for modern organizational life, a social learning perspective of self-management is developed and applied under the O.B. Mod. approach.

A SOCIAL LEARNING PERSPECTIVE OF SELF-MANAGEMENT

Social learning theory, as discussed in earlier chapters, emphasizes the reciprocal interaction of person, environment, and the behavior itself. This approach provides the basis for a comprehensive view of self-control. While it focuses on behavior and recognizes the impact of environmental consequences, as does the operant view, a social learning perspective also recognizes the role of cognitions and thus is more acceptable to humanists and cognitive theorists, who prefer to deal in terms of free will and self-determination. According to Bandura (1977b):

> "[A] distinguishing feature of social learning theory is the prominent role it assigns to self-regulatory capacities. By arranging environmental inducements, generating cognitive supports, and producing consequences for their own actions, people are able to exercise some measure of control over their own behavior" (p. 13).

This social learning perspective also differs from the operant view by including covert or personal events. "Antecedents as well as consequences can occur within the individual separately or in combination with overt responses" (Thoresen and Mahoney, 1974, p. 138). The purpose of this section is to pave the way for adequate understanding of the self-management techniques presented later by first analyzing the basic self-regulation process and then presenting the S-O-B-C model of self-management for O.B. Mod.

Kanfer's three-stage model of self-regulation

Frederick Kanfer (1980, pp. 334–389), a social learning theorist, formulated an instructive model for what he terms the self-regulation process. Kanfer's model is a good conceptual framework for the actual mechanics of self-managed behavior. As illustrated in Figure 7-2, his

FIGURE 7-2.   Kanfer's Self-regulation Model.

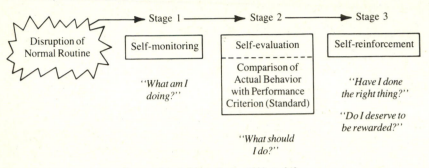

Source: Adapted from Kanfer, 1980, p. 340.

model has three stages: self-monitoring, self-evaluation, and self-reinforcement. This three-stage sequence is triggered by a disruption in
normal routine. Kanfer (1980) explains as follows:

> "Social learning theory assumes that much of everyday
> behavior consists of chains of reactions that have been built up
> so that a response is cued by completion of the immediately
> preceding response. For example, typing, driving a car, shav-
> ing, preparing breakfast, and many other activities do not con-
> sist of discrete acts which require continuous decisions among
> alternate responses based on the person's judgment of the ade-
> quacy of each discrete component. However, when these smooth
> activities are interrupted, or fail to produce the effects to which
> the person has become accustomed, the activity will stop and a
> *self-regulation* process will begin" (p. 338).

Because each is so important to the overall self-regulation process, the
subprocesses of self-monitoring, self-evaluation, and self-reinforcement
require closer examination.

Self-monitoring • When normal routine is disrupted or expectations are not met, the individual tends to pause and focus his or
her attention on what is happening. One's own behavior receives conscious attention during this reflective period. In effect, one asks the
question "What am I doing?" For example, in the middle of giving an
engineer routine performance appraisal feedback, a research and development manager might pause to reflect on why the engineer is getting
visibly angry. If things went as usual, the R & D manager would conduct and conclude the meeting according to an established and habitual

routine. But, for some unknown reason, this particular engineer is reacting strangely. So the R & D manager pauses for reflection and reviews a mental checklist of possible reasons. Inevitably, some of those possible explanations would involve things the R & D manager did or did not do. "Did I say something offensive?" "Maybe I didn't explain the purpose of the meeting." After this quick pause for reflection on why things are going wrong, the R & D manager turns to self-evaluation.

Self-evaluation • In the self-regulation process, the Stage 1 question "What am I doing?" gives way to the Stage 2 question "What *should* I do?" Inherent in this second question is a comparison between self-observed behavior and performance criteria or standards. Bandura (1976) contends that people learn the behavioral standards that they use as measuring sticks in two ways. First, a lifetime of shaping influences by parents, teachers, managers, and other authority figures gives individuals a good idea of what behavior is valued and what is not. Second, as discussed earlier in this chapter, behavior models inculcate standards of conduct. Bandura (1976) notes that successful social development gives people generic standards for self-reward that generalize across situations. Standards learned through shaping and modeling are symbolically coded in the memory in visual or verbal form.

Going back to our example of the R & D manager who is faced with the angry engineer, a mental picture of how the R & D manager's boss once defused the R & D manager's own anger might come into play as a performance standard. Alternately, the R & D manager might recall a verbal tip learned in a performance appraisal seminar (e.g., "When in doubt, talk it out"). Having compared self-observed behavior with a performance criterion or standard, the R & D manager judges his or her behavior to be either acceptable (and hence, self-rewardable) or unacceptable. If his or her behavior is judged unacceptable through self-evaluation, the R & D manager will be motivated to switch to an acceptable approach worthy of self-reinforcement.

Self-reinforcement • If people are capable of self-reinforcement, why don't they just say their behavior is fine and feel good about it? According to social learning theory, life isn't so simple. Again, shaping and modeling influences are said to provide standards for determining what it takes to *earn* self-reinforcement. This implies an ability to forego self-reinforcement when it is undeserved. Bandura (1976) has put this important factor into context by noting: "To self-reinforce one's own performances contingently requires adoption of a performance standard, evaluation of ongoing performance relative to the standard, and self-privation of freely available reinforcers when performances do not warrant self-reward" (p. 145). Doing without is a product of socialization: "Rewarding oneself for inadequate or undeserving performances is more likely than not to evoke critical reactions from others. And lowering one's performance standards is rarely considered praiseworthy" (Bandura, 1976, p 140).

Referring once again to the troubled R & D manager, if self-observed behavior does not measure up to the symbolic visual or verbal standard, then the standard will likely be applied in order to defuse the engineer's anger. On the other hand, should the R & D manager determine that he or she is not responsible for the engineer's anger, then self-satisfaction will signal that the meeting should proceed as planned or perhaps with some redirection to help the engineer curb his or her anger. Thus, the R & D manager can be said to be exercising self-regulation in the face of unexpected circumstances.

Importantly, Kanfer (1980) cautions that his three-stage self-regulation model, although derived from laboratory research, is not necessarily an actual or universal representation of discrete psychological processes. He adds:

> "In fact, it is quite likely that the total sequence of criterion setting, self-observation, evaluation, reinforcement, and planning of new actions proceeds rather quickly, often without much thought by the person. Nevertheless, it can help us to organize some of the essential features of the process by which an individual manages his own behavior" (p. 339).

With Kanfer's self-regulation model serving as a foundation, an expanded social learning model of self-management can be formulated.

An S-O-B-C model of self-management

As illustrated in the S-O-B-C model in Figure 7-3, both overt and covert self-controlled behaviors are determined by prior situational cues, subsequent environmental and personal consequences, and mediating cognitive processes. Central to this S-O-B-C model of self-management are two strategies described by Thoresen and Mahoney (1974, pp. 16-22): (1) environmental planning (often called stimulus control) and (2) behavioral programming. The former strategy involves managing circumstances prior to behaving, while the latter strategy involves behavior-contingent reinforcement or punishment. Under the "O" are cognitive self-management processes and mediators.

Environmental planning • This stimulus control strategy occurs when "the individual plans and implements changes in relevant situational factors *prior* to the execution of a target behavior" (Thoresen

FIGURE 7-3.   A Social Learning Model of Self-management

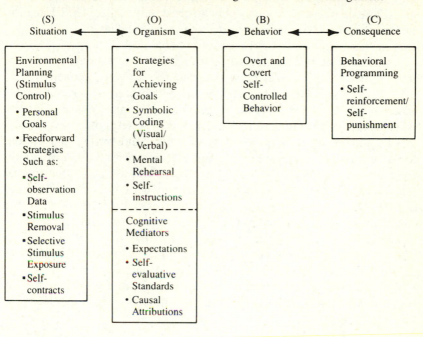

and Mahoney, 1974, p. 16). The idea is to avoid situations that encourage unwanted behaviors and create opportunities for the performance of desired behaviors. For instance, a manager on a diet would do well to stay away from the candy machine and pack only low-calorie health food for his or her lunch. Specific environmental planning techniques discussed later in this chapter are personal goals and feedforward strategies such as self-observation data, stimulus removal, selective stimulus exposure, and self-contracts.

Behavioral programming • This strategy involves self-administering positive or negative consequences *after* the behavior in question has been performed. For instance, you might treat yourself to an ice cream cone (or some other goody) *if*, and only if, you finish reading this chapter. Self-reinforcement and self-punishment are discussed in more detail later.

Cognitive self-control processes and mediators • As listed under the "O" in Figure 7-3, self-control can be enhanced cognitively. Strategies for achieving goals, symbolic representations, rehearsal, and self-instructions can help the individual respond to relevant cues in a timely and appropriate fashion. Moreover, the three cognitive mediators discussed in detail in Chapter 5—expectations, self-evaluative standards, and causal attributions—play a role in self-control by helping the person to properly interpret cues, to evaluate behavior, and to determine when and how to self-reinforce behavior.

Expectations, particularly self-efficacy expectations, and causal attributions are of central importance in the S-O-B-C model of self-control. As discussed in Chapter 5, efficacy expectations relate to one's belief in his or her own ability to get the job done. Low self-efficacy expectations constitute a serious roadblock for self-controlled performance. For example, a police sergeant will avoid setting appropriate goals, arranging supportive cues, and self-contracting for desired rewards if she believes that young male officers will not accept her critical feedback on their performance. Guided experience, modeling, and formal training would be needed in this case to enhance all three dimensions of the sergeant's self-efficacy expectations: (1) *magnitude*—a willingness to tackle difficult tasks; (2) *generality*—a willingness to adapt to new situations; and (3) *strength*—a willingness to persevere despite failure (Bandura, 1977a; Brief and Aldag, 1981).

Regarding the central importance of causal attributions in self-control, Kanfer (1980) has listed the advantages of self-attribution:

> "When a person believes that he has the responsibility for some action; that a successful outcome is due to personal competence; that the behavior is voluntary and not controlled by external threats or rewards; and that he has chosen voluntarily among alternative courses of action; the person tends to learn more easily, to be more highly motivated, and to report more positive feelings than when operating under perceived external pressures" (p. 346).

Once again, self-attribution can be bolstered by modeling as well as guided experience, involving exposure to progressively more challenging tasks so that success will be achieved.

BEHAVIORAL SELF-MANAGEMENT TECHNIQUES

Thanks to successful clinical and field experimentation, it is possible to catalog several practical and relatively easy-to-use self-management techniques for use in modern organizations (Thoresen and Mahoney, 1974; Luthans and Davis, 1979; Manz and Sims, 1980).

These practical applications can be part of the O.B. Mod. approach. As such, the self-management portion of O.B. Mod. can be formally defined as: "the manager's deliberate regulation of stimulus cues, covert processes, and response consequences to achieve personally identified behavioral outcomes" (Luthans and Davis, 1979, p. 43). Although this definition focuses on managerial behavior, self-management for organizational behavior modification is appropriate for managers and nonmanagers alike. In S-O-B-C terms, the techniques highlighted here come from the "S" (personal goals, self-observation data, stimulus removal, selective stimulus exposure, and self-contracts), the "O" (strategies for achieving goals, symbolic coding, rehearsal, and self-instructions), and the "C" (self-reinforcement and self-punishment).

Personal goals

As discussed in Chapter 5, goals are one of the most powerful antecedent cues available to direct and regulate behavior. They provide not only targets for improving performance, as Locke and his colleagues have clearly demonstrated (Locke, Shaw, Saari, and Latham, 1981), but also are measuring sticks for performance. This is especially true for self-management. To the extent that imposed goals are internalized or that employees formulate their own self-improvement goals, the direction, effort, and persistence of job behavior will be enhanced. Bandura (1977b) has explained the motivational aspect of goals in the following manner:

> "The motivational effects do not derive from the goals themselves, but rather from the fact that people respond evaluatively to their own behavior. Goals specify the conditional requirements for positive self-evaluation. Once individuals have made self-satisfaction contingent upon goal attainment, they tend to persist in their efforts until their performances match what they are seeking to achieve. Both the anticipated satisfactions of desired accomplishments and the negative appraisals of insufficient performances provide incentives for action. Most successes do not bring lasting satisfaction; having accomplished a given level of performance, individuals ordinarily are no longer satisfied with it and make further positive self-evaluation contingent upon higher attainments" (p. 161).

Specific and challenging, yet attainable, self-improvement goals are a necessary focal point for successful self-management under O.B. Mod.

Self-observation data

Some observational studies (e.g., see: Kotter, 1982; Mintzberg, 1971, 1973) have found that managers spend a considerable amount of time in reactive fire fighting rather than doing proactive planning, organizing, and controlling, as the traditional prescriptive approach to management advocates. But, behavioral self-management proponents take more of a middle position between these extremes. They believe that managers realistically are more *adaptive* rather than strictly reactive or proactive. An adaptive approach "involves the manager's adapting his or her behavior to the interactive stimulus environment as the situation unfolds" (Davis and Luthans, 1980, p. 70). Unfortunately, when busy managers react habitually to a steady stream of ringing phones, requests from co-workers, and unscheduled visitors, the situation controls the manager rather than vice versa. This is where the technique of collecting self-observation data can help managers turn things around. According to Thoresen and Mahoney (1974):

> "Self-monitoring provides a method by which a person can become quantifiably more aware of both his own behavior and the factors that influence it. As such it represents an important first step in the development and implementation of effective self-control techniques. Preliminary evidence suggests that self-observation functions both as a measurement and a preliminary self-change strategy" (p. 64).

Along with goals, valid self-observation data serve as necessary foundations for most of the other self-management techniques discussed in this section. It is difficult to gauge how much self-improvement is needed (or whether it is needed at all) if an objective measure of behavior is not in hand.

By using behavior frequency charts, as discussed in Chapter 4, to record their own selected behaviors, organizational participants can begin to regain control of their work lives. For example, it is important for an office manager who "never seems to get anything done" to learn that he answers an average of fifty questions a day from his staff about word processor problems. This type of objective self-observation data, when functionally analyzed relative to the "S" (cues), the "O" (cognitive mediation), and the "C" (consequences), can help managers become less reactive and more adaptive. In this case, the office manager could escape the bothersome questions by having the best word processor operator in the office serve as a troubleshooter who would field questions. This relatively simple adjustment in the office manager's cue system could make his work life much more productive and pleasant.

Stimulus removal

This self-management technique involves removing cues that prompt unproductive or unwanted behavior. For example, a manager could eliminate interruptions from passersby simply by closing his or her office door. Holding an important meeting in a room without a telephone or requesting the switchboard operator to hold all calls are also popular ways of removing a generally disruptive stimulus. Many diet programs recommend this technique under the heading of "remove temptations" (e.g., "don't have candy on your desk"). The same holds true for many dysfunctional organization behaviors—eliminate the cues for these behaviors.

Selective stimulus exposure

Sometimes, it is sufficient or desirable to limit rather than totally eliminate a disruptive cue. For instance, managers can keep from being swamped by interruptions by limiting their "open-door policy" to a two-hour period in the afternoon. Otherwise, managers with an un-restricted open-door policy typically find themselves shortchanging their peoples' concerns because they tend to come in at the "wrong time." Taking morning phone calls only between 9 and 10 A.M. is another example of selective stimulus exposure in action.

Self-contracts

A self-contract is a personal "if-then" contingency and can be an effective antecedent strategy for self-management. For example, a busy staff specialist may make an evening out with friends contingent upon the completion of an important quarterly report. In effect, self-contracts are an extension of personal goal setting. But not only is the goal specified, the contingent self-reward is specified as well. The power of self-contracts can be enhanced by writing them down or stating them publicly.

Strategies for achieving goals

While goal setting provides direction and regulation, the actual accomplishment of those goals is another matter. Goals themselves are a necessary but not sufficient condition for goal accomplishment in ef-fective self-management. One must think through and develop strategies relative to *how* specified goals will be accomplished. Personal action plans represent one such strategy. The person cognitively sorts out various alternative courses of action that will lead to goal accomplishment and then selects the best alternative. As with self-contracts, the power of personal action plans can be enhanced if they are eventually written down and publicly distributed to relevant parties and respected role models.

Symbolic coding (visual/verbal)

Visual and verbal memory aids are common. For example, some safety programs show employees films of grisly accidents to give them realistic and hopefully lasting visual images of the costs of unsafe practices. In a more positive vein, most management training and development films are intended to impart visual imagery of good management practice. Verbal symbolic codes are an efficient way of remembering important things. For example, by relying on the verbal code "red, right, returning," military and merchant sailors around the world know that red buoys should be on their right-hand side when they are returning to port from sea. No doubt, this simple code has prevented many costly collisions and groundings in dangerous waters. So, too, managers can create their own visual and verbal symbolic codes for self-management. Perhaps a mental image of an apple could serve as a cognitive cue for remembering Applegate, the name of an important new customer. Maybe the verbal code M & M could help a production manager remember to file the *maintenance* report at *mid*-month.

Rehearsal (mental/actual)

Rehearsal involves systematic practice, both covert and overt, of desired behaviors. By engaging in mental rehearsal, people can avoid being thrust into situations totally unprepared. For example, a young sales trainee, who wants to impress the sales manager with his or her carefully prepared product marketing plan, would do well to mentally rehearse possible scenarios (e.g., the boss will think the plan is too conservative, overly optimistic, or unjustified). Of course, mental rehearsal goes hand in hand with actual physical rehearsal such as that carried out by actors and athletes. Human competence is based squarely on practice, both in the privacy of one's mind and in empirical reality.

Self-instructions

The performance of both new and well learned behaviors can be enhanced by appropriate self-instructions. For a manager in a high-pressure job, self-instructions for relieving stress can help (e.g., "relax," "take your time and do it right," "will this project be significant ten years from now?"). Learning points from modeling-based training programs, discussed earlier, are an excellent basis for self-instruction. So are many of the coping strategies found in the stress management literature (e.g., see: Brief, Schuler and Van Sell, 1981; Cooper and Marshall, 1977; McLean, 1979) and the guidelines for time management (e.g., see: Lakein, 1973; MacKenzie, 1975; Schuler, 1979).

Self-reinforcement/self-punishment

Just as in the O.B. Mod. strategies discussed in previous chapters, overt and covert self-reinforcement is an essential technique for effective self-management. However, it is important to recognize the short- versus long-term aspects of self-management that tend to hamper self-reinforcement efforts (see: Bandura, 1977b, p. 145). In the short-term, for instance, procrastination has powerful reinforcing consequences (e.g., avoiding dreaded tasks) while anticipated benefits of becoming more prompt (e.g., promotions or raises) are slow in coming. Contingent self-rewards are needed to bridge the gap between short-term consequences that encourage undesirable behavior and long-term consequences that reinforce improved behavior. As many failed dieters and smokers will attest, self-control efforts often lose the tug-of-war with status quo payoffs. Consequently, self-reinforcement strategies need to be based on potent self-rewards and supported by other self-management techniques such as personal goals, self-observation data, stimulus removal, symbolic coding, and self-instructions.

In terms of administering this self-management technique, the opportunity for self-reinforcement is closely tied to the nature of the job itself. As explained by Brief and Aldag (1981):

> "Employees whose workdays are rigidly controlled by the sounding of a buzzer cannot contingently reward their job performance with a coffee break, but those employees who do control their work schedules are free to reward their accomplishments with self-designated breaks. More generally, employees occupying enriched jobs . . . would be expected to

more readily establish and maintain self-reinforcement systems
than those employees occupying short-cycle, simplified, routine
jobs. This would be the case in part because enriched jobs are
endowed with activities vested with self-enhancing properties"
(p. 79).

So work redesign, as discussed in Chapter 5 as an antecedent management strategy, is a prime vehicle for self-reinforcement because it provides for potentially reinforcing characteristics such as skill variety, task
identity, task significance, autonomy, and job feedback. If work redesign is not possible, more contrived forms of self-reinforcement will
have to be brought into play (e.g., travel, recreational equipment, food,
entertainment, etc.).

Regarding self-punishment, Manz and Sims (1980) have pointed
out that: "The apparent effectiveness of self-reinforcement does not
seem to be shared by self-punishment, which attempts to reduce undesired behavior by self-administering *aversive* consequences. Because
the aversive consequence for undesired behavior is self-administered, it
can be freely avoided" (p. 364). As when managing others' behavior, the
person is advised to rely on positive rather than negative consequences
for self-management.

In the final analysis, the best management may well be *self-*
management because people must bring their own behavior under control before they can expect to effectively manage others. In other words,
our discussion of O.B. Mod. has now come full circle, from managing
others more effectively to managing oneself more effectively. The next
chapter will describe in detail some applications of O.B. Mod. to performance problems in organizations and present some actual self-management cases.

Actual Application
of O.B. Mod. 8

Thus far in the book, the discussion has been somewhat conceptual, laying out the theory and principles of O.B. Mod. Realistic examples have been used as much as possible to illustrate the concepts presented, but concrete applications of O.B. Mod. used to improve employee performance in actual organizations remain to be discussed.

This chapter first summarizes the growing research literature on O.B. Mod.-type approaches to human resource management. However, the bulk of the chapter is devoted to specific applications of O.B. Mod. in manufacturing, non-manufacturing, and nonprofit organizations. At the end, some specific applications of self-management are also included. In total, this chapter details the actual application of O.B. Mod. to show that it *works*.

RESEARCH SUMMARY

There has been a growing amount of research on O.B. Mod. over the past ten years. When this book was first written, we had very little directly applicable research to fall back on. There was considerable research on the operant approach in experimental psychology and some applications in institutional settings (e.g., schools, prisons and mental hospitals). However, except for the widely publicized, but not research-based, application that Feeney made at Emery Air Freight and a few scattered studies of the operant approach to quality control (Adam,

1972; Adam and Scott, 1971), punctuality (Hermann, de Montes, Dominquez, Montes, and Hopkins, 1973) and absenteeism (Nord, 1970; Pedalino and Gamboa, 1974), there was a void in the research literature on this behavioral approach to human resource management. Now, ten years later, there is more reported research, yet still not as much as there is on the more cognitively based approaches to the management of people at work. The internal approach still predominates.

Wide range of application

Recent review articles of both practitioner surveys (Andrasik, McNamara, and Edlund, 1981; Frederiksen and Lovett, 1980) and the reported research literature (Andrasik 1979; Andrasik, Heimiberg and McNamara, 1981; Frederiksen, 1982; and Frederiksen and Johnson, 1981) indicate that O.B. Mod. has been applied in a wide range of organizations and human resource management functions. In particular, the performance-related applications have generally focused on the quality and quantity of work in production operations, absenteeism and tardiness, safety, and sales. Operant and social learning principles have also been widely applied in the training and development field (e.g., programmed instruction and modeling).

Methodological criticism of the research

Reported research is not without methodological criticism. For example, comprehensive reviews of the training literature have been mixed. McGhee and Tullar (1978) found no scientific evaluations of behavior modification as a training technique from 1967 to 1976. A more recent review concludes, however, that although admittedly meager, the research supports the efficacy of the behavior principles used in training (Frederiksen, 1982).

The methods used in researching the performance areas have also been criticized. In a review of about 20 studies, Andrasik (1979) found that only about a third performed reliability assessments, about two-thirds had systematic interventions, and only one-fifth bothered with postintervention assessments. Another review (Snyder, 1978) found that the majority of 63 published articles reporting some aspect of the application of behavior modification techniques to performance problems in organizations did not meet the minimal criteria for accepted research methodology proposed by Campbell and Stanley (1963).

Since these reviews were done, there have been some studies which have devoted considerable attention to accepted research methodology. For example, Luthans, Paul and Baker (1981) used a control-group experimental design and specifically addressed each of the Cook and Campbell (1976) threats to validity. As another example, Haynes, Pine and Fitch (1982) used a within-group reversal design (Komaki, 1977) plus a control group with random assignment of subjects to the experimental and control groups in their carefully designed study. Thus, like any other area of study, there have been some methodological problems, but they are being corrected and new perspectives and methods better suited to behavioral studies are being proposed (Komaki, 1982; Luthans and Davis, 1982).

Research results to date

So far, research results indicate that O.B. Mod. does indeed have a positive impact on performance in organizations. Lee Frederiksen, the editor of the *Journal of Organizational Behavior Management*, which is specifically devoted to reporting research on O.B. Mod., and the recent *Handbook of Organizational Behavior Management* (1982) summarizes these findings as follows:

1. *Employee productivity.* In this biggest area of application, the research clearly indicates that O.B. Mod. does increase worker productivity or task completion. A number of field studies report that the improvement of either quantity or quality of employee output cuts across virtually all organizational settings and all intervention techniques (Frederiksen, 1982).

2. *Absenteeism and tardiness.* Probably the second biggest area of application, these studies use some combination of rewards (e.g., small monetary bonuses or lottery incentive systems) for attendance (or for promptness) and/or punishers for nonattendance (or for tardiness). An extensive search of this literature by Kempen (1982) revealed very positive results. An 18- to 50-percent reduction in the absence rate and a 90-percent reduction in frequency of tardiness were reported in six of the most methodologically sound field studies.

3. *Safety.* Because accidents occur at such a relatively low frequency, most studies have concentrated on reducing identifiable safety hazards or increasing the performance of safe behaviors (e.g., wearing ear plugs or hard hats or keeping the safety guard in place on dangerous equipment). Figure 8-1

FIGURE 8-1.   A Behavioral Analysis of Model Safety Practices

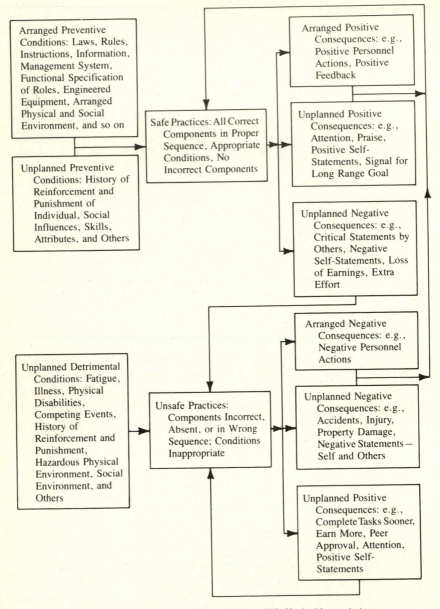

Source: Adapted from Sulzer-Azroff, 1982. p. 507. Used with permission.

shows how a comprehensive behavioral analysis can be made of safe and unsafe practices. A safety program that uses the O.B. Mod. approach outlined in Chapter 4 would follow the five steps of identifying the safe or unsafe behavior, measuring it, functionally analyzing it, setting up an intervention to reduce the unsafe behaviors and/or accelerate the safe behaviors, and evaluating the results. A recent review article by Sulzer-Azaroff (1982) indicates the considerable success that such an approach has had in a wide diversity of organizations.

4. *Sales.* An O.B. Mod. approach to improving sales performance is in marked contrast to the traditional internal approach used in typical sales training programs. For example, Connellan (1978) talks about one company that gave its sales people the typical high powered, multimedia training program intended to teach them effective selling skills. However, when these enthusiastic trainees went out and actually tried the things they had supposedly learned in the program, they received little if any feedback and reinforcement and within a few weeks the enthusiasm began to wane and, most importantly, sales performance began to decline. In other words, even though these sales people had acquired the appropriate effective selling skills during their training, the environment did not support the use of these skills. By focusing on an O.B. Mod. type of an approach, where important selling behaviors such as customer approach, suggestive statements, and closing statements are identified, measured, analyzed, intervened and evaluated, sustained improved sales can result. Mirman (1982) in a comprehensive review of the behavioral approach to sales in restaurants, retail stores, wholesale sales, and telephone sales found considerable success. By using a combination of antecedent and consequence management strategies (similar to those outlined in Chapters 5 and 6), dramatic improvements were shown in areas such as wine and dessert sales, average customer transactions, customer assistance, sales forecasting, sales call frequency, sales of telephone services, and airline reservations.

There are many areas of application that have been researched other than the four summarized above, but these are most closely associated with the performance orientation of this book. It must also be pointed out that the research summarized so far does not always directly reflect the O.B. Mod. model of Chapter 4. There are some differences in the various applications (for example, some of the studies use behavioral management techniques that do not have an explicit functional analysis). Yet, despite some differences, the general principles and approach as presented in this book were used in almost all the studies cited so far. The remainder of this chapter is devoted to a more in-depth treatment of several direct applications of O.B. Mod. as represented by the model in Chapter 4.

MANUFACTURING APPLICATIONS

To date, most of the direct applications of O.B. Mod. have been in manufacturing firms of all sizes. These manufacturing applications, of course, are readily adaptable to an O.B. Mod. approach because, at least on the surface, the performance problems are easy to identify in quantity and quality terms and relatively easy to measure and evaluate. In addition, production facilities are popular targets for performance improvement efforts in light of the highly publicized decline in productivity growth rates this country has experienced in recent years. However, in spite of this obvious and very important application, it should be pointed out right from the beginning that O.B. Mod. is not limited to manufacturing applications. We later present examples of the application of O.B. Mod. to non-manufacturing and nonprofit organizations as well. But for now, we will look at several examples of the application of O.B. Mod. to widely different manufacturing firms. These differ according to size, type of interventions, degree of application, and method of analysis.

Comprehensive analysis of O.B. Mod. in a medium-sized manufacturing plant[1]

One of the first attempts at using O.B. Mod., this application remains as one of the most comprehensive and methodologically sound evaluations available. This application took place in a medium-sized plant engaged in light manufacturing. Two groups of nine first-line supervisors from the production division participated in the study. One of the groups received training on and used an O.B. Mod. approach in supervising their departments. They served as the experimental group. The other group, which was matched with the experimental group on the basis of age, education, experience as supervisors, and mental test

[1] The data for this discussion are drawn from Ottemann and Luthans, 1975. We are indebted to Professor Robert Ottemann, University of Nebraska at Omaha, for his work on this case.

scores, did not undergo any training, did not use O.B. Mod., and served as the control group. Spans of control for the supervisors ranged from ten to thirty years. All had worked their way up from operative positions in the plant. For the most part, each had gained his managerial knowledge from the "school of hard knocks" rather than formal education or supervisory training.

The O.B. Mod. training sessions were held in the plant's training room for ten 90-minute sessions spread over ten consecutive weeks. In general, the content of these sesssions was preplanned and sequenced around the five steps of the O.B. Mod. model but was not rigidly structured during each session. Some of the assumptions made by the trainers included: it is easier to change trainees' behavior first and overall style later than the reverse; appropriate trainee responses must be reinforced immediately and frequently; complex trainee behaviors must be gradually shaped; and allowances must be made for individual differences in learning speed.

This "process" approach resulted in an informal and relaxed learning environment. Importantly, the trainers served as models of what they were teaching by first cuing and then contingently reinforcing appropriate trainee behavior. Among the reinforced trainee behaviors were attendance, contributions to discussion, and data presentation and analysis. In effect, the O.B. Mod. approach was taught to the trainees through the application of O.B. Mod. principles.

The steps of O.B. Mod., as taught to the trainees, were as follows:

1. *Identifying target behavior.* The focus was on objective behavior rather than on internal states. Initial reliance upon internal explanations such as "Joe has a bad attitude" was eventually replaced in the training sessions and on the job by an attention to observable behavior: "Joe is at least 20 minutes late every morning." Identification of performance-related behavior was stressed. The trainees in the study identified behaviors such as work-assignment completions, absences, quality and quantity problems, complaints, excessive breaks, and leaving the work area. Important performance outcomes such as rejects and scrap rates were also monitored.

2. *Measuring the frequency of behavior.* After learning the measuring techniques, the trainees charted real behavioral data on the job and from production data gathered from the engineering staff and discussed it during the training sessions. The resulting frequency charts provided both training session data and feedback for the trainees on their progress with implementing various intervention strategies.

3. *Functionally analyzing behavior.* The trainees were taught to identify the elements in the behavioral contingency (i.e., the A-B-C's). By analyzing antecedents and especially contingent consequences, the supervisors began to see for themselves how target behavior could be predicted and controlled. Emphasis was placed on managing contingent consequences to change on-the-job behavior.

4. *Developing intervention strategies.* Strengthening desirable performance behavior and weakening undesirable behavior were the goals of the intervention. All strategies of antecedent and consequence management were presented and discussed. Because of the difficulty of identifying reinforcers ahead of time, methods of selecting and establishing effective reinforcers were given a great deal of attention. Potential reinforcers that were proposed and used included attention, work scheduling, feedback on performance, approval, recognition, praise, responsibility, and contingent assignments to favorite tasks.

5. *Evaluating results.* The supervisors continually monitored their interventions through measurement to see whether the intended effects were in fact taking place. Evaluation was needed to determine if performance improvement was occurring.

Importantly, emphasis throughout the entire ten-week training program was on getting the supervisors to identify and solve behavioral problems on their own. As much as possible, the trainers resisted offering any direct prescriptions. Occasionally in the sessions, a problem would be brought up by trainees and solutions suggested by the trainers, but basically the trainees became problem-solving behavioral managers.

Results were evaluated on two levels. First, the supervisors using O.B. Mod. were evaluated in terms of their ability to change specific on-the-job behaviors. Representative cases of these behavioral changes are discussed next. Second, and more important, the overall, "bottom-line" performance of the O.B. Mod.-trained supervisors' departments was assessed.

Changes in specific on-the-job behaviors • Frequency of response was the dependent variable in this analysis and the intervention strategy (step 4 of O.B. Mod.) was the independent variable in measuring on-the-job behavioral changes. The supervisors/trainees measured the frequency of the target behavior of an individual subordinate or a group of subordinates during the baseline period and subsequently during the intervention period. Thus, data for the behavioral change analysis were contained on response frequency charts. Four representative illustrations of these behavioral change problems are:

1. The disruptive complainer • A particularly disruptive female machine operator was selected as a target for change by one supervisor. She often complained bitterly about the production standards to the supervisor. In addition, she seemed to adversely affect the productivity of her co-workers by talking to them about their rates and production sheets. According to her, everyone else in the plant had an easier job. Close review of her case revealed that her complaints were unfounded.

After identifying the complaining behavior, the supervisor gathered baseline data on this behavior during a ten-day period. No new contingencies were introduced during this "before" baseline measure. In conducting a functional analysis of the target response during the baseline period, the supervisor determined that he was probably serving as a reinforcing consequence by paying attention to the complaints.

Armed with the baseline data and information gathered in the functional analysis, the supervisor decided to use a combination extinction/positive reinforcement intervention strategy. Extinction took the form of his withholding attention when she complained. Satisfactory production and constructive suggestions were reinforced by feedback and attention in order to strengthen the incompatible desirable behavior. In addition, her constructive suggestions were implemented whenever possible.

The supervisor's chart, shown in Figure 8-2, illustrates that the combination intervention strategy did in fact have the desired effect.

FIGURE 8-2.   Frequency of Complaints

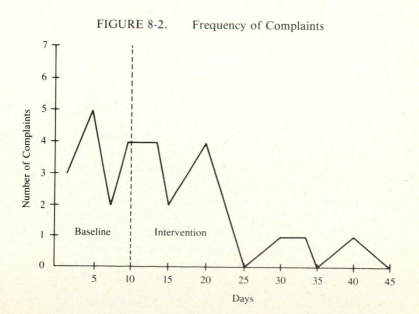

The complaining behavior decreased in frequency. For data collection, a time-sampling technique was used. Rather than carrying out time-consuming measures every day, the target behavior was charted on randomly selected days (the 1st, 5th, 7th, 10th, 13th, etc.). Implementing the machine operator's constructive suggestions turned out to be especially reinforcing in this case. The supervisor noted to the trainers that the rapid reduction in frequency of complaints was amazing because it had been such a long-standing problem.

2. Group scrap rate • Another supervisor identified group scrap rate as a growing performance problem in his department. Attempts at reducing the scrap by posting equipment maintenance rules and giving frequent reminders to his workers had not produced any noticeable improvement. The specific target response to be strengthened was identified as stopping the stamping mill when a defective piece was sighted and sharpening and realigning the dies.

During a two-week baseline period the supervisor kept a careful record of the group's scrap rate. Of course, consistent with good O.B. Mod., no new contingencies were introduced during this baseline period. The extent of the problem had to be determined before any intervention was attempted. After conducting a functional analysis, the supervisor intervened by installing a feedback system to inform group members of their scrap rates. This was accomplished by measuring, charting, and posting in the department work area the group scrap rate. The supervisor then actively solicited ideas from his workers on how to improve the scrap rate. Providing the feedback and implementing the suggestions turned out to be valid reinforcers.

Figure 8-3 shows the results of the intervention. In this case, group, not individual, behavior was charted. In addition to the improved scrap rate, the supervisor noted an increase in interaction between himself and his workers and among the workers themselves. Consequently, a number of social reinforcers were brought into play.

3. Group quality • A third supervisor identified quality in the paint line as a major performance problem in his department. The paint-line attendants' job consisted of hanging pieces on a paint-line conveyor, removing the painted pieces, and inspecting them for acceptance or rejection. "Getting on the men's backs" by the supervisor typically produced only temporary improvement in quality. Soon after the supervisor reprimanded the men, the defective pieces would again pass unnoticed. As defined by the supervisor, a desirable target behavior consisted of identifying and removing defective pieces from the paint line. Overlooking defective pieces also was targeted.

During the two-week baseline period, the average daily number of overlooked defective pieces was recorded for the entire work group.

FIGURE 8-3.   Group Scrap Rate

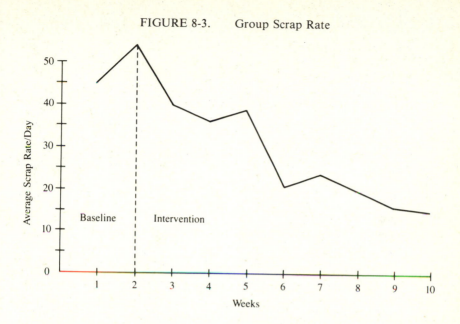

Figures were charted weekly during both the baseline period, where contingencies remained unchanged, and the intervention period. The supervisor noted to the trainers that after conducting a functional analysis he had concluded that he had a group of "clock watchers" on his hands, particularly around break time, lunch time, and quitting time.

The supervisor developed his intervention strategy during a discussion session with his work group. It was decided that a group rate of eight or fewer overlooked defective pieces a day would qualify the group for an extra five minutes for each of two coffee breaks the next day. To increase the value of the potential reinforcer, the paint-line attendants were told each morning if they had qualified for the extended breaks.

Figure 8-4 shows that the extra time off in the form of extended coffee breaks did in fact prove to be reinforcing. Contingency contracting, an antecedent management strategy, had been effectively used. With the average daily rate of defectives down to around two or three, the supervisor confided to the trainers that he couldn't see how they could improve any more.

4. Individual performance problem • A fourth supervisor was having a problem with the quality of assembled components in his department. During the problem identification (step 1 of O.B. Mod.), the supervisor discovered that most of the rejects were coming from a single assembler. Assembly work in this operation entailed the precise manipulation of intricate subcomponents. Records indicated that the

FIGURE 8-4.   Frequency of Overlooked Defective Pieces

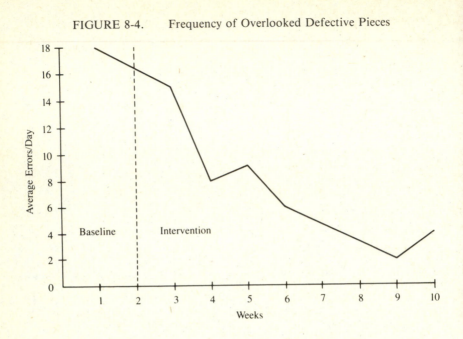

worker in question had satisfactory scores on screening tests for dexterity and coordination and had received the standard training in assembly and checking. After initial consideration, the supervisor rejected the alternative of running the assembler through more training. In his previous experience with similar cases, more training had failed to improve poor performance. Thus, he decided to use the O.B. Mod. approach with this particular employee.

The supervisor specifically identified undesirable behavior as more than two rejects per one hundred assembled components and desirable behavior as two or fewer. Without changing the existing contingencies, the supervisor obtained a two-week baseline measure. To facilitate measuring, boxes of assembled components were randomly sampled and the per box average recorded on a weekly basis. After a functional analysis, the supervisor decided that performance feedback and attention and praise for desirable behavior would be an appropriate positive reinforcement intervention strategy.

Beginning a shaping process at five or fewer errors, the supervisor contingently praised the assembler for any improved quality. As the reject level began to drop, the reinforcement schedule was gradually stretched. In other words, the worker had to have four, then three, and eventually only two rejects before attention and praise were given by the supervisor. Summarized reject statistics were charted and presented to the assembler as feedback on performance. Discussions of this feedback data between the assembler and the supervisor provided the opportunity for the supervisor to reinforce desirable behavior and ignore undesirable behavior.

Figure 8-5 illustrates the rapid improvement resulting from this positive reinforcement intervention strategy.

Overall performance improvement • The supervisors' ability to modify specific on-the-job individual and group behavior represents only one level of evaluation of O.B. Mod. A second and more important level is overall performance improvement. Although the supervisors worked on specific problems such as those discussed above during the training program, the trainers' ultimate objective was to have the O.B. Mod. approach generalize to the supervisors' total method of managing their departments. To evaluate the effectiveness of O.B. Mod. as an overall method of managing, a productivity measure of direct labor effectiveness (a ratio of actual to standard hours stated as a percent) was used for each of the supervisors' departments both in the experimental group (those who were using O.B. Mod.) and in the control group (those who were not using O.B. Mod.).

Figure 8-6 shows the results of the overall performance evaluation. Both the experimental group's and the control group's mean direct labor effectiveness curves were plotted for a six-month period subsequent to the start of the training program. The training itself lasted ten weeks (until the middle of December). Figure 8-6 clearly shows that the overall performance of the control group remained relatively stable during the six-month period, but the performance of the experimental

FIGURE 8-5.   Assembly Reject Rate

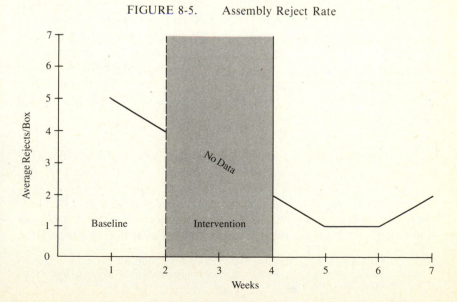

FIGURE 8-6.   Overall Performance Results of O.B. Mod. in a
               Manufacturing Application

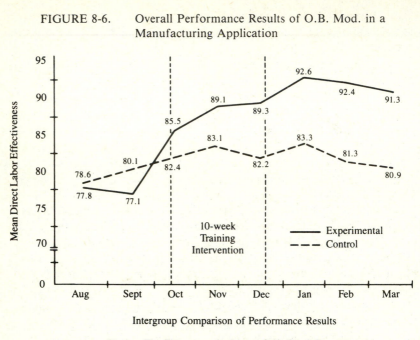

Intergroup Comparison of Performance Results

Note: The Figures on the Lines of the Graph Represent
         the Mean for the Respective Months.

Source: Ottemann and Luthans, 1975.

group significantly improved and remained high even after the training
period was over. This evaluation demonstrated that the O.B. Mod.
approach had generalized and paid off in terms of overall performance
improvement. Applying experimental design, one can justifiably conclude that the O.B. Mod. approach *caused* the improved performance in
this study. In contrast, the widely publicized Emery Air Freight application cited in earlier chapters did not involve such an evaluation. But
with this type of methodologically sound research design, the evidence
seems quite clear that O.B. Mod. does indeed work.

Application of O.B. Mod. in a very large production operation[2]

Although subsequent studies on the application of O.B. Mod.
have not been as comprehensive nor use as rigorous a research design as
the case just discussed, there is accumulating evidence to support the

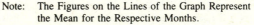

[2]The data for this discussion are drawn from Luthans, Maciag and Rosenkrantz, 1983. We would like to give special recognition to Walter S. Maciag for
his work on this case.

conclusion that O.B. Mod. works. For example, we recently applied the O.B. Mod. approach to eleven major product areas of a very large, labor-intensive firm.

O.B. Mod. was applied in this case by first training 135 first-line supervisors on its background and steps in a 12-hour program spaced over a couple of weeks. These trained supervisors were then closely monitored by the trainers to observe the implementation of O.B. Mod. This training and implementation involved the five steps outlined in Chapter 4. In particular, these supervisors first made a detailed analysis/audit of the specific, observable, and measurable employee behaviors in their respective departments that contributed to quality and/or quantity of output. Examples included behaviors such as performing a particular operation more efficiently or delivering a certain piece of material in a more timely manner. Next, the supervisors quantitatively measured and then charted the frequency of occurrence of the identified behavior. Analyzing the antecedents and consequences of the critical behavior (i.e., doing an A-B-C analysis) was the third step. Step four involved providing performance feedback and social reinforcement (attention and recognition) for progress and attainment. Finally, an evaluation of the results was made to determine the exact impact on performance.

The 135 supervisors using O.B. Mod. in this case were in charge of unionized, hourly production employees in two shifts at one large plant (identified as Groups A and B in Figure 8-7) and one shift at another large plant in the same firm (identified as Group C). Quantity

FIGURE 8-7.   The Impact of O.B. Mod. on the Quantity and Quality of Performance in a Large Production Operation

Product	Group	Quality Improvement	Quantity Improvement
1	B	50%	
2	A		2%
3	A	15%	
4	A	23%	
	C	64%	
5	A	35%	
	C	51%	
6	A		1.4%
7	B		15%
8	B		16%
9	B	42%	
10	B	39%	
11	B		52%

Source: Adapted from Luthans, Maciag, and Rosenkrantz, 1983.

and quality of performance data for these employees had been carefully gathered by industrial engineers over the years. These measures consisted of the overall number of units produced per week or the number of units produced per employee per hour. Quality was measured by the engineers in terms of the percentage of defective units produced per week or by the percent of time that unit quality was at or above standard. In some product areas, quality was the target for an O.B. Mod. approach while quantity was the target for other products.

Figure 8-7 illustrates the results. As shown, O.B. Mod. had a positive impact on all the product areas. While only small *percentage* gains appear for Products 2 and 6, it is important to note that the 2-percent gain in Product 2 translated to an annual value of nearly $900,000 and the 1.4-percent gain in Product 6 equated to an annual value of about $750,000. Projected annual value of the gains from other product areas were estimated by this company as follows: Product 1, $259,000; Product 3, $510,000; Product 4, $371,000; and Product 5, an impressive $2,276,000. Data for computing the actual dollar values of the improvements for Products 7 through 11 were not available, but they were judged to be very comparable to those already described. Besides this tremendous impact on added dollar value (i.e., several million dollars in this company), it is important to note that in no case did the O.B. Mod. approach result in a decrease in quantity or quality of performance.

In addition to the dramatic improvement on the quantity and quality of performance in this large production operation, the O.B. Mod. approach seemed to also have had a stabilizing effect on the variability of performance in these product areas. Low performance variability is a tremendous help to more effective planning and control. Figure 8-8 indicates the baseline (pre-intervention) and post-intervention

FIGURE 8-8.   Performance Variability Under O.B. Mod.

Product	Group	Baseline Variance	Post-Intervention Variance	Improvement Factor
1	B	3.53	0.20	18
2	A	0.012	0.0004	30
3	A	0.28	0.56	0.5
4	A	1.99	0.46	4
	C	14.9	1.34	11
5	A	6.42	0.905	7
	C	16.8	1.07	16
6	A	0.016	0.0095	1.7

Source: Adapted from Luthans, Maciag, and Rosenkrantz, 1983.

variance for quality and quantity of Products 1–6 among the three work groups in the program. Of the eight product-work group combinations for which data were available, seven indicated performance consistency improvement of 1.7 to 30 times (as measured by the proportion of baseline to intervention variance). Only Product 3 exhibited less than its original production consistency after the intervention, but still increased in output by 15 percent after the O.B. Mod. program was implemented. Reduced variability for the other products was expected to greatly improve resource allocation and inventory control problems facing this company.

It should be noted that this case does not contain the rigorous methodology of the previously discussed case and thus cannot lead to the same causal conclusions concerning the impact of O.B. Mod. Yet, there is still considerable evidence that O.B. Mod. did lead to the improved performance in this case and not some alternative explanation. For instance, Figure 8-9 shows the effects of the O.B. Mod. program, implemented at different points in time, on the quantity and quality of products. Although the amounts of change are not to scale, the performance changes following the staggered starting dates of the program support the conclusion that the effects were indeed caused by the O.B. Mod. approach rather than some other factor. This is a simplified version of a multiple baseline design (Komaki, 1977; Van Ness and Luthans, 1979) from which causal conclusions can be drawn. In every product area tracked in this part of the analysis, the start of the O.B. Mod. program was followed almost immediately by a clear improvement in the quality or quantity of performance.

Application of O.B. Mod. in an entire small manufacturing firm[3]

The two manufacturing applications of O.B. Mod. discussed above were limited to samples of first-line supervisors drawn from their respective firms. To give evidence of its generalizability, O.B. Mod. was also applied as a performance improvement strategy for an entire small manufacturing firm.

In this case, the entire managerial staff consisting of the owner/manager, his four department heads of production, shipping, quality control and specials, and their eight first-line supervisors all used the O.B. Mod. approach. This company had grown over the last decade

[3]The data for this discussion are drawn from Luthans and Schweizer, 1979. We would like to acknowledge the work done on this case by Professor Jason Schweizer of Northern Arizona University.

FIGURE 8-9.   Effects of a Staggered O.B. Mod. Interventions (A Simplified Multiple Baseline)

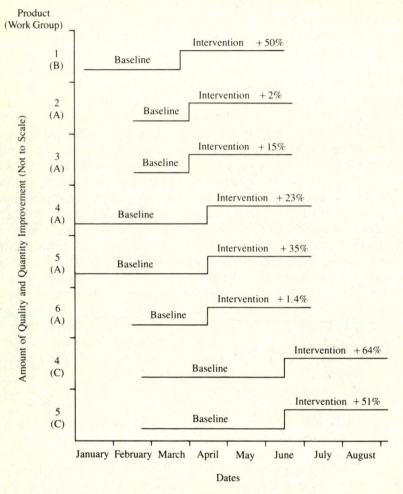

Source: Adapted from Luthans, Maciag, and Rosenkrantz, 1983.

from a five-man "back of a building operation" into a 50 employee national supplier of waterbed liners to wholesale and retail outlets. Management was unusually concerned about the well-being of its employees (who were mostly in their early twenties) and were very open to innovation and change.

O.B. Mod. was implemented in three major phases in this small firm. First, a training program consisting of several sessions outlining the background and steps of O.B. Mod. were held initially with the owner/manager, then the department heads, and finally the first-line supervisors. Phase two initially utilized fictional/disguised cases and role playing exercises to analyze and apply O.B. Mod. principles and steps. This simulation/experiential approach was then followed by an assignment to identify an actual performance-related behavior problem in each manager's area of responsibility and then to measure, analyze, intervene and evaluate it (following the steps of O.B. Mod.). This allowed each trainee to practice O.B. Mod. on a real but small scale problem to pave the way for later use on an organization-wide basis.

In the third and final phase of implementation, a total organizational performance management system was developed. Specifically, a new feedback system was instituted. Before this new system, performance information was only available if the employees sought it out. For example, the employees had a general idea of how many mistakes they caught themselves, but they did not receive formal feedback from the quality control system. Their only formal feedback on performance was a vague monthly evaluation form and their paycheck which supposedly reflected the amount of their incentive pay, but which no one could figure out.

In summary, the old feedback system was vague, non-contingent, provided only negative information from quality control, and was not timely. Under the new feedback system, these deficiencies were corrected. Each supervisor provided objective data obtained from quality control, first on a daily basis and then, more conveniently, on a weekly basis. Supervisors tried to keep this feedback as positive as possible. For example, they talked about up-time instead of down-time and percentage of standard instead of amount below standard. In addition to the new feedback system, the supervisors also used contingent positive reinforcers. They used both natural reinforcers such as praise, attention, recognition, and working with favored coworkers as well as contrived reinforcers such as special assignments and contingent time off.

Although the managers/supervisors were able to concentrate on some individual change projects during the second phase of their training, all of them aimed the O.B. Mod. approach at overall quality and quantity in the third phase. The multiple baseline design (Komaki, 1977; Van Ness and Luthans, 1979) was used to evaluate these overall results. Under such a design, baseline measures are taken on two or more dependent variables and then an intervention is made on one of the variables while baseline measures are continued on the others. These staggered interventions continue until all the dependent variables are af-

FIGURE 8-10.   Results of the Application of O.B. Mod. in an Entire Small Manufacturing Firm

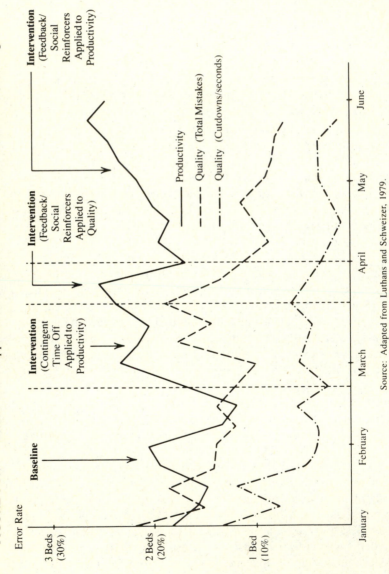

Source: Adapted from Luthans and Schweizer, 1979.

fected. This design eliminates most of the threats to internal validity and allows causal conclusions (Komaki, 1977).

Figure 8-10 shows that there were significant improvements in both the quantity and quality of performance after implementing an O.B. Mod. approach in this small manufacturing firm. In fact, the peaks on the quantity curve and the valleys on the quality curves represent *record* performance in this company—they had never produced this number of beds with so few errors. Statistical analysis verified what simple inspection shows—O.B. Mod. had a significant positive impact on both quantity and quality of overall performance.

The left-hand portion of the graph in Figure 8-10 depicts the baseline (pre-intervention) levels of a quantity measure (solid line) and two quality measures (dashed and dotted lines). The second segment of the graph shows the positive impact that O.B. Mod. had on quantity performance using a contingent time-off intervention. Nothing was done with quality performance and the curves remained at the same level as in the baseline period. In the third part of the graph O.B. Mod. was also applied to quality performance. Instead of the contingent time-off intervention strategy which appears to have been wearing off on the quantity performance in this period, a feedback/social reinforcement strategy was applied to the two dimensions of quality performance. This resulted in significant improvement. (Remember, the quantity curves must be going up and the quality curves going down to show improvement in this graph.)

Even though the contingent time off (if the employees had met the established standard by Thursday at quitting time they got Friday off with pay) worked very well initially (see period 2), its effect did seem to eventually wear off. Therefore, in the last period (on the far right), the feedback/social reinforcement strategy that was being used on quality was also applied to quantity. The results show a less variable, steady climb in performance improvement in both quantity and quality using the feedback/social reinforcement intervention strategy.

Although this study is not as rigorous an evaluation as the first manufacturing case cited, by using the multiple baseline design, causal conclusions can be made concerning the positive impact that O.B. Mod. had on the overall performance of this small firm. In addition, this case brings out the positive, long-run effects that a feedback/social reinforcement intervention strategy seems to have on performance. It seemed to have, at least with these employees in the long run, an even more positive effect on performance than the potentially powerful contingent time-off strategy. Next, another contingent time-off application is examined in more detail.

Application of contingent time off in a large manufacturing firm[4]

In tight economic times, such as those during the early 1980s, nonmonetary reward systems for employees become especially attractive to management. Largely overlooked to date have been contingent time off (CTO) plans. CTO falls right in line with an O.B. Mod. approach. For example, as the last case indicated, at least in the short run, CTO may be a very powerful intervention strategy in O.B. Mod.

Although there is no precise format for CTO plans, the general approach is for employees to attain "earned time" (i.e., leisure time or time off from the job) once performance (both quantity and quality) standards are met. Breaking from the traditional incentive plans, CTO focuses on results, not hours worked. Time off, not just the pay, becomes the reward. Although labor costs do not decrease under the CTO plan, performance may substantially increase at no additional cost to the employer. To test the potential impact of CTO on performance, it was recently applied in a manufacturing plant.

The fairly large plant employed about 2000 hourly workers, split up into non-interdependent work groups that assembled different types of products. Following an O.B. Mod. approach, it was determined by a combined team of in-house staff and researchers that quantity and quality of performance were the problems in this plant. Measurement revealed that one representative group was producing at about 160 units with about 10 percent rejects. Functional analysis suggested that this group could probably produce at about 200 units with better quality, if there were reinforcing consequences for doing so. Since this firm did not have funds available for wage incentives, a CTO intervention was applied.

The following contingency contract was put into effect: if the group produced at 200 units with three additional good units for every defective unit, then they could leave the work site for the rest of the day. Within a week of implementing this CTO intervention, the group was producing 200+ units with an average of 1.5-percent rejects. These employees, who had formerly *put in* an 8 hour day, were now *working* an average of 6-1/2 hours per day and, importantly, they increased their performance by 25 percent.

Except for some minor problems with parts availability, the employees reacted very favorably to the CTO plan and, of course, management was very happy with achieving record performance while incurring no additional labor costs. It was a "win-win" strategy.

[4]The data for this discussion are drawn from Lockwood and Luthans, 1983. We would like to recognize the work done on this case by Professor Diane L. Lockwood of Seattle University.

An interesting but disturbing postscript to this case, however, was that after things had been going along very well (e.g., there were plans to implement CTO in the entire plant), there was an unanticipated changeover in top management. Upon coming on board the new general manager reviewed the CTO plan and concluded: "If employees can produce 200 units in 6 hours, then they were 'gold-bricking' before. Given that we pay them for an 8 hour day, they should be able to produce at least 240 units." He then proceeded to terminate the CTO plan and admonished the group to "get with it." Production immediately dropped in this group to 140 units, 20 units below the original productivity rate. The lesson to be learned from this case, of course, is that there must be a strong commitment from management to carry through and support contingency contracts, such as the CTO plan, if the desired results are to be achieved. Punishing employees for living up to their end of a contingency contract can obviously have disastrous results.

NONMANUFACTURING APPLICATION[5]

The applications of O.B. Mod. discussed so far took place in relatively structured manufacturing environments. These manufacturing applications also involved relatively easy-to-measure quantity and quality performance outcomes. Can O.B. Mod. also be successfully applied to less structured nonmanufacturing organizations with less obvious measures of performance? Fortunately, because of recent hard evidence, this question does not have to be answered on the basis of extrapolation or speculation.

O.B. Mod. was applied in a large metropolitan retail store that offered a full line of products and merchandise in about 100 departments. For the evaluation study, 16 departments were randomly selected; 8 of those departments, containing a total of 41 salespersons, served as the experimental group that was managed by the O.B. Mod. approach and the other 8 departments, also containing 41 salespersons, served as the control group and was not managed by the O.B. Mod. approach. All salespeople in both groups had completed the store's standard orientation and job training programs and were repeatedly told what was expected of them in terms of performance standards such as waiting on customers and keeping shelves stocked. They had all worked for the store for at least 6 months.

In order to identify critical performance behaviors, information was gathered by the research team from written job descriptions, direct

[5]Data for this discussion are drawn from Luthans, Paul and Baker, 1981. We would like to give recognition to Professor Robert Paul of Kansas State University for his work on this case.

observation of the salespersons in action, and input from managerial personnel and staff specialists from the store. Consequently, five categories of a salesperson's performance behavior were identified:

> 1. *selling* — talking with customers, showing merchandise, assisting with selection and fitting, ringing up the sale, and filling out charge slips;
> 2. *stockwork* — arranging and displaying merchandise, folding and straightening merchandise stacks or racks, tagging, replenishing stacks or racks, and packing and unpacking merchandise;
> 3. *miscellaneous* — directing customers to other departments, checking credit ratings, handling returns, receiving instructions, business-related conversations with supervisors or co-workers;
> 4. *idle time* — socializing with friends or co-workers and standing or sitting around doing nothing;
> 5. *absence* — being absent from the work station or from the assigned work area.

For ease of computation and graphic presentation of the data, the behavioral categories of selling, stockwork, and miscellaneous were collapsed into a single category called aggregate retailing behavior. Absence from the work station and idle time were similarly combined.

After these critical performance behaviors were identified (Step 1 of O.B. Mod.), they were measured to determine their baseline frequency. These baseline measures and subsequent post-intervention measures were obtained by direct observation. Trained observers were as unobtrusive as possible and appeared at random times throughout the day.

Functional analysis was used to determine the antecedents and consequences of the identified behaviors and to develop appropriate goals/standards (i.e., antecedents) for these behaviors. It was determined that (1) the salespersons, except when they had an excused absence, should be present in the department, within three feet of displayed merchandise, during assigned working hours; (2) when customers enter the department they should be offered assistance or acknowledged and given immediate help within 5 seconds; and (3) the display shelf should be filled to at least 70-percent capacity.

Intervention in the 8 departments exposed to the O.B. Mod. approach consisted of time off with pay or equivalent cash and an opportunity to draw for a paid vacation for two. These contrived rewards were administered contingent upon attaining the performance standards and were on a graduated scale. For example, 1 hour per week was given for a record of 10 percent (or lower) absence from the work area and 2 hours for attaining this absence standard plus reaching the standard for the sales activity. If all the performance standards were met, a half-day off with pay or equivalent cash was awarded and the salesperson's name was entered into the vacation drawing that was awarded at the end of the 4-week intervention period.

The results of this application of O.B. Mod. are shown in Figures 8-11 and 8-12. It can be seen (and statistical analysis verifies) that the baseline frequencies of both the aggregate retailing behaviors and the idle time/absence behaviors were basically the same for both groups. However, immediately after the intervention, the group managed by the O.B. Mod. approach showed a dramatic improvement in the performance behaviors (i.e., the frequency of the aggregate retailing behaviors shot up and the absence/idle time behaviors shot down). The

FIGURE 8-11.   Aggregate Retailing Behavior

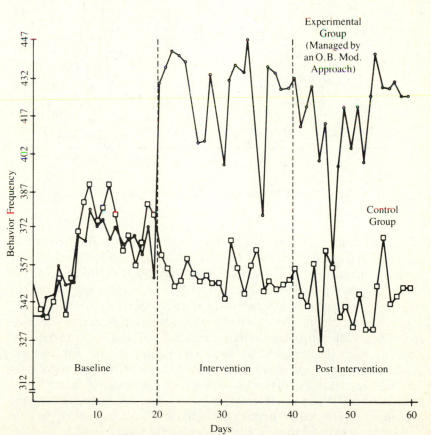

Source: Adapted from Luthans, Paul, and Baker, 1981.

FIGURE 8-12.   Absence from the Work Station and Idle Time

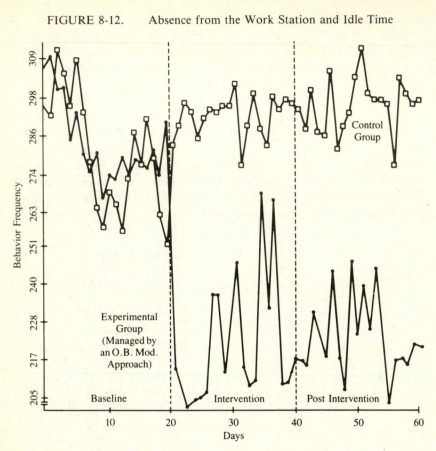

Source: Adapted from Luthans, Paul, and Baker, 1981.

equivalent control groups that were not managed with the O.B. Mod. approach remained at the same level of performance behaviors. Like the first manufacturing case discussed, this rigorous experimental design provided powerful evidence that the O.B. Mod. approach caused the improved performance behaviors of the salespersons in this study.

Interestingly, the high performance levels of behavior remained in the O.B. Mod.-managed group even after the contingent rewards of time off/equivalent pay and the vacation drawing ceased (see the right-hand portion of Figures 8-11 and 8-12). One would normally expect that the frequencies of behavior would return to baseline levels during this "reversal." There are several possible reasons why they did not. One reason, of course, could be that the behaviors were not under the control of the rewards offered during the intervention period. However, because of the control group design, this explanation can be ruled out.

A more plausible explanation is that other, more natural contingencies in the environment took over to maintain the frequencies of the targeted behavior at the intervention level. As explained by Miller (1973): "If the original environment had a consequence that was too weak to initiate a behavioral change but that is strong enough to maintain such a response once initiated, the behavior should not be expected to revert" (p. 535). In other words, the injection of the contrived rewards may have been necessary to get these salesperson's behaviors tracking in the right direction, but then other, more powerful, natural reinforcers such as feedback from supervisors, self-satisfaction, and social rewards from customers, co-workers, and supervisors took over to maintain the desired behaviors. As in the case of the small manufacturing firm discussed earlier, feedback and social reinforcement may be more important to performance behaviors in the long run than are contrived reinforcers such as time off and free vacations.

APPLICATION IN A NONPROFIT ORGANIZATION[6]

Besides the application to both manufacturing and nonmanufacturing business firms, O.B. Mod. has been applied and evaluated in nonprofit organizations as well. As in the previous case of the application of O.B. Mod. to sales performance in a department store, performance behaviors and measures are not as easily identifiable in nonprofit organizations as they are in manufacturing environments. Nevertheless, we strongly feel that the principles and applicability of O.B. Mod. hold across all types of organizational environments, including those in the nonprofit, public sector. In order to test this assumption, O.B. Mod. was applied to a large health care organization.

Today's large hospitals are "under the public gun" because of rapidly escalating costs and resulting demands for increased accountability. It must be recognized that the modern hospital is a very labor intensive operation. In terms of number of employees, health care is the third largest industry in the U.S. Yet, the traditional concerns and approaches to increasing employee productivity that have preoccupied manufacturing firms over the years have largely been ignored by both hospital administrators and the public. Fortunately, this hospital's management was looking for innovative ways to increase the productivity of its people and was willing to give O.B. Mod. a try.

[6]Data for this discussion are drawn from Synder and Luthans, 1982. We would like to recognize Professor Charles A. Snyder of Auburn University for his work on this case.

Although behavior modification techniques have been widely used on patients in the mental health area, the O.B. Mod. approach has not been used to any significant degree for managing hospital employees. In this application, the supervisory staff from several medical and administrative units in the hosptial were trained in O.B. Mod. Job titles for these supervisors included: emergency room clerk supervisor, hardware engineer group supervisor, assistant director of medical records, supervisor of the transcription area, technical director of the heart station, nurse in charge of the eye clinic, pharmacy technician supervisor, technical administrator of radiology, director of patient accounting, assistant manager of the admitting office, and operations manager of the hospital data center. These 11 supervisors were trained in eight sessions over a two-month period. Their training was structured along the five steps of the O.B. Mod. model. Everyone sat around a big table, which facilitated trainee interaction and participation.

Similar to the first manufacturing case reported earlier, each of these supervisors worked on individual behavioral change projects throughout the training, but the program was mainly geared toward using O.B. Mod. as a total approach to managing their people and improving some critical performance measures in their respective departments. An example of an individual behavioral change project was the approach that a supervisor in the admissions department took toward a problem employee. This particular female employee had been giving him fits over the last few years. She was definitely having a negative impact on the performance of the department. He had tried all the traditional ways to "motivate" her. For instance, he enriched her job by giving her more responsibility (performing direct liaison with third-party insurers) and an upgraded title of "Staff Assistant." None of these techniques had worked and he was ready to take the risk of firing her even though she was related to a powerful member of the governing board of the hospital and reportedly had gotten the last supervisor fired when he had tried to get her dismissed. With the objective of getting out of this difficult but important dilemma, the supervisor decided to use an O.B. Mod. approach.

As a first step in managing this employee, he identified the following problem behaviors that seemed to most affect her performance: absence from the work station, extended coffee and lunch breaks, not completing work assignments on time, emotional outbursts, complaints to co-workers, use of a restricted telephone for private calls, and personal visits from members of her large family. He then attacked each of these behaviors one at a time by measuring its frequency of occurrence, functionally analyzing the antecedents and consequences, intervening primarily with feedback and social reinforcement, and, finally, evaluating to insure that the problem behavior was improving.

This approach had a tremendous impact on changing his problem employee's behavior. For example, absence from the work station went from 70 percent to 30 percent; extended coffee and lunch breaks went from 100 percent to 0; and the number of uncompleted assignments went from an average of 1.2 to 0. Emotional outbursts and the problems with excessive telephone use and visits from family members disappeared when this employee improved on the other performance behaviors. Her supervisor was amazed that this very poor employee, who he was about to fire and suffer the potentially dire consequences, had become an excellent worker and was making an important contribution to the performance of the department.

Almost all the supervisors going through the O.B. Mod. training program had success stories similar to the admissions supervisor. Importantly, these individual projects generalized into the way these supervisors managed their whole department.

The results that the O.B. Mod. approach had on key performance areas from each of these supervisors' respective departments are shown in Figure 8-13. This evaluation does not employ an experimental design and thus cause-and-effect conclusions are not warranted. However, the simple before-and-after analysis reveals such dramatic results that one could argue that O.B. Mod. played a significant role in modifying a broad range of performance-related behaviors in this hospital. In other words, the O.B. Mod. approach does indeed seem to be as appropriate for nonprofit organizations as it is for profit ones.

SELF-MANAGEMENT APPLICATIONS[7]

Our final representative application of O.B. Mod. moves away from managing others, as in the cases discussed so far, and examines how the approach has been applied to more effective self-management. Significantly, this application draws more heavily from the expanded social learning material discussed in earlier chapters, the S-O-B-C four-term contingency, and the discussion of self-management in Chapter 7.

A number of managers have utilized behavioral self-management techniques that are based on O.B. Mod. principles. These managers have come from a wide variety of organizations (e.g., in advertising, retailing, manufacturing, and public service) and from both line and staff jobs. Examples of the types of behaviors targeted for change and improvement include leaving the office without informing anyone, time

[7]Data for this discussion are drawn from Luthans and Davis, 1979. We would like to recognize Professor Tim R. V. Davis of Cleveland State University for his work on these cases.

FIGURE 8-13.   Productivity Changes in a Large Hospital After the Application of O.B. Mod.

Unit	Measure(s)	Pre-Intervention	Post-Intervention	Percent Change
Emergency room clerks	Registration errors (per day)	19.16	4.580	76.10
Hardware engineer group, HIS	Average time to repair (minutes)	92.53	33.250	61.40
Medical records file clerks	Errors in filing (per person per audit)	2.87	0.078	97.30
Medical records	Complaints	8.00	1.000	875.00
Transcriptionists	Average errors	2.07	1.400	33.00
	Average output	2,258.00	2,303.330	2.00
Heart station	EKG procedures accomplished (Ave.)	1,263.00	1,398.970	11.00
	Overdue procedures	7.00*	4.000	42.80
Eye clinic	Daily patient throughput	19.00	23.000	21.00
	Daily patient teaching documentation	1.00	2.800	180.00
	Protocols produced	0.00	2.000	200.00
Pharmacy technicians	Drug output (doses)	348.80	422.100	21.00
	Posting errors	3.67	1.480	59.70
	Product waste (percent)	5.80	4.350	25.00
Radiology technicians	Average patient throughput (procedural)	3,849.50	4,049.000	5.00
	Retake rate (percent)	11.20	9.950	11.20
Patient accounting	Average monthly billings	2,561.00	3,424.500	33.70
Admitting office	Time to admit (minutes)	43.73	13.570	68.97
	Average cost	$ 15.05	$ 11.730	22.00
Data center operations	Systems log-on (time)	1:54	1:43	13.40

*Estimate   All averages are arithmetic means

Source: Adapted from Snyder and Luthans, 1982.

spent on the phone, leaving one's own daily work to assist others, filling out a daily expense form, visiting with salespersons without appointments, getting to work on time, writing a plan, following a plan, processing paperwork more efficiently, decreasing the dependence of subordinates, visiting with subordinates and co-workers, and reducing stress when interacting with others or meeting deadlines. The O.B. Mod. approach to these problems has resulted in impressive changes. Systematic evaluations employing experimental and/or reversal/multiple-baseline designs indicate that the O.B. Mod. techniques led to improvement in targeted behaviors, thus making these managers more effective in their jobs. A couple of representative examples will demonstrate how the O.B. Mod. approach to self-management was actually carried out by a manager and how the analysis and evaluations were conducted by the researchers.

Decreasing dependence on the boss

A major problem facing many managers is that they are overdependent on their bosses. An assistant retail store manager who had major responsibilities (such as supervising sales clerks, pricing and displaying merchandise, managing the stockroom, and checking in and reordering goods for suppliers) identified this problem as affecting her performance. She felt that most of her questions and visits with the boss were unnecessary and he agreed. Her boss was enlisted to record the number of visits.

Figure 8–14 shows the baseline frequency. In this case, the intervention consisted of the assistant manager being instructed in the background and principles of O.B. Mod., with special emphasis given to self-management and the S-O-B-C framework of analysis. By using this framework she was able to clarify the contingencies of overdependence. For instance, the following S-O-B-C functional analysis was made:

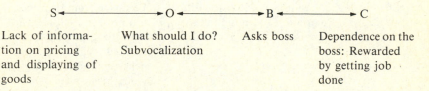

S	O	B	C
Lack of information on pricing and displaying of goods	What should I do? Subvocalization	Asks boss	Dependence on the boss: Rewarded by getting job done

To change the overdependent behavior, she used a feedforward/feedback intervention strategy. She carried an index card, began a notebook record, and subvocalized not to ask her boss questions as an

FIGURE 8-14.   Results of Self-management of Overdependence on the Boss

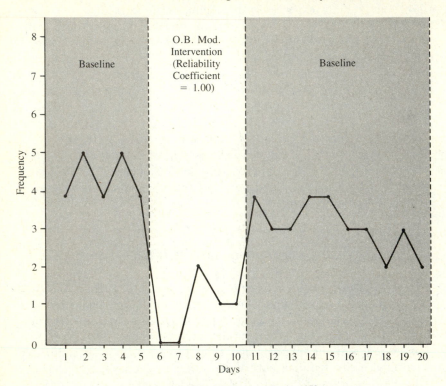

Source: Adapted from Luthans and Davis, 1979.

antecedent management strategy to prompt taking action on her own instead of asking the boss. She also used a consequence management strategy of self-generated feedback and good feelings as reinforcing consequences. In S-O-B-C terms, this feedforward/feedback intervention amounted to:

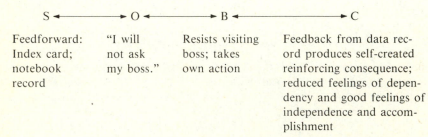

S	O	B	C
Feedforward: Index card; notebook record	"I will not ask my boss."	Resists visiting boss; takes own action	Feedback from data record produces self-created reinforcing consequence; reduced feelings of dependency and good feelings of independence and accomplishment

As Figure 8–14 shows, this intervention led to a significant decline in the number of visits with the boss. When the intervention ceased, there was an appreciable increase in the number of visits. Thus, this reversal design shows that the O.B. Mod. self-management approach had a causal impact. Reliability analysis indicated these data were accurate throughout the study period. Armed with these results, this manager was reinforced for using the O.B. Mod. approach and she set out to use it on other problem areas that she felt eroded her performance as a manager.

Reducing dysfunctional behaviors

Another representative example of the application of O.B. Mod. principles to self-management is an advertising manager of a newspaper who used self-management to improve several behaviors that were affecting his performance. He was in a very hectic job involving constant requests and interruptions from his staff, queries from employees in other departments in the printing plant, and calls and visits from and to customers. Although many of his behaviors could be better managed, he identified processing paperwork, leaving the office without informing anyone, and failure to fill out a daily expense form as especially critical behaviors that needed to be improved to make him more effective.

Participant observers (his secretary and a clerk) were used to record the frequencies of the targeted behaviors. In addition, actual measures such as where the manager left "traces" of his behavior (e.g., how many pieces of paper were left on his desk and in-box when he left at the end of the day) were also carefully kept.

This manager used the S-O-B-C framework to functionally analyze each of the behaviors. Particular attention was given to both the S-O antecendents and, of course, the consequences. Based on this analysis, this manager developed and implemented a feedforward/feedback intervention strategy. The purpose of this intervention was to change each behavior in the desired direction. For example, the strategy, in S-O-B-C terms, for the paperwork problem consisted of the following:

S   O   B   C

S	O	B	C
Reduce paper inflow; Feedforward data display	Paper cognitively differentiated by category	Act on or note in diary or box file	Feedback from data display produces self-reinforcing consequences

For the problem of leaving the office without telling anyone, the following strategy was used:

S ◄────────► O ◄────────► B ◄────────► C

| Feedforward: In-Out board | "Must leave message" Sub-vocalization | Exits from office after leaving message | Feedback from in-board and data displays produces self-created reinforcing consequence. Whereabouts known; no staff embarrassment |

Finally, for the problem of incompleted expense claims, the following strategy was employed:

S ◄────────► O ◄────────► B ◄────────► C

| Feedforward; Expense form placed on desk; data display | "Oh yes, the expense form" Subvocalization | Fills out the form | Feedback from data display produces self-created reinforcing consequences |
| | | | Expenses complete; no financial loss; accurate picture of costs |

The results of this self-management effort are shown in Figure 8-15. All three behaviors were dramatically improved by the self-management intervention strategies. By using a multiple baseline design (staggering the interventions), there was powerful evidence that the O.B. Mod. approach to self-management caused the dysfunctional behaviors to lessen and made this advertising manager more effective.

Overall, this chapter has shown that O.B. Mod. works! We have had this type of success on performance whenever and wherever O.B. Mod. has been systematically applied. The next chapter, however, will explore some actual and anticipated criticisms, misconceptions, and ethical problems with O.B. Mod.

FIGURE 8-15.   Results of Self-management of Dysfunctional Behaviors of an Advertising Manager

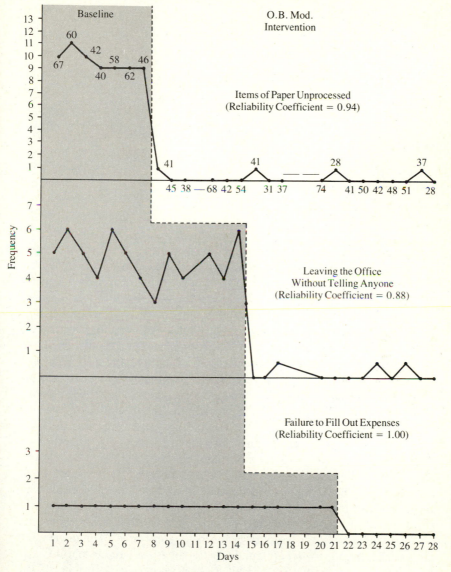

Source: Adapted from Luthans and Davis, 1979.

Misconceptions and Ethical Issues

9

Genuine concern has arisen about real or imagined concepts and applications of behavior modification. We come across people who in effect say, "I'm not exactly sure what behavior modification involves, but I don't want any part of it." Interestingly, however, this concern may not be widespread among practicing managers. For example, one study of 210 practicing managers found that they were more concerned with the relative success of an O.B. Mod.-type program than whether or not it was labeled behavior modification (Kreitner, 1981). This study suggests that managers, who tend to be pragmatic, are interested in *results* rather than academic controversies. Nonetheless, widespread misconceptions exist about what behavior modification and, by association, O.B. Mod. involve. These issues and accompanying ethical questions can and most probably have hampered the actual application of O.B. Mod. to human resource management.

Although the concepts and applications of O.B. Mod. have changed and been expanded since the first edition of this book was written nearly ten years ago, misconceptions and potential underlying ethical issues have persisted. But, because O.B. Mod. is still a comparatively recent approach, scholars in the behavioral area of management are just beginning to debate fundamental questions of its nature, appropriateness, and ethics (see: Gray, 1979; Kreitner, 1982; Locke, 1977, 1979; Luthans, 1980, Parmerlee and Schwenk, 1979; and Smith, 1980). This chapter addresses major misconceptions about O.B. Mod. and by implication relevant ethical issues and related controversy.

THE CONTROVERSY SURROUNDING RADICAL BEHAVIORISM

An enduring source of controversy relative to O.B. Mod. centers on the validity of radical behaviorism. This becomes largely a philosophical issue because fundamental assumptions about human functioning are involved. On one side, Skinner (1974, pp. 16–18) and his conceptual adherents are called *radical* behaviorists because they prefer to focus on the mechanics of how environmental (and genetic) factors control behavior. Introspection and internal cognitions are rejected by the radical behaviorists. They find these interesting, but comparatively useless, for predicting and controlling behavior. Cognitive and humanistic psychologists and philosophers, on the other side, contend that radical behaviorism sells human capabilities short and runs roughshod over the notion of free will. They feel that radical behaviorism oversimplifies and is too mechanistic. In this section, each side of this debate is briefly highlighted and a workable compromise is offered in the form of social learning theory.

Skinner's radical behaviorism

In his classic text, *Science and Human Behavior*, B. F. Skinner noted that:

> "The objection to inner states is not that they do not exist, but that they are not relevant in a functional analysis. We cannot account for the behavior of any system while staying wholly inside it; eventually we must turn to forces operating upon the organism from without" (1953, p. 35).

This view of human behavior has stirred a storm of controversy and opposition among both behavioral scientists (Rogers and Skinner, 1956) and philosophers (see, for example: Audi, 1976).

Philosophic opposition to radical behaviorism

Edwin A. Locke (1979), a cognitive theorist whose work on goal setting was discussed in Chapter 5, adamantly explains why he is philosophically opposed to radical behaviorism:

"I am unalterably opposed to behaviorism, not because I am biased, but because it flies in the face of the most elementary and self-evident facts about human beings: that they possess consciousness and that their minds are their guides to action, or more fundamentally: their means of survival. I am not against the judicious use of contingent rewards and punishments; it is the behaviorist philosophy of man that I oppose" (p. 135).

While, at first glance, Skinner's and Locke's positions seem to be irreconcilable, social learning theory can offer a workable compromise.

Social learning theory: A compromise

Rather than fanning the flames of emotional debate and thus polarizing the behaviorist and cognitive perspectives, a more conciliatory position may be best for at least the long-run effectiveness of behavioral management. Fortunately, many management scholars are beginning to see the theoretical and practical value of synthesizing these disparate views, as opposed to continuing a divisive and largely unproductive polemic. Fedor and Ferris (1981), for example, have taken a constructive step by observing that: "one of the most notable and effective attempts at integrating the cognitive and behavioral perspectives with respect to motivation is social learning theory." Social learning theorist Albert Bandura (1977b) has outlined such a compromise as follows:

"Social learning theory approaches the explanation of human behavior in terms of a continuous reciprocal interaction between cognitive, behavioral, and environmental determinants. Within the process of reciprocal determinism lies the opportunity for people to influence their destiny as well as the limits of self-direction. This conception of human functioning neither casts people into the role of powerless objects controlled by environmental forces nor free agents who can become whatever they choose. Both people and their environments are reciprocal determinants of each other" (p. vii).

This integrative approach should be at least partially acceptable to both behaviorists and cognitive theorists because (1) objective behavior and environmental influences are included and (2) the role of cognitive mediation is recognized. By integrating operant and social learning theory throughout this book, we have hopefully operationalized this approach for the understanding, prediction, and control of organizational behavior for effective performance.

THE GENERAL ISSUE OF BEHAVIORAL CONTROL

With respect to operant conditioning theory and the principles and application of behavior modification, the issue of behavior *control* is a source of lively controversy. Because social learning theory is comparatively new, it has so far escaped becoming embroiled in the same controversy. Therefore, as a topical side note, the issues raised and discussed in the balance of this chapter relate primarily to operant theory and its applied derivative, behavior modification. By virtue of its heritage, O.B. Mod., as presented in this book, is automatically affected by these issues.

One source of controversy about behavioral control relates to basic behavioral research with lower animals (e.g., white rats and pigeons) in highly controlled experiments. Another controversy stems from popular accounts of behavioral control. George Orwell's widely read classic, *Nineteen Eighty-Four*, and the best-selling novel and critically acclaimed movie, *A Clockwork Orange*, have contributed to a type of "Big Brother" syndrome associated with the term behavior modification. Finally, some basic ethical questions are continually being raised concerning the use of behavior control techniques, in general, and behavior modification, in particular. Some misconceptions that can hinder effective understanding and application of O.B. Mod. are dispelled by analyzing in some detail each of these sources of controversy.

From animal research to human application

Behavior modification is frequently criticized for being too "rat-centered." This criticism is derived from the extensive use of rats as subjects in operant conditioning experiments. The logic runs as follows: the principles and techniques associated with behaviorism were largely formulated by experimenters using pigeons and rats as subjects; humans possess capabilities much greater than those of pigeons or rats;

therefore, the principles and techniques of behaviorism are not applicable to humans.

At least on the surface, this syllogism appears to make sense. But a closer look suggests otherwise. As Hammer (1971) argued in opposition to the operant conditioning application that Adam and Scott (1971) made to quality control, "Any theory of behavior which effectively equates man with lower animals will . . . be incapable of dealing with the vast majority of human behavior that has no parallels in the subhuman world." Hammer then went on to label the O.B. Mod.-type approach as "applied ratamorphism." In another criticism of O.B. Mod., Fry's (1974) article titled "Operant Conditioning and O.B. Mod.: Of Mice and Men" noted that the behaviorist principle of minimizing the time between behavior and consequence may be important for animals, but irrelevant for humans, since they have developed an ability to remember the past and to expect the future. Conceivably, by now integrating a social learning approach, O.B. Mod. would be less offensive to these critics because it includes distinctly human cognitive processes such as symbolic retention and expectations.

Obviously, an O.B. Mod. approach does not assume that humans can or should be equated with rats or pigeons. What the critics fail to realize is that despite the tremendously more complex behavior of humans relative to animals, the controlling mechanisms and derived principles for both are basically the same. This is much different from saying that rats and people are the same. While behavior and consequences are certainly different between humans and animals, the fact remains that behavior, animal and human, is basically a function of antecedents and consequences. Many people are uncomfortable paralleling animals and humans in any sense, proven laws of behavior or not. Yet, what would happen to the frequency of a critic's article-writing behavior if it was not reinforced by occasional publication? The law of effect applies to people as much as it does to animals.

Further light is shed on the animal research/human application controversy by appreciating how modern behaviorism developed. Initially, experimentation in behaviorism greatly depended on animals because they were readily accessible, cheaply maintained, and easily controlled (Skinner, 1969, pp. 100–101). Pigeons were particularly popular because they could emit an easily observed and hence countable response (pecking) at a very high frequency, sometimes exceeding thirty thousand pecks an hour (see: Ferster and Perrott, 1968, p. 280).

Scientific endeavors, including building a science of human behavior, typically start off with relatively simple subjects and objects and then evolve toward the more complex. For example, as Skinner (1969) noted: "Those who study living organisms—say, in genetics, embryology, or medicine — usually start below the human level, and students of behavior have quite naturally followed the same practice" (p. 100). No one seemed to think it was unnatural when the Soviet and American space scientists rocketed lower animals into orbit around the earth prior to doing so with human astronauts (concern for cruelty to animals notwithstanding). The basic scientific research model dictates that early efforts be carried out with relatively simple organisms under highly controlled conditions.

Eventually, the transition was made from animals to humans in behaviorism, both in research and application. History is filled with examples of scientists who turned to new and often radically different solutions to difficult or unsolved human problems. For example, until Fleming's discovery of penicillin, no one saw the pharmacological value of common mold. Destructive self-mutilation by autistic children, behavioral problems with the mentally retarded, and dysfunctional classroom behavior of special and normal children also required new solutions. Techniques derived from operant conditioning used in the past primarily with animal subjects were successfully applied to these behavior problems.

Of course, autistic children, the mentally retarded, and special and normal schoolchildren also should not be equated with fully functioning adults working in modern, complex organizations. The point is not that they are the same but that animal, mentally retarded, immature, and normal adult behavior is a function of contingent antecedents and consequences. While the nature of the behavior and the cues and consequences may be drastically different, the mechanisms and principles of behavior control remain the same. Actual applications of O.B. Mod. reported in the last chapter indicate that the translation of behavior principles from lower animals to immature human behavior and, ultimately, to full-blown human resource management is both possible and desirable.

The "big brother" syndrome

A theme in popular literature is to characterize behavior modification as some sort of tyrannical tool suited for the destruction of democracy and erosion of human rights. This view can be labeled the "Big Brother" syndrome. It is largely based on misconceptions of what is involved in the positive as well as negative control of behavior.

Because of Orwell's (1949) frightening depiction of the future in his classic book, *Nineteen Eighty-Four*, the term behavior modification often conjures up visions of his principal character Winston Smith being unmercifully truncheoned and electrocuted in the Ministry of Love. Others think of the book and movie version of *A Clockwork Orange* (Burgess, 1963) in which the character Alex, an overly aggressive and sexually promiscuous teenager, is turned into a "nice" boy with drugs and torturous aversive conditioning.

While popular depictions of this type make for exciting entertainment, the behavioral control techniques they describe have nothing in common with an O.B. Mod. approach to human resource management. First of all, the techniques referred to by popular novelists and screenwriters involve aversion therapy. These techniques involve two basic strategies, punishment and classical aversive conditioning (Sherman, 1973).

For example, Orwell's Winston Smith was aversively conditioned with punishment while Burgess's Alex was aversively conditioned through classical conditioning. When Smith answered "No" to the question, "Do you love Big Brother," he was struck on the tips of his elbows and in other sensitive spots with a truncheon. As one would expect, the "No" responses diminished in frequency. Eventually, Smith declared that he really did love the symbolic dictator, Big Brother. Loving Big Brother was an avoidance response — verbal allegiance to Big Brother enabled Smith to avoid further cruel physical torture. It goes without saying that this type of inhuman treatment is inexcusable in civilized society.

In *A Clockwork Orange*, Alex's fate was somewhat different. After being injected with a nausea-inducing drug, he was strapped into a seat with his eyelids propped open and forced to watch films of bloody beatings, war atrocities, and hard-core pornography. Through simple classical conditioning, Alex learned to associate violence and sex with nausea. After conditioning Alex, his trainers proudly displayed their "new Alex" who became nauseous at mere references to violence or at the sight of a nude female. The ethics of such methods of treating even the most anti-social behavior has been questioned, as well it should be.

Unfortunately for the legitimate approaches to constructive behavior control, the Orwells and Burgesses have done more than make their literary point; they have created a generalized fear of anything that remotely suggests systematic behavior control. This, coupled with the fact that aversive conditioning is sometimes used in behavior therapy (e.g., quit-smoking clinics), has led to a great deal of confusion surrounding behavior modification in general. It should be remembered that O.B. Mod. is *not* behavior therapy; rather, it is an outgrowth of applied behavior analysis, and more recently, social learning theory. O.B. Mod. is based mainly on *positive* rather than negative control and makes no use of aversive conditioning. Hopefully, the preceding chapters have eradicated the Big Brother fears surrounding behavior modification.

The ethics of behavior control

Another ethical issue is the whole concept of *control*, per se. For some, the word "control" connotes a serious threat to individuality and freedom. While decrying a shift in the prevailing American value system from what they call the individual imperative to the organizational imperative, Scott and Hart (1979) criticized those who have embraced the philosophy of behaviorism because it assumes that humans are inherently malleable:

> "Since managers control all modern organizations, they can write programs of social control for people who cannot hope to accede to managerial power but whose support is absolutely necessary for maintaining the managerial regime. . . . The inescapable fact remains that management scholars and practitioners accepted the premise of innate human malleability without a trace of philosophical reflection. That demonstrates an appalling philosophical bankruptcy" (p. 61).

Scott and Hart's point is well taken; indeed, it is socially undesirable to view individuals as little more than moldable cogs for impersonal organizational wheels. However, to imply that managers are malevolent dictators bent on self-serving control seems to be stretching the point way too far. Behavioral managers, while believing that behavior principles are useful for shaping effective human performance, do not claim to be able to mechanically bend employees to their whim. O.B. Mod. assumes that it is possible and desirable to systematically manage behavioral processes that are already a natural part of overt social interaction and/or covert functioning. Moreover, an O.B. Mod. approach that strives for improved productivity in a positively reinforcing environment promises a greater measure of individual freedom and dignity than contemporary work settings where the work is dull, working conditions are less than desirable, and negative control is everpresent.

Control by any other name • The fact remains that behavioral control, in one form or another, has always existed, continues to exist, and probably will remain with us for the foreseeable future.

Popular human resource management terms such as discipline, leadership, direction, persuasion, communication, motivation, and influence all revolve ultimately around behavior control. Apparently, behavior control is more acceptable to people when carried out in the name of leadership or motivation. McGinnies and Ferster (1971) succinctly outlined the ethical dilemma associated with behavior control as follows:

> "Social situations have long been manipulated both practically and deliberately. Ever since Machiavelli, and perhaps before, there has been a fear of the control and manipulation of one person's behavior for the benefit of another. With the development of a laboratory science of social psychology, where social phenomena are developed in prototype form and actually shaped and manipulated, a technology is becoming available to influence social situations rationally and self-consciously. This raises questions concerning the ethics of such manipulation" (p. 432).

Skinner (1953) commented that, "We all control, and we are all controlled" (p. 438). But to say that behavior control is ethical because everyone does it is not sufficient. Yet, recognizing that we are all behavior modifiers (albeit rather unsystematic ones), constantly attempting to change the behavior of those around us by manipulating antecedents and consequences, we have a point of departure for an ethical analysis.

When we smile, nod approval, frown, make a critical remark, or pretend not to notice someone who is annoying us, we are experiencing normal, daily social interaction. Each of these social exchanges has the effect, or at least is intended to have the effect, of bringing the behavior of others under control. Admittedly, such social activity often occurs with little or no formal understanding of the underlying behavioral principles. However, such activity raises an interesting analytical question: is the unwitting use of behavior modification ethical while the purposeful, systematic use of the same techniques is unethical?

Who benefits? • The crux of the ethical issue surrounding behavior control in O.B. Mod. seems to lie in identifying the true beneficiary of the altered behavior. McGinnies and Ferster's earlier statement mentions the manipulation of one person's behavior for the *benefit of another*. Control of someone else's behavior for purely selfish reasons is, of course, based on questionable ethics. In Skinner's classic debate with the noted humanist Carl Rogers, Skinner made the point that, "Man's natural inclinations to revolt against selfish control has

been exploited to good purpose in what we call the philosophy and literature of democracy" (Rogers and Skinner, 1956, p. 1057). Hand in hand
with the ethical question of who benefits is one concerning the end(s) to
which O.B. Mod. is used.

To what end? • Certainly, behavior modification and O.B.
Mod. can, like any other technology or tool (e.g., cars, guns, or nuclear
fission), be misused. There is always the danger that social behavior
control techniques will be subverted to purely selfish, irresponsible, or
destructive ends. Accompanying the benefits of any scientific advance is
the professional responsibility for ensuring socially responsible application. From an ethical standpoint, tools are ethically neutral until put
into use. The point is that behavior modification and O.B. Mod. cannot
justly be labeled unethical per se, but they may be applied in unethical
ways.

It has been pointed out (Kreitner, 1982) that an ethical loophole
is created when O.B. Mod. is called an ethically neutral tool that subsequently can be used to pursue ethical or unethical ends:

> "The question of ends is really an economic one. At least
> within the private business sector, the marketplace is the ulti-
> mate arbiter of which products and services are sold and which
> are not. Firms producing salable goods and services tend to sur-
> vive to do business another day, while those left with unsalable
> items face bankruptcy. But closer examination shows the situa-
> tion to be less than clear-cut. Unfortunately, mass advertising,
> government subsidies, and other exogenous factors have a ten-
> dency to bias the free market mechanism, so that organizations
> can end up pursuing some rather unwholesome and socially
> irresponsible ends. For example, as a long-time proponent of
> [O.B. Mod.], I had serious second thoughts after hearing a
> glowing report about the enhancement of productivity through
> behavior modification in a cigarette manufacturing firm. Con-
> sidering that cigarette smoking is a proven health hazard, the
> reader is left to ponder along with the author the societal value
> of this particular means-ends arrangement. From an ethical
> standpoint, it is imperative that every prospective user of [O.B.
> Mod.] consider the ultimate ends of its use in terms of the
> general well-being of society rather than from solely the myopic
> standpoint of 'will it sell?' " (p. 88).

Thus, those who are concerned with the ethics of O.B. Mod. are urged
to focus their attention on the ends to which it is used.

Controlling the controllers

Those who criticize Skinner's (1971) suggestion that we modify our culture with behavior technology are concerned with who will retain the *final* power to decide what behavior is strengthened and what behavior is weakened. In other words, who will control the controllers?

On an organizational level, at least from a management perspective, the problem of controlling the controllers is largely settled because all private and public sector organizations operate within larger spheres of control. For example, top corporate management is responsible to the board of directors and is controlled by organizational consequences such as growth, increased share of the market, improved rate of return on investment, and survival. In addition, direct and indirect control is exercised by stockholders, unions, customers, suppliers, government, the press, and general social, political, economic, and technological conditions. Business managers who are unable to meet required performance criteria or who abuse their behavior control prerogatives are typically replaced. The same is basically true of government agency, hospital, military, church, and educational administrators.

Control carries all the way down the organization. Managerial controllers of subordinates' behavior are themselves subject to many controlling consequences. A hierarchy of consequences thus leads to a hierarchy of control. Improved performance of an employee at the operative level, as a result of systematic shaping with positive reinforcement by a manager, contributes to organizational success, which ultimately reinforces top management through favorable organizational outcomes.

A unique behavior modification application in education (Gray, Graubard, and Rosenberg, 1974) suggests a pragmatic solution to controlling the controllers. In one case, troublesome students were instructed in the basics of differential positive reinforcement (selecting and positively reinforcing only certain responses). For experimental control purposes, this procedure was carried out without the teacher's knowledge. Needless to say, teachers who were used to handling "incorrigible" students showed great surprise when those same students started reinforcing them with compliments and other positive reinforcers for helpful and understanding behaviors. By "turning the reinforcement tables" through *countercontrol*, the troublemakers began to gain a measure of control over the controllers and simultaneously change their own behavior. As a result of this unique approach, teacher effectiveness improved and the troublesome students became models of good behavior in the eyes of their teachers.

O.B. Mod.'s antecedent management, positive reinforcement, shaping, and modeling techniques are all two-way streets. Just as communication flows up and down the organizational ladder, O.B. Mod. can do the same. There is no reason why this countercontrol cannot work in today's organizations. For example, subordinates can change the behavior of a particularly cranky boss into friendly, supportive behavior through the use of compliments, rapid and efficient compliance, and other relevant forms of social reinforcement made *contingent upon* desirable supervisory behavior. In other words, O.B. Mod. can be used to manage the boss's behavior as well as subordinates' behavior. When paired with the self-control techniques discussed in Chapter 7, all organizational members—superiors, subordinates, and those interested in more effective self-management—can use O.B. Mod. to create an environment of reciprocal positive reinforcement for personal and organizational goal attainment.

A COROLLARY ISSUE: MEASURING ON-THE-JOB BEHAVIOR

Thinking back to Chapter 4, the second step in the O.B. Mod. model involves measuring the performance-related behavior targeted in step one. This baseline measure is vital to the subsequent steps of analysis, intervention, and evaluation. Further measurement is carried out after intervention to determine if the intervention strategy is having its intended effect. This measurement, a vital aspect of any scientific endeavor, plays an important role in O.B. Mod. However, a lingering question arises: "Is it ethical to observe and record organizational behavior without the person's knowledge?"

As pointed out in Chapter 4, there should never be a veil of secrecy surrounding O.B. Mod. Managers are advised to be aboveboard and to fully describe what they are doing to affected parties. But awareness of being measured can in some cases affect the behavioral data being gathered. As a result, managers attempting to obtain objective baseline data are often caught in a dilemma. As Brandt (1972) pointed out:

> "Merely close observation of someone, with or without the use of gadgetry, and recording his behavior inconspicuously, when such observation or recording is not expected, can certainly be viewed as an invasion of privacy and perhaps as deceitful also" (p. 40).

Two realities seem relevant to this ethical issue. First, observation and measurement of behavior in a work context is nothing new. In spite of the formal protection of employees' rights afforded by government legislation and collective bargaining agreements, a great deal of employee behavior in today's organizations is under very close scrutiny. This situation is largely the result of industrial engineering procedures that have timed, paced, recorded, charted, and analyzed minute details of human work behavior in the name of increasing productive efficiency. As a result, over the last sixty years, industrial workers in particular have become desensitized to being measured. They are remarkably tolerant of (or, perhaps, resigned to) managerial scrutiny. As Chapter 4 pointed out, most of the measures used in the O.B. Mod. approach are derived from existing, archival data already being gathered by industrial engineers and accountants. Where data are not available, then systematic recording of key *performance-related behavioral events* will be a new factor in the observation of employees. Subjective observation of nonperformance behavior will thus be replaced by objective observation and measurement of behavior that is critical to performance improvement.

A second reality is the public outcry over invasions of privacy through tape-recording and the indiscriminate use of personal information stored in computer data banks. Federal law now strictly interprets what constitutes an illegal invasion of privacy. While managers are limited as to what they can and cannot do with information from employee personnel records, privacy laws do not preclude the traditional managerial prerogative of retrieving and using employee performance data. But it is important to realize that the passage of privacy legislation signaled growing public discontent with "Big Brother" scrutiny.

In the final analysis, the question of how observation and measurement in O.B. Mod. can be effectively and responsibly accomplished must be answered by each professional manager. Obviously, a manager should not surreptitiously peer from behind filing cabinets or machines, measuring subordinates' behavior. This is "snoopervision," not responsible supervision. A manager can collect valid behavioral data with an employee's complete awareness by using existing records, various forms of behavior sampling, key performance results, contingency contracting, and self-recording methods.

An Integrative Model for O.B. Mod.

10

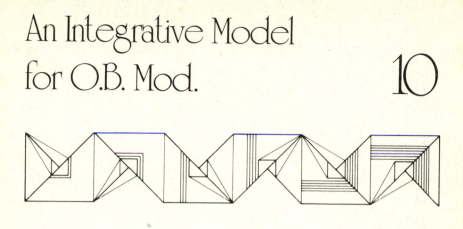

Early chapters laid down the theory and principles of an operant and social learning perspective. Attention then turned to a model for the application of antecedent and consequence management strategies, the background and techniques for modeling and self-control, and a detailed summary of actual applications of O.B. Mod. in a wide variety of organizations. Finally, some real and anticipated misconceptions and ethical issues were discussed. Now, in this final mini-chapter, it is necessary and instructive to come full circle by pulling everything together. The model shown in Figure 10-1 represents this attempt to integrate all of these issues.

This integrative attempt goes *beyond* the original operant O.B. Mod. approach with its three-term (A-B-C), overt environmental contingencies. Our integrative model incorporates both *operant and social learning* approaches to O.B. Mod. It accepts and employs all the operant assumptions, but goes beyond by using the four-term (S-O-B-C) contingency framework. In particular, covert as well as overt antecedents and consequences are recognized, and the role of cognitive mediating processes and self-control are specifically incorporated.

As shown, the situation for O.B. Mod. incorporates four major categories: goal cues, social cues, task and structural cues, and self-control cues. As in the operant paradigm, these cues do not *cause* subsequent behavior. Instead, they serve as cues that set the occasion for the behavior to be emitted. Goal cues include both personal/self-evaluative goals and imposed goals (as found in most organizational standards or quotas). In addition, the mere *opportunity* to participate in goal-setting can be an important cue. Social cues come from group membership and

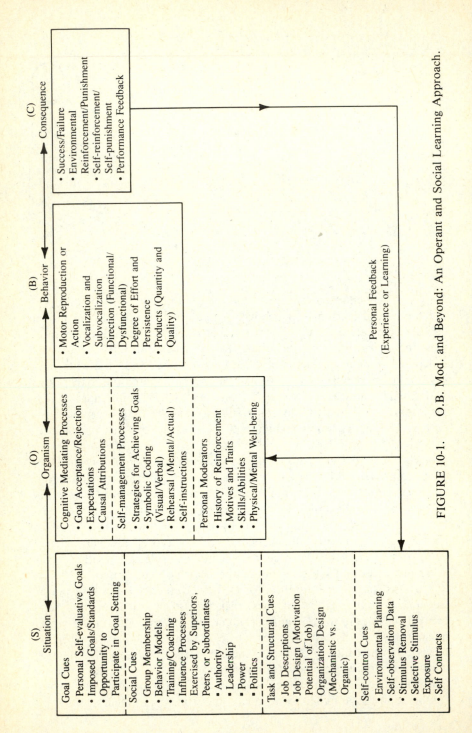

FIGURE 10-1.   O.B. Mod. and Beyond: An Operant and Social Learning Approach.

all of its dynamics, behavior models (e.g., supervisors or co-workers), training/coaching, and important influence processes such as authority, leadership, power or politics. Task and structural cues come from simple job descriptions as well as from the design of the job (e.g., task characteristics such as significance, identity, skill variety, autonomy and feedback) and the structural design of the organization (e.g., mechanistic or organic). The final category of cues found in the "situation" portion of this integrative model of O.B. Mod. deals with self-control. These self-control cues include environmental planning strategies, self-observation data, stimulus removal, selective stimulus exposure (e.g., through screening) and self contracts.

The "O" or organism/person portion of the integrative model represents the role that cognitive mediating and self-control processes play, as influenced by personal characteristics. The cognitive mediating processes include goal acceptance/rejection, expectations (as explained by expectancy approaches to motivation), and causal attribution (as explained by emerging attribution theories); among the self-control processes are strategies for achieving goals, symbolic coding (both visual and verbal), rehearsal (both mental and actual), and self-instruction. The importance of these mediating processes between the situation and the behavior is being recognized, as is the moderating effect of personal characteristics such as history of reinforcement, motives and traits, skills/abilities and physical/mental well-being. Thus, the concise A-B-C model is traded off for the more complex S-O-B-C approach to provide a better understanding of the complexities of human behavior in organizations. However, such understanding need not detract from the other O.B. Mod. goals of prediction and control which are essential for successful application.

Behavior remains central to this integrative model. First of all, it includes the obvious physical movement of motor reproduction or action. However, behavior also can be depicted as words spoken or subvocalized. Also, behavior exhibits a certain *direction* (either functional or dysfunctional for organizational purposes/outcomes) and *degree* of effort and persistence. Finally, at least for O.B. Mod. purposes, it is useful to represent behavior in terms of its direct products (e.g., quality or quantity outcomes or products in an organizational performance sense). For example, while it is not useful in most applications of O.B. Mod. to talk in terms of hand movements, it is helpful to deal with the direct *products* of these behaviors such as quality or quantity of performance.

In this model, as in the basic operant model, behavior is still a function of its consequences. For practical application, contingent consequences remain critical to the prediction and control of behavior. The personal feedback loops indicate that consequences also greatly influence mediating cognitions, self-management processes and personal moderators, and give power to situational cues. These consequences can be thought of as success or failure or, more precisely, environmental- or self-reinforcement/punishment. Also, the important role that performance feedback plays in the application of O.B. Mod. is given specific recognition in the consequence portions of the model.

Importantly, this is a summary, integrative model. It is not intended to replace nor revise what has been presented in previous chapters. However, this summary model does go *beyond* the original operant approach by integrating social learning and hopefully can serve as a foundation and point of departure for O.B. Mod. in the future.

REFERENCES

Adam, E. E., Jr. "An Analysis of Changes in Performance Quality with Operant Conditioning Procedures." *Journal of Applied Psychology* 56 (1972) 480–486.

Adam, E. E., Jr., & Scott, W. E., Jr. "The Application of Behavioral Conditioning Procedures to the Problems of Quality Control." *Academy of Management Journal* 14 (1971) 175–193.

Adams, J. S. "Inequity in Social Exchange." In L. Berkowitz (Ed.), *Advances in Experimental Social Psychology*. New York: Academic Press, 1965.

Addison, R. M., & Homme, L. E. "The Reinforcing Event (RE) Menu." *National Society for Programmed Instruction Journal* 5 (1966) 8–9.

Alderfer, C. P. "An Empirical Test of a New Theory of Human Needs." *Organizational Behavior and Human Performance* 4 (1969) 142–175.

Alderfer, C. P. *Existence, Relatedness and Growth: Human Needs in Organizational Settings*. New York: Free Press, 1972.

Anderson, C. R., Hellriegel, D., & Slocum, J. W. "Managerial Response to Environmentally Induced Stress." *Academy of Management Journal* 20 (1977) 260–272.

Anderson, C. R., & Schneier, C. E. "Locus of Control, Leader Behavior and Leader Performance Among Management Students." *Academy of Management Journal* 21 (1978) 690–698.

Andrasik, F. "Organizational Behavior Modification in Business Settings: A Methodological and Content Review." *Journal of Organizational Behavior Management* 2 (1979) 85–102.

Andrasik, F., Heimberg, J. S., & McNamara, J. R. "Behavior Modification of Work and Work-Related Problems." In M. Hersen, R. M. Eisler, & P. M. Miller (Eds.), *Progress in Behavior Modification*. New York: Academic Press, 11 (1981) 118–161.

Andrasik, F., McNamara, J. R., & Edlund, S. R. "Future Directions for OBM." *Journal of Organizational Behavior Management* 3 (1981) 1–3.

Argyris, C. *Personality and Organization*. New York: Harper & Row, 1957.

"At Emery Air Freight: Positive Reinforcement Boosts Performance." *Organizational Dynamics* (Winter 1973) 41–50.

Audi, R., "B. F. Skinner on Freedom, Dignity, and the Explanation of Behavior," *Behaviorism* 4 (1976) 163–186.

Bandura, A. "Modeling Theory." In W. S. Sahakin (Ed.), *Psychology of Learning: Systems, Models, and Theories*. Chicago: Markham, 1970.

Bandura, A. *Principles of Behavior Modification*. New York: Holt, Rinehart, & Winston, 1969.

Bandura, A. (Ed.). *Psychological Modeling: Conflicting Theories*. Chicago: Adline-Atherton, 1971.

Bandura, A. "Self-Efficacy: Toward a Unifying Theory of Behavioral Change." *Psychological Review* 84 (1977a) 191–215.

Bandura, A. "Self-Reinforcement: Theoretical and Methodological Considerations." *Behaviorism* 4 (1976) 135–155.

Bandura, A. *Social Learning Theory*. Englewood Cliffs, NJ: Prentice-Hall, 1977b.

Bandura, A. "Social Learning Theory." In J. T. Spence, R. C. Carson, & J. W. Thibaut (Eds.). *Behavioral Approaches to Therapy*. Morristown, NJ: General Learning Press, 1976, 1–46.

Bandura, A., & Walters, R. *Social Learning and Personality Development*. New York: Holt, Rinehart, & Winston, 1963.

Beatty, R., & Schneier, C. E. "Training the Hard-Core Unemployed Through Positive Reinforcement." *Human Resource Management* (Winter 1972) 11–17.

Berger, C. J., Cummings, L. L., & Heneman, H. G., III. "Expectancy Theory and Operant Conditioning Predictions of Performance Under Variable Ratio and Continuous Schedules of Reinforcement." *Organizational Behavior and Human Performance* 14 (1975) 227–243.

Blackman, G. J., & Silberman, S. *Modification of Child Behavior*. Belmont, CA: Wadsworth, 1971.

Brandt, R. *Studying Behavior in Natural Settings*. New York: Holt, Rinehart, & Winston, 1972.

Brief, A. P., & Aldag, R. J. "The 'Self' in Work Organizations: A Conceptual Review." *Academy of Management Review* 6 (1981) 75–88.

Brief, A. P., Schuler, R. S., & Van Sell, M. *Managing Job Stress*. Boston: Little, Brown, 1981.

Burgess, A. *A Clockwork Orange*. New York: W. W. Norton, 1963.

Burnaska, R. F. "The Effects of Behavior Modeling Training Upon Managers' Behaviors and Employees' Perceptions." *Personnel Psychology* 29 (1976) 329–335.

Burns, T., & Stalker, G. *The Management of Innovation*. London: Tavistock Publications, 1961.

Byham, W. C. "Transfer of Modeling Training to the Job." *Personnel Psychology* 29 (1976) 345–349.

Calder, B. J. "An Attribution Theory of Leadership." In B. Staw & G. Salancik (Eds.). *New Directions in Organizational Behavior*. Chicago: St. Clair Press, 1977, 179–204.

Campbell, D. T., & Stanley, J. C. *Experimental and Quasi-Experimental Designs for Research*. Chicago: Rand McNally, 1963.

Cantalanello, R. F., & Kirkpatrick, D. L. "Evaluating Training Programs — The State of the Art." *Training and Development Journal* 22 (May 1968) 2–9.

Carrell, M. R., & Dittrich, J. E. "Equity Theory: The Recent Literature, Methodological Considerations, and New Directions." *Academy of Management Review* 3 (1978) 202–210.

Cherrington, D. J., Reitz, H. J., & Scott, W. E. "Effects of Contingent and Noncontingent Rewards on the Relationship Between Satisfaction and Task Performance." *Journal of Applied Psychology* 55 (1971) 531–536.

Connellan, T. K. *How to Improve Human Performance: Behaviorism in Business and Industry*. New York: Harper and Row, 1978.

"Conversation with B. F. Skinner." *Organizational Dynamics* (Winter 1973) 31–40.

Cook, T. D., & Campbell, D. T. "The Design and Conduct of Quasi-Experimental and True Experiments in Field Settings." In M. D. Dunnette (Ed.), *Handbook of Industrial and Organizational Psychology*. Chicago: Rand McNally, 1976, 223–326.

Cooper, C. L., & Marshall, J. *Understanding Executive Stress*. London: Macmillan, 1977.

Cummings, L. L., & Schwab, D. P. *Performance in Organizations: Determinants and Appraisal*. Glenview, IL: Scott, Foresman, 1973.

Davis, T. R. V., & Luthans, F. "Leadership Re-Examined: A Behavioral Approach." *Academy of Management Review* 4 (1979) 237–248.

Davis, T. R. V., & Luthans, F. "Managers in Action: A New Look at Their Behavior and Operating Modes." *Organizational Dynamics* (Summer 1980a) 64–80.

Davis, T. R. V., & Luthans, F. "A Social Learning Approach to Organizational Behavior." *Academy of Management Review* 5 (1980b) 281–290.

Deci, E. L. "Paying People Doesn't Always Work the Way You Expect It To." *Human Resource Management* (Summer 1973) 28–32.

Decker, P. J. "The Enhancement of Behavior Modeling Training of Supervisory Skills by the Inclusion of Retention Processes." *Personnel Psychology* 35 (1982) 323–332.

Dossett, D. L., & Greenberg, C. I. "Goal Setting and Performance Evaluation: An Attributional Analysis." *Academy of Management Journal* 24 (1981) 767–779.

Dunnette, M. D., Campbell, J. P., & Hakel, M. D. "Factors Contributing to Job Satisfaction and Job Dissatisfaction in Six Occupational Groups." *Organizational Behavior and Human Performance* 2 (1967) 143–174.

Evans, W. A. "Pay for Performance: Fact or Fable." *Personnel Journal* 49 (September 1970) 726–731.

Fedor, D. B., & Ferris, G. R. "Integrating O.B. Mod. with Cognitive Approaches to Motivation." *Academy of Management Review* 6 (1981) 115–125.

Ferster, C. B., & Perrott, M. C. *Behavior Principles*. New York: New Century, 1968.

Ferster, C. B., & Skinner, B. F. *Schedules of Reinforcement*. New York: Appleton-Century-Crofts, 1957.

Ford, R. N. "Job Enrichment Lessons from AT&T." *Harvard Business Review* 51 (January-February 1973) 96–106.

Frederiksen, L. W. (Ed.), *Handbook of Organizational Behavior Management*. New York: Wiley, 1982a.

Frederiksen, L. W. "Organizational Behavior Management: An Overview." In L. W. Frederiksen (Ed.), *Handbook of Organizational Behavior Management*. New York: Wiley, 1982b, 3–20.

Frederiksen, L. W., & Johnson, R. P. "Organizational Behavior Management." In M. Hersen, R. Eisler, & P. Miller (Eds.), *Progress in Behavior Modification*. New York: Academic Press, 12 (1981) 67–118.

Frederiksen, L. W., & Lovett, S. B. "Inside Organizational Behavior Management: Perspectives on an Emerging Field." *Journal of Organizational Behavior* 2 (1980) 193-203.

French, W. "Organization Development Objectives, Assumptions, and Strategies." *California Management Review* 12 (Winter 1969) 23–24.

Fry, F. "Operant Conditioning and O.B. Mod.: Of Mice and Men." *Personnel* 51 (1974) 17–24.

Goldstein, A. P., & Sorcher, M. *Changing Supervisor Behavior*. New York: Pergamon Press, 1974.

Goodall, K. "Shapers at Work." *Psychology Today* (November 1972) 53–62 & 132–138.

Goode, R. V. "Complications at the Cafeteria Checkout Lines." In M. G. Miner & J. B. Miner (Eds.), *Policy Issues in Contemporary Personnel and Industrial Relations*. New York: Macmillan, 1977, 563–566.

Gray, F., Graubard, P., & Rosenberg, J. "Little Brother Is Changing You." *Psychology Today* 7 (1974) 42–46.

Gray, J. L. "The Myths of the Myths About Behavior Mod in Organizations: A Reply to Locke's Criticisms of Behavior Modification." *Academy of Management Review* 4 (1979) 121–129.

Greene, C. N. "Causal Connections Among Managers' Merit Pay, Job Satisfaction, and Performance." *Journal of Applied Psychology* 58 (1973) 95–100.

Gyllenhammar, P. G. "How Volvo Adapts Work to People." *Harvard Business Review* 55 (July-August 1977) 102–113.

Hackman, J. R., & Oldham, G. R. *Work Redesign*. Reading, MA: Addison-Wesley, 1980.

Hammer, M. "The Application of Behavioral Conditioning Procedures to the Problems of Quality Control: Comment." *Academy of Management Journal* 14 (1971) 529–532.

Haynes, R. S., Pine, R. C., & Fitch, H. G. "Reducing Accident Rates with Organizational Behavior Modification." *Academy of Management Journal* 25 (1982) 407–416.

Heider, F. *The Psychology of Interpersonal Relations*. New York: Wiley, 1958.

Hermann, J. A., de Montes, A. I., Dominguez, B., Montes, F., & Hopkins, B. L. "Effects of Bonuses for Punctuality on the Tardiness of Industrial Workers." *Journal of Applied Behavior Analysis* 6 (1973) 563–570.

Herzberg, F. "One More Time: How Do You Motivate Employees?" *Harvard Business Review* 46 (January-February 1968) 53–62.

Herzberg, F. "Orthodox Job Enrichment." In L. E. Davis & J. C. Taylor (Eds.), *Design of Jobs* (2nd ed.). Santa Monica: Goodyear, 1979.

Herzberg, F., Mausner, B., & Snyderman, B. *The Motivation to Work* (2nd ed.). New York: Wiley, 1959.

Hilgard, E. R. *Introduction to Psychology* (3rd ed.). New York: Harcourt, Brace, Jovanovich, 1962.

Hilgard, E. R., & Marquis, D. G. *Conditioning and Learning*. New York: Appleton-Century-Crofts, 1940.

Hill, W. F. *Learning: A Survey of Psychological Interpretations*. Scranton, PA: Chandler Publishing Company, 1963.

"How to Get More From Your Employees." *INC.* (November, 1981) 59–62.

Hulin, C. L., & Smith, P. A. "An Empirical Investigation of the Implication of the Two-Factor Theory of Job Satisfaction." *Journal of Applied Psychology* 51 (1967) 396–402.

"Imitating Models: A New Management Tool." *Business Week* (May 8, 1978) 119–120.

Johnston, J. M., Duncan, P. K., Monroe, L., Stephenson, H., & Stoerzinger, A. "Tactics and Benefits of Behavioral Measurement in Business." *Journal of Organizational Behavior Management* 1 (1978) 164–178.

Jorgenson, D. O., Dunnette, M. D., & Pritchard, R. D. "Effects of the Manipulation of a Performance-Reward Contingency on Behavior in a Simulated Work Setting." *Journal of Applied Psychology* 57 (1973) 271–280.

Kanfer, F. H. "Self-Management Methods." In F. H. Kanfer & A. P. Goldstein (Eds.), *Helping People Change: A Textbook of Methods* (2nd ed.). New York: Pergamon, 1980.

Kanfer, F. H., & Karoly, P. "Self-Control: A Behavioristic Excursion into the Lion's Den." In M. J. Mahoney & C. E. Thoresen (Eds.), *Self-Control: Power to the Person*. Monterey, CA: Brooks/Cole, 1974, 200–217.

Kazdin, A. E. *Behavior Modification in Applied Settings*. Homewood, IL: Dorsey Press, 1975.

Keller, F. S. *Learning: Reinforcement Theory*. New York: Random House, 1954.

Kelley, H. H. "Attribution Theory in Social Psychology." In D. Levine (Ed.), *Nebraska Symposium on Motivation* (Vol. 15). Lincoln: University of Nebraska Press, 1967, 192–237.

Kelley, H. H. "The Process of Causal Attribution." *American Psychologist* 28 (1973) 107–128.

Kelley, H. H., & Michela, J. L. "Attribution Theory and Research." *Annual Review of Psychology* 31 (1980) 457–501.

Kempen, R. W. "Absenteeism and Tardiness." In L. W. Frederiksen (Ed.), *Handbook of Organizational Behavior Management*. New York: Wiley, 1982, 365–392.

Komaki, J. L. "Alternative Evaluation Strategies in Work Settings: Reversal and Multiple-Baseline Designs." *Journal of Organizational Behavior Management* 1 (1977) 53–77.

Komaki, J. L. "The Case for the Single Case: Making Judicious Decisions About Alternatives." In L. W. Frederiksen (Ed.), *Handbook of Organizational Behavior Management*. New York: Wiley, 1982, 145–176.

Kondrasuk, J. N. "Studies in MBO Effectiveness." *Academy of Management Review* 6 (1981) 419–430.

Koontz, H., & Bradspies, R. W. "Managing Through Feedforward Control." *Business Horizons* 15 (June 1972) 25–36.

Kotter, J. *The General Managers*. New York: Free Press, 1982.

Kraut, A. I. "Developing Managerial Skills Via Modeling Techniques: Some Positive Research Findings—A Symposium." *Personnel Psychology* 29 (1976) 325–328.

Kreitner, R. "Controversy in OBM: History, Misconceptions, and Ethics." In L. Frederiksen (Ed.), *Handbook of Organizational Behavior Management*. New York: Wiley, 1982, 71–91.

Kreitner, R. "The Feedforward and Feedback Control of Job Performance Through Organizational Behavior Management (OBM)." *Journal of Organizational Behavior Management* 3 (1981/1982) 3–20.

Kreitner, R. *Management* 2/E. Boston: Houghton Mifflin, 1983.

Kreitner, R. "Managerial Reaction to the Term Behavior Modification." *Journal of Organizational Behavior Management* 3 (1981) 53–58.

Kreitner, R. "People Are Systems Too: Filling the Feedback Vacuum." *Business Horizons* 20 (December 1977) 54–58.

Krumhus, K. M., & Malott, R. W. "The Effects of Modeling and Immediate and Delayed Feedback in Staff Training," *Journal of Organizational Behavior Management* 2 (1980) 279–293.

Kuhn, D. G., Slocum, J. W., Jr., & Chase, R. B. "Does Job Performance Affect Employee Satisfaction?" *Personnel Journal* 50 (June 1971) 455–459.

Lakein, A. *How to Get Control of Your Time and Your Life*. New York: Signet, 1973.

Latham, G. P., & Dossett, D. L. "Designing Incentive Plans for Unionized Employees: A Comparison of Continuous and Variable Ratio Reinforcement Schedules." *Personnel Psychology* 31 (1979) 47–61.

Latham, G. P., Mitchell, T. R., & Dossett, D. L. "Importance of Participative Goal Setting and Anticipated Rewards on Goal Difficulty and Job Performance." *Journal of Applied Psychology* 63 (1978) 163–171.

Latham, G. P., & Saari, L. M. "Application of Social-Learning Theory to Training Supervisors Through Behavioral Modeling." *Journal of Applied Psychology* 64 (1979) 239–246.

Latham, G. P., & Yukl, G. A. "The Effects of Assigned and Participative Goal Setting on Performance and Job Satisfaction." *Journal of Applied Psychology* 61 (1976) 166–171.

Lawler, E. E. *Pay and Organizational Development*. Reading, MA: Addison-Wesley, 1981.

Lawler, E. E. *Pay and Organizational Effectiveness*. New York: McGraw-Hill, 1971.

Lindsay, E. M., & Gorlow, L. "The Herzberg Theory: A Critique and Reformulation." *Journal of Applied Psychology* 51 (1967) 330–339.

Locke, E. A. "The Myths of Behavior Mod in Organizations." *Academy of Management Review* 2 (1977) 543–553.

Locke, E. A. "Myths in 'The Myths of the Myths About Behavior Mod in Organizations.'" *Academy of Management Review* 4 (1979) 131–136.

Locke, E. A., Shaw, K. N., Saari, L. M., & Latham, G. P. "Goal Setting and Task Performance: 1969–1980." *Psychological Bulletin* 90 (1981) 125–152.

Lockwood, D. L., & Luthans, F. "Contingent Time Off (CTO): A Win-Win Nonfinancial Reward Strategy for the 1980's." Working paper, University of Nebraska, Lincoln, 1983.

Lockwood, D. L., & Luthans, F. "Multiple Measures to Assess the Impact of Organization Development Interventions." *The 1980 Annual Handbook for Group Facilitators*. San Diego: University Associates, 1980, 233–245.

Luthans, F. "Improving Performance: A Behavioral Problem-Solving Approach." In L. W. Frederiksen (Ed.), *Handbook of Organizational Behavior Management*. New York: Wiley, 1982.

Luthans, F. *Introduction to Management: A Contingency Approach*. New York: McGraw-Hill, 1976.

Luthans, F. "Leadership: A Proposal for a Social Learning Theory Base and Observational and Functional Analysis Techniques to Measure Leadership Behavior." In J. G. Hunt & L. L. Larson (Eds.), *Crosscurrents in Leadership*. Carbondale: Southern Illinois University Press, 1979, 201–208.

Luthans, F. *Organizational Behavior*. New York: McGraw-Hill, 1973.

Luthans, F. *Organizational Behavior* (2nd ed.). New York: McGraw-Hill, 1977.

Luthans, F. *Organizational Behavior* (3rd ed.). New York: McGraw-Hill, 1981.

Luthans, F. "Resolved: Functional Analysis Is the Best Technique for Diagnostic Evaluation of Organizational Behavior." In B. Karmel (Ed.), *Point and Counterpoint in Organizational Behavior*. Hinsdale, IL: Dryden, 1980, 48–60; 81–83; 87–90.

Luthans, F., & Davis, T. R. V. "Behavioral Self-Management: The Missing Link in Managerial Effectiveness." *Organizational Dynamics* 8 (Summer 1979) 42–60.

Luthans, F., & Davis, T. R. V. "Beyond Modeling: Managing Social Learning Processes in Human Resource Training and Development." *Human Resource Management* 20 (Summer 1981) 19–27.

Luthans, F., & Davis, T. R. V. "An Idiographic Approach to Organizational Behavior Research: The Use of Single Case Experimental Designs and Direct Measures." *Academy of Management Review* 7 (1982) 380–391.

Luthans, F., & Kreitner, R. "The Management of Behavioral Contingencies." *Personnel* (July-August 1974) 7–16.

Luthans, F., & Kreitner, R. "The Role of Punishment in Organizational Behavior Modification (O.B. Mod.)." *Public Personnel Management* 2 (May-June 1973) 156–161.

Luthans, F., & Lyman, D. "Training Supervisors to Use Organizational Behavior Modification." *Personnel* (September-October 1973) 38–44.

Luthans, F., Maciag, W. S., & Rosenkrantz, S. A. "O.B. Mod.: A Human Resources Management Answer to the Productivity Challenge." *Personnel* 60 (March–April 1983) 28–36.

Luthans, F., & Maris, T. L. "Evaluating Personnel Programs Through the Reversal Technique." *Personnel Journal* 58 (1979) 692–697.

Luthans, F., & Martinko, M. "An Organizational Behavior Modification Analysis of Absenteeism." *Human Resource Management* 15 (Fall 1976) 11–18.

Luthans, F., & Ottemann, R. "Motivation vs. Learning Approaches to Organizational Behavior." *Business Horizons* (December 1973) 55–62.

Luthans, F., Paul, R., & Baker, D. "An Experimental Analysis of the Impact of Contingent Reinforcement on Salespersons' Performance Behavior." *Journal of Applied Psychology* 66 (1981) 314–323.

Luthans, F., & Schweizer, J. "How Behavior Modification Techniques Can Improve Total Organization Performance." *Management Review* 68 (September 1979) 43–50.

Luthans, F., & White, D. "Behavior Modification: Application to Manpower Management." *Personnel Administration* (July-August 1971) 41–47.

McConkie, M. L. "A Clarification of the Goal Setting and Appraisal Processes in MBO." *Academy of Management Review* 4 (1979) 29–40.

McElroy, J. C. "A Typology of Attribution Leadership Research." *Academy of Management Review* 7 (1982) 413–417.

McGhee, W., & Tullar, W. L. "A Note on Evaluating Behavior Modification and Behavior Modeling as Industrial Training Techniques." *Personnel Psychology* 31 (1978) 477–484.

McGinnies, E. *Social Behavior: A Functional Analysis*. Boston: Houghton, Mifflin, 1970.

McGinnies, E., & Ferster, C. *The Reinforcement of Social Behavior.* Boston: Houghton, Mifflin, 1971.

McLean, A. A. *Work Stress.* Reading, MA: Addison-Wesley, 1979.

McManis, D. L., & Dick, W. G. "Monetary Incentives in Today's Industrial Setting." *Personnel Journal* 52 (May 1973) 387–392.

MacKenzie, A. *The Time Trap.* New York: McGraw-Hill, 1973.

Manz, C. C., & Sims, H. P. "Self-Management as a Substitute for Leadership: A Social Learning Theory Perspective." *Academy of Management Review* 5 (1980) 361–367.

Manz, C. C., & Sims, H. P. "Vicarious Learning: The Influence of Modeling on Organizational Behavior." *Academy of Management Review* 6 (1981) 105–113.

Mawhinney, T. C. "Intrinsic vs. Extrinstic Work Motivation: Perspectives from Behaviorism." *Organizational Behavior and Human Performance* 24 (1979) 411–440.

Maslow, A. H. "A Theory of Human Motivation." *Psychological Review* (July 1943) 370–396.

Meacham, M., & Wiesen, A. *Changing Classroom Behavior: A Manual for Precision Teaching.* Scranton, PA: International Textbook Company, 1969.

Milkovich, G. T., & Delaney, M. J. "A Note on Cafeteria Pay Plans." *Industrial Relations* 14 (1975) 112–116.

Millenson, J. R. *Principles of Behavioral Analysis.* New York: Macmillan, 1967.

Miller, D., Kets de Vries, M. F. R., & Toulouse, J. M. "Top Executive Locus of Control and Its Relationship to Strategy-Making, Structure, and Environment. *Academy of Management Journal* 25 (1982) 237–253.

Miller, L. K. "Methodological and Assessment Considerations in Applied Settings: Reviewers' Comments." *Journal of Applied Behavior Analysis* 6 (1973) 532–539.

Mintzberg, H. "Managerial Work: Analysis from Observation." *Management Science* 18 (1971) B 97–B 110.

Mintzberg, H. *The Nature of Managerial Work.* New York: Harper & Row, 1973.

Mirman, R. "Performance Management in Sales Organizations." In L. W. Frederiksen (Ed.), *Handbook of Organizational Behavior Management.* New York: Wiley, 1982, 427–475.

Mitchell, T. R., Smyser, C. M., & Weed, S. E. "Locus of Control: Supervision and Work Satisfaction." *Academy of Management Journal* 18 (1975) 623–631.

Mitchell, T. R., & Wood, R. E. "Supervisor's Responses to Subordinate Poor Performance: A Test of an Attribution Model." *Organizational Behavior and Human Performance* 25 (1980) 123–138.

Moses, J. L. "Behavior Modeling for Managers." *Human Factors* 20 (1978) 225–232.

Moses, J. L., & Ritchie, R. J. "Supervisory Relationships Training: A Behavioral Evaluation of a Behavior Modeling Program." *Personnel Psychology* 29 (1976) 337–343.

Nord, W. R. "Beyond the Teaching Machine: The Neglected Area of Operant Conditioning in the Theory and Practice of Management." *Organizational Behavior and Human Performance* 4 (1969) 375–401.

Nord, W. R. "Improving Attendance Through Rewards." *Personnel Administration* 33 (1970) 37–41.

O'Banion, D. R., & Whaley, D. L. *Behavior Contracting*. New York: Springer, 1981.

Odiorne, G. S. "MBO: A Backward Glance." *Business Horizons* 21 (October 1978) 14–24.

Orwell, G. *Nineteen Eighty-Four*. New York: Harcourt, Brace, Jovanovich, 1949.

Ottemann, R., & Luthans, F. "An Experimental Analysis of the Effectiveness of an Organizational Behavior Modification Program in Industry." In A. G. Bedeian, A. A. Armenakis, W. H. Holley, Jr., & H. S. Field (Eds.), *Proceedings of the 35th Annual Meeting of the Academy of Management*, New Orleans, 1975, 140–142.

Ouchi, W. G. *Theory Z*. Reading, MA: Addison-Wesley, 1981.

Parmerlee, M., & Schwenk, C. "Radical Behaviorism in Organizations: Misconceptions in the Locke-Gray Debate." *Academy of Management Review* 4 (1979) 601–607.

Pavlov, I. P. *Conditioned Reflexes: An Investigation of the Physiological Activity of the Cerebral Cortex*. Translated and edited by G. V. Anrep. London: Oxford University Press, 1927.

Pedalino, E., & Gamboa, V. U. "Behavior Modification and Absenteeism: Intervention in One Industrial Setting." *Journal of Applied Psychology* 59 (1974) 694–698.

"Performance Audit, Feedback, and Positive Reinforcement." *Training and Development Journal* (November 1972) 8–13.

Podsakoff, P. M., Todor, W. D., & Skov, R. "Effects of Leader Contingent and Noncontingent Reward and Punishment Behaviors on Subordinate Performance and Satisfaction." *Academy of Management Journal* 25 (1982) 810–821.

Porter, L. W., & Lawler, E. E. *Managerial Attitudes and Performance*. Homewood, IL: Irwin, 1968.

Premack, D. "Reinforcement Theory." In D. Levine (Ed.), *Nebraska Symposium on Motivation*. Lincoln, NE: University of Nebraska Press, 1965, 123–180.

Premack, D. "Toward Empirical Behavior Laws: I. Positive Reinforcement." *Psychological Review* 66 (1959) 219–233.

Prue, D. M., & Fairbank, J. A. "Performance Feedback in Organizational Behavior Management: A Review." *Journal of Organizational Behavior Management* 3 (1981) 1–16.

Pryer, M. W., & Distenfano, M. K. "Perceptions of Leadership, Job Satisfaction, and Internal-External Control Across Three Nursing Levels." *Nursing Research* 2 (1971) 534–537.

Raia, A. "Goal Setting and Self Control." *Journal of Management Studies* 2 (1965) 34–53.

Raushenberger, J., Schmitt, N., & Hunter, J. E. "A Test of the Need Hierarchy Concept by a Markov Model of Change in Need Strength." *Administrative Science Quarterly* 25 (1980) 654–670.

Razran, G. "Russian Physiologists' Psychology and American Experimental Psychology: A Historical and Systematic Collation and a Look into the Future." *Psychological Bulletin* 63 (1965) 42–64.

Reitz, H. J. "Managerial Attitudes and Perceived Contingencies Between Performance and Organizational Response." *Academy of Management Proceedings* (1971) 227–238.

Rogers, C., & Skinner, B. F. "Some Issues Concerning the Control of Human Behavior." *Science* 124 (1956) 1057–1066.

Rotter, J. B., Liverant, S., & Crowne, D. P. "The Growth and Extinction of Expectancies in Change Controlled and Skilled Tasks." *Journal of Psychology* 52 (1961) 161–177.

Rush, H. M. F. *Organization Development: A Reconnaissance* Report 605. New York: The Conference Board, 1973.

Schneider, J., & Locke, E. A. "A Critique of Herzberg's Incident Classification System and A Suggested Revision." *Organizational Behavior and Human Performance* 6 (1971) 441–457.

Schonberger, R. *Japanese Manufacturing Techniques*. New York: Free Press, 1982.

Schuler, R. S. "Time Management: A Stress Management Technique." *Personnel Journal* 24 (1979) 40–48.

Schuster, J. R., Clark, B., & Rogers, M. "Testing Portions of the Porter and Lawler Model Regarding the Motivational Role of Pay." *Journal of Applied Psychology* 55 (1971) 187–195.

Schwab, D. P. "Conflicting Impacts of Pay on Employee Motivation and Satisfaction." *Personnel Journal* 53 (1974) 196–200.

Schwab, D. P., DeVitt, H. W., & Cummings, L. L. "A Test of the Adequacy of the Two-Factor Theory as a Predictor of Self-Report Performance Effects." *Personnel Psychology* 24 (1971) 293–303.

Scott, W. G., & Hart, D. K. *Organizational America*. Boston: Houghton Mifflin, 1979.

Sherman, A. R. *Behavior Modification: Theory and Practice*. Belmont, CA: Brooks/Cole, 1973.

Sims, H. P., & Manz, C. C. "Modeling Influences on Employee Behavior." *Personnel Journal* 61 (January 1982) 58–65.

Sims, H. P., & Manz, C. C. "Social Learning Theory: The Role of Modeling in the Exercise of Leadership." *Journal of Organizational Behavior Management* 3 (1981/82) 55–63.

Skinner, B. F. *About Behaviorism*. New York: Knopf, 1974.

Skinner, B. F. *The Behavior of Organisms*. New York: Appleton-Century-Crofts, 1938.

Skinner, B. F. *Beyond Freedom and Dignity*. New York: Bantam, 1971.

Skinner, B. F. *Contingencies of Reinforcement*. New York: Appleton-Century-Crofts, 1969.

Skinner, B. F. "Operant Behavior." In W. Honig (Ed.), *Operant Behavior: Areas of Research and Application*. New York: Appleton-Century-Crofts, 1966.

Skinner, B. F. *Science and Human Behavior*. New York: The Free Press, 1953.

Smith, P. C. "Resolved: Functional Analysis Is the Best Technique for Diagnostic Evaluation of Organizational Behavior." In B. Karmel (Ed.), *Point and Counterpoint in Organizational Behavior*. Hinsdale, IL: Dryden, 1980, 60–81; 83–87; 90–91.

Smith, P. E. "Management Modeling Training to Improve Morale and Customer Satisfaction." *Personnel Psychology* 29 (1976) 351–359.

Snyder, C. A. "Application of Organizational Behavior Modification in the Public Sector: Case Studies in a Hospital Environment" (Doctoral Dissertation, University of Nebraska, 1978). *Dissertation Abstracts International* 39 (1978) 5036A.

Snyder, C. A., & Luthans, F. "Using O.B. Mod. to Increase Hospital Productivity." *Personnel Administrator* (August 1982) 67–73.

Spector, P. E. "Behavior in Organizations as a Function of Employee's Locus of Control." *Psychological Bulletin* 91 (1982) 482–497.

Sulzer-Azaroff, B. "Behavioral Approaches to Occupational Health and Safety." In L. W. Frederiksen (Ed.), *Handbook of Organizational Behavior Management*. New York: Wiley, 1982, 505–538.

Thoresen, C. E., & Mahoney, M. J. *Behavioral Self-Control*. New York: Holt, Rinehart, & Winston, 1974.

Thorndike, E. L. *Educational Psychology: The Psychology of Learning, Vol. II.* New York: Columbia University, Teachers College, 1913.

Turner, A. N., & Lawrence, P. R. *Industrial Jobs and the Worker.* Cambridge: Harvard Graduate School of Business, 1965.

Van Ness, P. W., & Luthans, F. "Multiple Baseline Designs: An Alternative Strategy for Organizational Behavior Research." In E. L. Miller (Ed.), *Proceedings of the 22nd Annual Conference of the Midwest Academy of Management* (1979) 336–350.

Vroom, V. H. *Work and Motivation.* New York: Wiley, 1964.

Wahba, M. A., & Bridwell, L. G. "Maslow Reconsidered: A Review of Research on the Need Hierarchy Theory." *Organization Behavior and Human Performance* 15 (1976) 212–240.

Wanous, J. P. "Effects of a Realistic Job Preview on Job Acceptance, Job Attitudes, and Job Survival." *Journal of Applied Psychology* 58 (1973) 327–332.

Wanous, J. P. "Realistic Job Previews: Can a Procedure to Reduce Turnover Also Influence the Relationship Between Abilities and Performance?" *Personnel Psychology* 31 (1978) 249–258.

Watson, J. B. *Behaviorism.* New York: Norton, 1924.

Watson, J. B., & MacDougall, W. *The Battle of Behaviorism.* New York: Norton, 1929.

Watson, J. B., & Rayner, R. "Conditioning Emotional Reactions." *Journal of Experimental Psychology* 3 (1920) 1–14.

Webb, E. J., Campbell, D. T., Schwartz, R. D., & Sechrest, L. *Unobtrusive Measures: Nonreactive Research in the Social Sciences.* Chicago: Rand McNally, 1966.

Weiner, B. *Theories of Motivation.* Chicago: Rand McNally, 1972.

Weiss, H. M. "Social Learning of Work Values in Organizations." *Journal of Applied Psychology* 63 (1978) 711–718.

Weiss, H. M. "Subordinate Imitation of Supervisor Behavior: The Role of Modeling in Organizational Socialization." *Organizational Behavior and Human Performance* 19 (1977) 89–105.

Wexley, K. N., & Latham, G. P. *Developing and Training Human Resources in Organizations.* Glenview, IL: Scott Foresman, 1981.

"Where Skinner's Theories Work." *Business Week* (December 2, 1972) 64–65.

Wolpe, J. *Psychotherapy by Reciprocal Inhibition.* Palo Alto, CA: Stanford University Press, 1958.

"Worker-Training Cost Tops $30 Billion." *Arizona Republic* (June 28, 1981) c–9.

Yukl, G. A., & Latham, G. P. "Consequences of Reinforcement Schedules and Incentive Magnitudes for Employee Performance: Problems Encountered in an Industrial Setting." *Journal of Applied Psychology* 60 (1975) 294–298.

Yukl, G. A., Latham, G. P., & Pursell, E. D. "The Effectiveness of Performance Incentives Under Continuous and Variable Ratio Schedules of Reinforcement." *Personnel Psychology* 29 (1976) 221–231.

Yukl, G. A., Wexley, K. N., & Seymore, V. D. "Effectiveness of Pay Incentives Under Variable Ratio and Continuous Reinforcement Schedules." *Journal of Applied Psychology* 56 (1972) 19–23.

Zuckerman, M. "Actions and Occurrences in Kelley's Cube." *Journal of Personality and Social Psychology* 36 (1978) 647–656.

NAME INDEX

SUBJECT INDEX

ACKNOWLEDGMENTS   **Figure 3–5.** Adapted from *Organizational Behavior*, 3rd edition by Fred Luthans. Copyright © 1981, 1977, 1973 by McGraw-Hill, Inc. Reprinted by permission of McGraw-Hill Book Company.   **Figure 4–3.** F. Luthans and R. Kreitner, "The Management of Behavioral Contingencies," *Personnel*, July-August (New York: AMACOM, a division of American Management Associations, 1974) p. 13. Reprinted by permission.   **Figure 4–7.** From "An Organizational Behavior Modification Analysis of Absenteeism" by Fred Luthans and Mark Martinko in *Human Resource Management*, Fall 1976, Vol. 15, No. 3, Page 15. Copyright © 1975 by The University of Michigan. Reprinted by permission.   **Figure 5–2.** Adapted from Robert Kreitner: *Management* Second Edition, Copyright © 1983 Houghton Mifflin Company. Adapted with permission.   **Figure 5–5.** J. Hackman and G. Oldham, *Work Redesign*, © 1980, Addison-Wesley, Reading, Massachusetts. Pg. 90, Fig. 4.6. Reprinted with permission.   **Figure 7–1.** From Albert Bandura, *Social Learning Theory*, copyright © 1977, pp. vii, 13, 23, 25, 79, 160, 161. Reprinted by permission of Prentice-Hall, Inc., Englewood Cliffs, NJ   **Figure 7–2.** From "Self-Management Methods" by F. H. Kanfer in *Helping People Change: A Textbook of Methods*, edited by F. H. Kanfer and A. P. Goldstein. Copyright © 1980 by Pergamon Press Inc. Reprinted by permission.   **Figure 8–1.** From "Behavioral Approaches to Occupational Health and Safety" by Beth Sulzer-Azaroff in *Handbook of Organizational Behavior Management*, edited by L. W. Frederiksen. Copyright © 1982 by John Wiley & Sons, Inc. Reprinted by permission of John Wiley & Sons, Inc.   **Figure 8–6.** From "An experimental analysis of the effectiveness of an organizational behavior modification program in industry" by R. Ottemann and F. Luthans in *Proceedings of the 35th Annual Meeting of the Academy of Management*, A. G. Bedeian, A. A. Armenakis, W. H. Holley, Jr., and H. S. Field, eds., 1975, p. 141.   **Figures 8–7, 8–8, 8–9.** Fred Luthans, Walter S. Maciag, and Stuart A. Rosenkrantz, "O.B. Mod.: Meeting the Productivity Challenge with Human Resources Management," *Personnel*, March-April (New York: AMACOM Periodicals Division, 1983) pp. 31–3. Reprinted by permission.   **Figure 8–10.** Luthans and Schweizer, "How Behavior Modification Technique Can Improve Total Organizational Performance," *Management Review*, September, (New York: AMACOM, a division of American Management Associations, 1979) p. 49. Reprinted by permission.   **Figures**

8–11, 8–12. From "An Experimental Analysis of the Impact of Contingent Reinforcement on Salesperson's Performance Behavior" by Fred Luthans, Robert Paul, and Douglas Baker in *Journal of Applied Psychology*, June 1981, Vol. 66, No. 3, pp. 319 and 320. Copyright © 1981 by the American Psychological Association. Adapted by permission of the publisher. **Figure 8–13.** Reprinted from the August 1982 issue of *Personnel Administrator*, copyright, 1982, The American Society for Personnel Administration, 606 North Washington Street, Alexandria, VA 22314. **Figures 8–14, 8–15.** F. Luthans and T. Davis, "Behavioral Self-Management—The Missing Link in Managerial Effectiveness," *Organizational Dynamics*, Summer (New York: AMACOM, a division of American Management Associations, 1979) pp. 53 and 56. Reprinted by permission.

"Modeling Influences on Employee Behavior," by Henry P. Sims, Jr. & Charles C. Manz, copyright January 1982. Reprinted with the permission of *Personnel Journal*, Costa Mesa, California; all rights reserved. From "The Effects of Behavior Modeling Training Upon Managers' Behaviors and Employees' Perceptions" by Robert F. Burnaska in *Personnel Psychology*, Vol. 29, No. 3, 1976. Copyright © 1976 by Personnel Psychology, Inc. Reprinted by permission. From *Changing Supervisor Behavior* by A. Goldstein and M. Sorcher. Copyright © 1974 by Pergamon Press Inc. Reprinted by permission. From "The Feedforward and Feedback Control of Job Performance Through Organizational Behavior Management," by Robert Kreitner. 1982, The Haworth Press, pp. 7–8. From "Social Learning Theory: The Role of Modeling in the Exercise of Leadership," by H. P. Sims and C. C. Manz. 1982, The Haworth Press, pp. 56, 61. From "Application of Social-Learning Theory to Training Supervisors Through Behavioral Modeling," by G. P. Latham and L. M. Saari. 1979, American Psychological Association, Inc., p. 241. From "Controversy in OBM" by Robert Kreitner. 1982, John Wiley & Sons, p. 88. From "At Emery Air Freight." 1973, AMACOM, p. 43.